Networks of Trade in Raw Materials and Technological Innovations in Prehistory and Protohistory

an Archaeometry Approach

Proceedings of the XVII UISPP World Congress
(1–7 September 2014, Burgos, Spain)

Volume 12/Session B34

Edited by

Davide Delfino, Paolo Piccardo,
and João Carlos Baptista

Archaeopress Archaeology

ARCHAEOPRESS PUBLISHING LTD
Gordon House
276 Banbury Road
Oxford OX2 7ED

www.archaeopress.com

ISBN 978 1 78491 423 3
ISBN 978 1 78491 424-0 (e-Pdf)

© Archaeopress, UISPP and authors 2016

VOLUME EDITORS: Davide Delfino, Paolo Piccardo, João Carlos Baptista

SERIES EDITOR: The board of UISPP

SERIES PROPERTY: UISPP – International Union of Prehistoric and Protohistoric Sciences

The editing of this volume was funded by the Instituto Terra e Memória, Centro de Geociências UID/Multi/00073/2013, with the support of the Fundação para a Ciência e Tecnologia FCT/MEC

KEY-WORDS IN THIS VOLUME: Archaeometry, Networks, Raw Materials, Technological Inovation, Prehistory & Protohistory

UISPP PROCEEDINGS SERIES is a printed on demand and an open access publication, edited by UISPP through Archaeopress

BOARD OF UISPP: Jean Bourgeois (President), Luiz Oosterbeek (Secretary-General),
François Djindjian (Treasurer), Ya-Mei Hou (Vice President), Marta Arzarello (Deputy Secretary-General).
The Executive Committee of UISPP also includes the Presidents of all the international scientific commissions (www.uispp.org)

BOARD OF THE XVII WORLD CONGRESS OF UISPP: Eudald Carbonell (Secretary-General),
Robert Sala I Ramos, Jose Maria Rodriguez Ponga (Deputy Secretary-Generals)

All rights reserved. No part of this book may be reproduced, or transmitted, in any form or by any means, electronic, mechanical, photocopying or otherwise, without the prior written permission of the copyright owners.

This book is available direct from Archaeopress or from our website www.archaeopress.com

Contents

List of Figures and Tables ii

Foreword to the XVII UISPP Congress Proceedings Series Edition iv
Luiz OOSTERBEEK

Networks of trade in raw materials and technological innovations in Prehistory & Protohistory: an archaeometry approach Introduction v
Davide DELFINO, Paolo PICCARDO, João Carlos BAPTISTA

Middle Bronze Age metalworking in the cave of Monte Meana (South-western Sardinia, Italy) 1
Marco SERRA, Stefano NAITZA, Carla CANNAS, and Giacomo PAGLIETTI

Bronze Age silver artifacts from Romania – an archaeo-metallurgical study 13
Bogdan CONSTANTINESCU, Daniela CRISTEA-STAN and Anca-Diana POPESCU

Prehistoric gold metallurgy in Transylvania – an archaeometrical study 27
Daniela CRISTEA-STAN and Bogdan CONSTANTINESCU

Passage of technologies – an archaeometric case study of iron artifacts of a Scythian Age grave from the Carpathian Basin 39
B. TÖRÖK, A. GYUCHA, Á. KOVÁCS, P. BARKÓCZY, and Gy. GULYÁS

An indigenous pottery production strategy in the late Early Bronze Age site of Mursia, Pantelleria, Italy. Perspectives on social complexity and indigenous interaction patterns 51
Matteo CANTISANI

Bronze Age ceramics from Sardinia (Italy) – a technological study 69
Maria Giuseppina GRADOLI

A preliminary archaeometric study of eneolithic anthropomorphic statues from Nurallao (central Sardinia, Italy) 81
Marco SERRA, Valentina MAMELI and Carla CANNAS

Early Iron Age pottery in south-western Iberia – archaeometry and chronology 95
Michał KRUEGER, Dirk BRANDHERM

List of Figures and Tables

M. SERRA et al.: **Middle Bronze Age metalworking in the cave of Monte Meana (South-western Sardinia, Italy)**

FIGURE 1. MAP OF SOUTH-WEST SARDINIA (ITALY) AND LOCATION OF THE MONTE MEANA CAVE AND CLOSE MINES OF COPPER 2
FIGURE 2. THE INTERIOR OF THE CAVE WITH THE INDICATION OF THE FINDING OF THE SLAGS AND THE DAGGER 3
FIGURE 3. SLAGS AND DATED CHARCOAL FOUND AREA 3
FIGURE 4. THE SLAGS AND THE DAGGER 4
FIGURE 5. pXRF QUALITATIVE ELEMENTAL DATA OBTAINED ON THE METALLURGICAL SLAGS (A-B) AND THE DAGGER (C-D) 7
FIGURE 6. MICROSCOPIC FEATURES OF THE METALLURGICAL SLAG 2042. THIN SECTION (TRANSMITTED LIGHT) 9
FIGURE 7. A, B. MAIN CRYSTALLOGRAPHIC PHASES OF THE SLAG 2042 10
TABLE 1. ^{14}C DATES OF THE MONTE MEANA CAVE'S SMELTING FURNACE AND SA TURRICULA DOMESTIC AREA 4
TABLE 2. ANALITICAL CONTENTS (PPM AND %) FROM THE SLAG 2042 AND THE DAGGER 1694 8

B. CONSTANTINESCU et al.: **Bronze Age silver artifacts from Romania – an archaeo-metallurgical study**

FIGURE 1. MAP OF SILVER ARTIFACTS PROVENANCE SITES 15
FIGURE 2. SILVER HAIR RINGS AND BEADS: 1. VERBIȚA; 2A-B. PLENIȚA; 3-6. ZIMNICEA; 7-8. ARICEȘTII RAHTIVANI 16
FIGURE 3. THE COMPOSITION OF THE ANALYZED SILVER HAIR RINGS 17
FIGURE 4. ARICEȘTII RAHTIVANI GILDED SPIRAL RING 18
FIGURE 5. THE SILVER-COPPER DAGGER FROM PODURI 19
FIGURE 6. PERȘINARI SILVER SHAFT-HOLE AXES 20
FIGURE 7. XRF ANALYSES OF A BROKEN AXE 20
FIGURE 8. GOLD NUGGET 21
FIGURE 9. VULCHITRUN-TYPE DISC FOUND IN CĂLĂRAȘI 21
TABLE 1. ELEMENTAL COMPOSITION OF PODURI DAGGER ALLOY 19

D. CRISTEA-STAN and B. CONSTANTINESCU: **Prehistoric gold metallurgy in Transylvania – an archaeometrical study**

FIGURE 1. MAP OF GOLD GEOLOGICAL SOURCES INVESTIGATED BY OUR GROUP 28
FIGURE 2. MAP OF ARCHAEOLOGICAL GOLD ARTIFACTS INVESTIGATED BY OUR GROUP 28
FIGURE 3. GOLD BRONZE AGE ARTIFACTS FROM SMIG, BIIA, CAUAS, SACUIENI, PECICA-ROVINE, CACOVA 29
FIGURE 4. HAIR RINGS (LOCK RINGS) FROM: A. CACOVA (AIUD) AND B. SIBIU 30
FIGURE 5. TAUTEU HOARD 31
FIGURE 6. TAUTEU RING 1 – MICRO-SR-XRF SPECTRUM 32
FIGURE 7. GOLD BRACELET BOARTA 32
FIGURE 8. A SPIRALED GOLD DACIAN BRACELET 33
FIGURE 9. FREQUENCY DISTRIBUTION FOR THE AU/AG RATIO AND THE AU CONTENT [%] IN DACIAN BRACELETS 34
FIGURE 10. GOLD DACIAN KOSON STATERS 35
TABLE 1. ELEMENTAL COMPOSITION OF ARTIFACTS FROM SMIG, CAUAS, SACUIENI, PECICA, CACOVA, TAUTEU 30
TABLE 2. ELEMENTAL COMPOSITION OF ARTIFACTS FROM CACOVA (AIUD) AND SIBIU 31
TABLE 3. DACIAN BRACELETS COMPOSITION 34
TABLE 4. ELEMENTAL CONCENTRATION VARIATIONS IN KOSON STATERS WITH MONOGRAM 36
TABLE 5. ELEMENTAL CONCENTRATION VARIATIONS IN KOSON STATERS WITHOUT MONOGRAM 36

B. TÖRÖK et al.: **Passage of technologies – an archaeometric case study of iron artifacts of a Scythian Age grave from the Carpathian Basin**

FIGURE 1. THE EXAMINED IRON ARTIFACTS – LONG AXE, TRUNNION AXE, SHAFT-HOLE AXE, ADZE-AXE, SPEARHEAD AND SHEATH ... 41
FIGURE 2. SEM MICROGRAPH OF THE LONG AXE – NEAR THE SURFACE OF ITS STEM 42
FIGURE 3. P-RICH SLAG INCLUSIONS IN THE INNER AREA OF THE LONG AXE ARRANGED IN THE DIRECTION OF FORMATION 43
FIGURE 4. WIDMANSTÄTTEN-FERRITE ON A SEM MICROGRAPH OF THE TRUNNION AXE 43
FIGURE 5. OM MICROGRAPH OF THE LOOP OF THE SHAFT-HOLE AXE 44
FIGURE 6. PEARLITIC-FERRITIC LAYERS IN ALTERNATING SERIES WITH INCLUSION IN THE INNER AREA OF
    THE LOOP OF THE SHAFT-HOLE AXE 45
FIGURE 7. FRACTURED CEMENTITE OF THE EDGE OF THE SHAFT-HOLE AXE 45
FIGURE 8. PEARLITE AND NET LIKE FERRITE (WIDMANNSTÄTTEN-STYLE IN SOME PLACES) ON SEM MICROGRAPH OF
    THE EDGE PERPENDICULAR TO THE HOLE OF THE ADZE AXE 46
FIGURE 9. PEARLITE AND SECONDARY CEMENTITE ON AN OM MICROGRAPH OF THE EDGE-RING PARALLEL TO
    THE HOLE OF THE ADZE AXE 47
FIGURE 11. ELEMENT SPECTRUM OF A SLAG INCLUSION OF THE SHEATH 48
FIGURE 10. SEM MICROGRAPH OF THE SPEARHEAD 48

M. Cantisani: An indigenous pottery production strategy in the late Early Bronze Age site of Mursia, Pantelleria, Italy. Perspectives on social complexity and indigenous interaction patterns

Figure 1. Planimetry and excavation areas 52
Figure 2. The ceramic types assemblage from Mursia 52
Figure 3. Geographical settings and Mursia site location 54
Figure 4. Particular of the investigated areas [A) the location of B area; B) the North zone;
    C) the South zone with location of the structure B3] 55
Figure 5. Pantelleria isle location within the SCRZ 57
Figure 6. Faults and Caldera areas in Pantelleria 58
Figure 7. The eruptive cycles and the volcanic structures above; Under the main geological lithotypes
    are represented 59
Figure 8. Raw material sources location; A) the geological context; B) the lake basin with secondary
    clay sediments; C) Fossa del Rosso and the two Gibbile Mounts within the Vecchia Caldera 62
Figure 9. Thin section micrographs of the late Early Bronze Age pottery from Mursia 63
Table 1. Sample. Petrographic characterization 60

M. G. Gradoli: Bronze Age ceramics from Sardinia (Italy) – a technological study

Figure 1. The area under study. From Lilliu C. 1985; and Badas et al. 1989 70
Figure 2. Complex Nuraghe Genna Maria at Villanovofarru. Photo Municipality of Villanovaforru 71
Figure 3. Middle and Recent Bronze Age pottery from the studied area 73

M. Serra et al.: A preliminary archaeometric study of eneolithic anthropomorphic statues from Nurallao (central Sardinia, Italy)

Figure 1. Geographic setting of Nurallao 82
Figure 2. Aiodda-Nurallao: southern view of the nuragic burial (a); menhir statues called Aiodda I (b),
    Aiodda IV (c) and Aiodda 13 (d) 83
Figure 3. Eastern view (a), layout plan and cross sections (b) of the Perda Tellada's limestone quarry 84
Figure 4. Geological setting of Nurallao 85
Figure 5. Geological sampling plan of the Villagreca limestone 86
Figure 6. Comparison between palaeontological and mineralogical characters recognized on
    the geological samples of Villagreca (a-c) and on the eneolithic sculptures of Aiodda (d) 90
Table 1. ED-XRF spectra of a Villagreca geological sample (a) and a menhir statue of Aiodda (b) 89
Table 2. Geochemical intra-source variability of the Villagreca Unit: scatter plots of
    the ED-XRF intensities ratios (a) and ICP-OES/ICP-MS concentrations (b) 89
Table 3. PXRD patterns of the Villagreca geological samples 91
Table 4. Source provenance of the anthropomorphic sculptures of Aiodda 92

M. Krueger and D. Brandherm: Early Iron Age pottery in south-western Iberia – archaeometry and chronology

Figure 1. Main sites of the Lower Guadalquivir studied within the project 96
Figure 2. Chronological range for cremation burials from the Setefilla flat cemetery and tumuli A and B 98
Figure 3. The XRF spectrometer in the Faculty of Chemistry of the Adam Mickiewicz University in Poznań ... 100

Foreword to the XVII UISPP Congress Proceedings Series Edition

Luiz OOSTERBEEK
Secretary-General

UISPP has a long history, starting with the old International Association of Anthropology and Archaeology, back in 1865, until the foundation of UISPP itself in Bern, in 1931, and its growing relevance after WWII, from the 1950's. We also became members of the International Council of Philosophy and Human Sciences, associate of UNESCO, in 1955.

In its XIVth world congress in 2001, in Liège, UISPP started a reorganization process that was deepened in the congresses of Lisbon (2006) and Florianópolis (2011), leading to its current structure, solidly anchored in more than twenty-five international scientific commissions, each coordinating a major cluster of research within six major chapters: Historiography, methods and theories; Culture, economy and environments; Archaeology of specific environments; Art and culture; Technology and economy; Archaeology and societies.

The XVIIth world congress of 2014, in Burgos, with the strong support of Fundación Atapuerca and other institutions, involved over 1700 papers from almost 60 countries of all continents. The proceedings, edited in this series but also as special issues of specialized scientific journals, will remain as the most important outcome of the congress.

Research faces growing threats all over the planet, due to lack of funding, repressive behavior and other constraints. UISPP moves ahead in this context with a strictly scientific programme, focused on the origins and evolution of humans, without conceding any room to short term agendas that are not root in the interest of knowledge.

In the long run, which is the terrain of knowledge and science, not much will remain from the contextual political constraints, as severe or dramatic as they may be, but the new advances into understanding the human past and its cultural diversity will last, this being a relevant contribution for contemporary and future societies.

This is what UISPP is for, and this is also why we are currently engaged in contributing for the relaunching of Human Sciences in their relations with social and natural sciences, namely collaborating with the International Year of Global Understanding, in 2016, and with the World Conference of the Humanities, in 2017.

The next two congresses of UISPP, in Melbourne (2017) and in Geneva (2020), will confirm this route.

Networks of trade in raw materials and technological innovations in Prehistory & Protohistory: an archaeometry approach
Introduction

Davide DELFINO, Paolo PICCARDO, João Carlos BAPTISTA
Session coordinators

Key-words: *Archaeometry, Networks, Raw Materials, Technological Inovation, Prehistory & Protohistory*

Archaeometry is a multidisciplinary research field, where archaeologists, chemists, physicists, materials scientists and geologists cooperate for a better understanding of the past under the point of view of materials and context. It makes clear that no natural scientists can fully understand the materials evidences of the past, despite all precise measurements, without the competent and experienced support of the archaeologists in ancient human dynamics. Besides that, the skills and knowledge of the above mentioned scientists about mineralogy (e.g. ores, rocks, sediments and their characteristics), materials properties, and chemical-physical dynamics are essentials for the archaeological studies in order to put light on provenances, technology and absolute chronology of ancient materials and contexts.

Thanks to archaeometry in the last nearly four decades archeologists have had a simplified access to physical and chemical investigation methods suitable to better study the materials and their archaeological contexts, as witnessed by several authors who published manuals, such as: Renfrew and Bahn (1991 and further editions), Ellis (2000), and Brothwell and Pollard (2001). The existance of such references does not make archaeologists independent, but simply helps them to easier collaborate with chemists, physicists and geologists. What could be today questioned is the unique of the 'archeometer', since a team made of the needed specialists would be more efficient than any individual claiming to have a suitable knowledge in both arhcaeologic and scientific disciplines.

The paper collected in this book corresponds to the lectures held during session B34 of UISPP conference in Burgos (June 2014) where the presentation of multidisciplinary works were encouraged. The main goal of bringing together specialists from various disciplines (humanities and natural sciences) was to debate by different perspectives the networks in raw materials and technological innovation in Prehistory and Protohistory, involving investigation topics typical of archaeometry: archeometallurgy, petrography, and mineralogy.

C. Hawkes in 1958 coined the term 'Archaeometry', two years later, in 1960, W. F. Libby wins the Nobel prize after discovery, in 1950, the possibility to use the Carbon isotopes ratio as a dating method for organic materials. Since the number of researches involving archaeometry as an approach to the study of ancients' materials increased considerably. The technological know-how of ancient peoples and the provenance studies were carried out in two directions:
1. characterization of ancient technologies and materials, since the fundamental works by Hodges (1964 and 1971) and Forbes (1966) about technologies in ancient world; by Kempe and Harvey (1983); by Clough and Cummins (1988) about petrology and axe stone study; by Sieveking and Hart (1986), in flint and chert technology and production; by Torrrence (1986) about production and exchange of stone tools; by Shepard (1985) and by Rice (1987), about ceramic analysis and technology; by Craddock and Hughes (1985) and by Tylecote (1962, 1987) about early metallurgy in Europe followed by Pollard and Heron (1996), and by Lambert (1997) about general aims of archaeometry. The most recent works are are by Hurcombe (2007), about manufacturing methods of archaeological artefatcs; by Cuomo di

Caprio (2008) and by AlbieroSantacreu (2014) for the study of ceramic, and by Montero Ruiz (2010) for archaeometallurgy, with very comprehensive manuals. Concerning petrology, it is worth remembering Shakley (2008) for all lithic materials and Quinn (2013) for ceramic petrology.
2. provenance of materials and artifacts, carried out by, citing the most important works only, Earle and Ericson (1977) in a general view and about problems of production, circulation and provenance; by Ericson and Purdy (1984) about the production and circulation of lithic tools; by Stoss Gale (1991), Stoss Gale *et al.* (1995) (1998) and Gale (2011), about provenance of copper alloys objects in Mediterranean Bronze Age using lead isotopes; by Peacock (1969) about provenance of Neolithic pottery; by Mannoni (1968) about the contribution of mineralogy and ceramic technology to archaeology; by Wilson (1978) discussing about the meaning of chemical composition in pottery; by Glascock, Neff and Vaughn (2004) about physical methods in Nazca pottery provenance; by Tite (2008), about current state of research in ceramic production, provenance and use.

In virtue of the state of research, the limits of the classical approaches and of the new frontiers further disciplines were added to the available one as anthropology for the interpretation of ancient productions and exchanges. One aim is to sustain the discussion about trade in raw materials unveiling the few improper practices made in past researches by chemical methods (e.g. simply relying on the chemical composition of bronzes to suggest their area of origin) and introducing new approaches and methods. Another aim is to underline the importance of the technological innovations from Pre- and Proto-history in order to understand which reasons were behind the innovation.

Within these specific issues the present volume treats three main materials: metals, ceramic and stones with the following papers divided by materials kind:
1. Metals
    1.1. Paglietti *et al.*, about a finding of an object from Monte Meana-Santadi cave representative of early bronze technology in Sardinian Bronze Age;
    1.2. Cristea-Stan and Constantinescu, about the continuity of gold metallurgy between Neolithic and Bronze Age in Transilvania;
    1.3. Constantinescu and Cristea-Stan, about researches on silver metallurgy in Bronze Age of Lower Danube;
    1.4. Török *et al.*, about metals from a First Iron Age grave postioned at Bátmonostor-Szurdokthat reflects shared cultural traditions and commercial activities between different regions of Scythian Culture, Great Hungarian Plain and Transdanubian Hallstatt Culture
2. Ceramic
    2.1. Cantisani presenting a research about Bronze Age pottery from a settlement sited in Mursia (Pantelleria island) with the related issues about local production or imported goods;
    2.2. Gradoli refers about technological and production studies in nuragic Bronze Age ceramic;
    2.3. Krueger and Brandherm, write about a tecno-chronological study in Tartessian ceramic (South-West Iberia) with the aim to better define the chronology of the First Iron Age based also on the discovery of imported (Phoenician)
3. Stones
    3.1. Serra *et al.*, presenting the provenance study of 13 menhir-stelae by the Calcolithic site of Aiodda-Nurallao

References

ALBERO SANTACREU, D. 2014. *Material, Technics and Society in Pottery Production*, Warsaw and Berlin: De Gruyter Open, Ltd.
BROTHWELL, D. R.; POLLARD, A. M. 2001. *Handbook of Archaeological Sciences*, Chichester, West Sussex: John Wiley & Sons Ltd.

CLOUGH, T.; CUMMINS, W. 1988. *Stone Axes Studies 2*, Research Report 67, London: Council for the Bristish Archaeology.

CRADDOCK, P. T.; HUGHES, M. J. 1985. *Funaces and smelting technology in Antiquity*, British Museum Occasional Papers, 48, London: Trust of British Museums.

CUOMO DI CAPRIO, N. 2008. *Ceramica in arqueologia 2*, Roma: L'Erma di Bretschneider.

EARLE, T. K.; ÉRICSON, J. E. (eds.) *Exchenge System in Prehistory*, New York: Accademic Press.

ELLIS, L. 2000. *Archaeological Methods and Teory*, New York and London: Garland Publishing.

ERCSON, J.; PURDY, B. 1984. *Prehistoric Quarries and Lithic Production*, Cambridge: Cambridge University Press.

FORBES, R. J. 1966. *Studies in Ancient Technology*, Leiden; E. J. Brill.

GALE, N. H. 2011. Copper Oxhide Ingots and Lead Provenancing, In Betancourt, P.; Ferrence, S. C. (eds.) *Metallurgy: understanding how, learning why. Studies in Honour of James D. Muhly*, Philadelphia, Pennsylvania: Instap Academic Press, 213-221.

HURCOMBE, L. M. 2007. *Archaeological artefacts as material culture*, London and New York: Routledge.

KEMPE, D.; HARVEY, A. 1983. *The Petrology of Archaeologcial Artefacts*, Oxford: Clarenton Press.

LAMBERT, J. B. 1997. *Traces of the past: Unreveling the secrets of Archaeology through Chemistry*, Reading, Massachusetts: Helix Books/Wesley Longman.

HODGES, H. 1964. *Artifacts: an introduction to Early Materials and Technology*, London: John Backer.

HODGES, H. 1971. *Technology in the Ancient World*, Harmondsword and Baltimore: Penguin Books.

MANNONI, T. 1968. Mineralogia e tecnologia della ceramica al servizio dell'archeologia, *Atti e memorie della Deputazione di Storia Patria per le antiche Provincie Modenesi*, X, vol. III, pp. 249-258.

MONTERO RUIZ, I. (ed.) 2010. *Manual de* Arqueometallurgia, Madrid: Alaclá de Enares.

NASCOCK, M. D.; NEFF, H.; VAUGHN, K. J. 2004. Instrumental Neutron Activation Analysis and Multivariate Statistic for Pottery Provenance, *Hyperfine Interaction*, vol. 154, Issue 1, pp. 95-105.

PEACOCK, D. P. S. 1969. Neolithicpottery production in Cornwall, *Antiquity*, vol. 43, Issue 170, pp. 145-149.

POLLARD, A. M.; HERON, C. (eds.) 1996. *Archaeological Chemistry*, Cambridge: Royal Society of Chemistry.

QUINN, P. S. 2013. *Ceramic Petrography: The Interpretation of Archaeological Pottery & Related Artefacts in Thin Section*, Oxford: Archaeopress.

RENFREW, C.; BAHN, P. 1991. *Archaeology: Theory, Methods and Pratices*, London: Thames and Hudson.

RICE, P. M. 1987. *Pottery Analysis: a Sourcebook*, Chicago: Chicago University Press.

SHAKLEY, M. S. 2008. Archaeological Petrology and the Archaeometry of Lithic Materials, *Archaeometry*, vol. 50, Issue 2, April 2008, pp. 194-215, DOI:10.1111/j.1475-4754.2008.00390.x

SHEPARD, A. O. 1985. *Ceramic for the Archaeologist*, Washington, D.C.: Carnegie Institute.

SIEVEKING, G.; HART, M. B. 1986. *The Scientific Study of Flint and Chert*, Cambridge: Cambridge University Press.

STOS-GALE, Z. A. 1990. Lead isotope studies of metals and the metals trade in the Bronze Age Mediterranean, In Henderson, J. (ed.) *Scientific Analysis in Archaeology*, Oxford: Oxford University Committee for Archaeology and the UCLA Institute of Archaeology, pp. 274-301.

STOS-GALE, Z. A.; GALE, N. H.; HOUGHTON, J.; SPEAKMAN, R. 1995. Lead isotope analyses of ores from the Western Mediterranean, *Archaeometry* 37, 2, pp. 407-415.

STOS-GALE, Z. A.; GALE, N. H.; BASS, G.; PULAK, C; GALILI, E.; SHARVIT, J. 1998. The copper and tin ingots of the Late Bronze Age Mediterranean: New scientific evidence. In *Proceedings of The Fourth International Conference on the Beginning of the Use on Metals and Alloys (BUMA-IV)*, Aoba: The Japan Institute of Metals, pp. 115-126.

TITE, M. A. 2008. Ceramic production, provenance and use- a review, *Archaeometry*, vol. 50, Issue 2, pp. 216-231.

TORRENCE, R. 1986. *The Production and Exchange of Stone Tools*, Cambridge: Cambridge University Press.

TYLECOTE, R. F. 1962. *Metallurgy in Archaeology,* London: Edward Arnolds.

TYLECOTE, R. F. 1987. *The Early History of Metallurgy in Europe*, London and White Plains: Longman.

WILSON, A. L. 1978. Elemental Analysis of Pottery in the study of its provenance: a review, *Journal of Archaeological Sciences*, vol. 5, Issue 3, pp. 219-236.

Middle Bronze Age metalworking in the cave of Monte Meana (South-western Sardinia, Italy)

Marco SERRA
Dipartimento di Storia, Beni Culturali e Territorio, Università degli Studi di Cagliari, Italy;
Consorzio per la Promozione delle Attività Universitarie del Sulcis-Iglesiente (AUSI), Italy;
Centro di Ricerca per l'Energia, l'Ambiente e il Territorio (C.R.E.A.TE), Italy
marco.serra@unica.it

Stefano NAITZA
Dipartimento di Ingegneria Civile, Ambientale e Architettura Università degli Studi di Cagliari, Italy
snaitza@unica.it

Carla CANNAS
Dipartimento di Scienze Chimiche e Geologiche, Università degli Studi di Cagliari, Italy
Consorzio Interuniversitario Nazionale per la Scienza e Tecnologia dei Materiali (Cagliari Unit), Italy
ccannas@unica.it

Giacomo PAGLIETTI[*]
Dipartimento di Storia, Beni culturali e Territorio Università degli Studi di Cagliari, Italy
gpaglietti@unica.it

Abstract

A metalwork station and metal artifacts were found in 2012 during the excavation of a south western Sardinia cave, in Italy. Numerous charcoals, smelting slags and a dagger, coming from a probable bowl furnace, were found. These remains are typologically related to the middle bronze age manufacturing, as confirmed by ^{14}C dating. To reconstruct the ancient metallurgical technology, an archaeometric study was performed by chemical (pXRF, ICP-OES) and mineralogical (PXRD, microscopy) techniques. The results showed that all finds are made primarily of Cu, Fe and Pb with several trace elements. The main part of these analytes is due to the mineral charge. Microscopic analyses show gangue fragments and minerals comparable to the ones noticed in the mixed sulphides ores close to the cave. PXRD patterns and polarizing microscopy indicate metallurgical temperatures ranging from 600-700°C to 1100°C.

Key-words: *Sardinia, Middle Bronze Age, archaeometry, copper artifacts, technological properties*

Résumé

Une station de métallerie et un objets en métal ont été trouvés en 2012 lors de la fouille d'une grotte en Sardaigne sud ouest, en Italie. De nombreux fusains, de la fusion et des scories d'un poignard, provenant d'un bol four probable, ont été trouvés. Ces restes sont typologiquement liés à la fabrication de l'âge de bronze du milieu, tel que confirmé par ^{14}C jour. Pour reconstruire l'ancienne technologie métallurgique, une étude a été réalisée par archéométrique (PXRD, microscopie) techniques chimiques (pXRF, ICP-OES) et minéralogie. Les résultats ont montré que toutes les découvertes sont faites principalement de Cu, Fe et Pb avec nombreux traces éléments. La partie principale de ces analytes est due à la charge minérale. Microscopique analyse des fragments et des minéraux de gangue montrent comparables à ceux constatés dans les sulfures mixtes minerais à proximité de la grotte. des motifs PXRD et la microscopie de polarisation indiquent des températures allant de la métallurgie 600-700°C à 1100°C.

Mots-clés: *Sardaigne, Moyen Age du Bronze, archéométrie, artefacts de cuivre, propriétés technologiques*

---

[*] Corresponding author.

1. Introduction

The Archaeometallurgical studies in Sardinia are a new field of investigation. In a recent study some Sardinian Early and Middle Bronze Age metal swords and daggers have been analyzed by EDS-AAS and by ICP-MS for lead isotope ratios (Sanna, Valera, Lo Schiavo 2011). Until today this work represented the only research on Early and Middle Bronze Age metal artifacts of Sardinia.

In 2012, a metalwork station and some metal artifacts of Middle Bronze Age were found by the Dipartimento di Storia, Beni Culturali e Territorio of Cagliari University (Sardinia, Italy), during the excavation of the karst cave of Monte Meana-Santadi (south-western Sardinia). With the aim to reconstruct the ancient technological aspects of metallurgy (as the use of alloys and the raw materials used by local prehistoric people) by spectroscopic and X-ray techniques and polarizing microscope we determined the qualitative and quantitative chemical characterization and the mineralogical composition of the found materials.

2. The archaeological site

The area covered by this research is the historical region of Sulcis in south-western Sardinia (Italy). The geological context is characterized by Cambrian limestones, dolostones and shales, and by Ordovician clastic metasediments; these geological sequences host several types of ore deposits, including sphalerite, galena, chalcopyrite and other silver–lead rich copper sulphide ores, along with

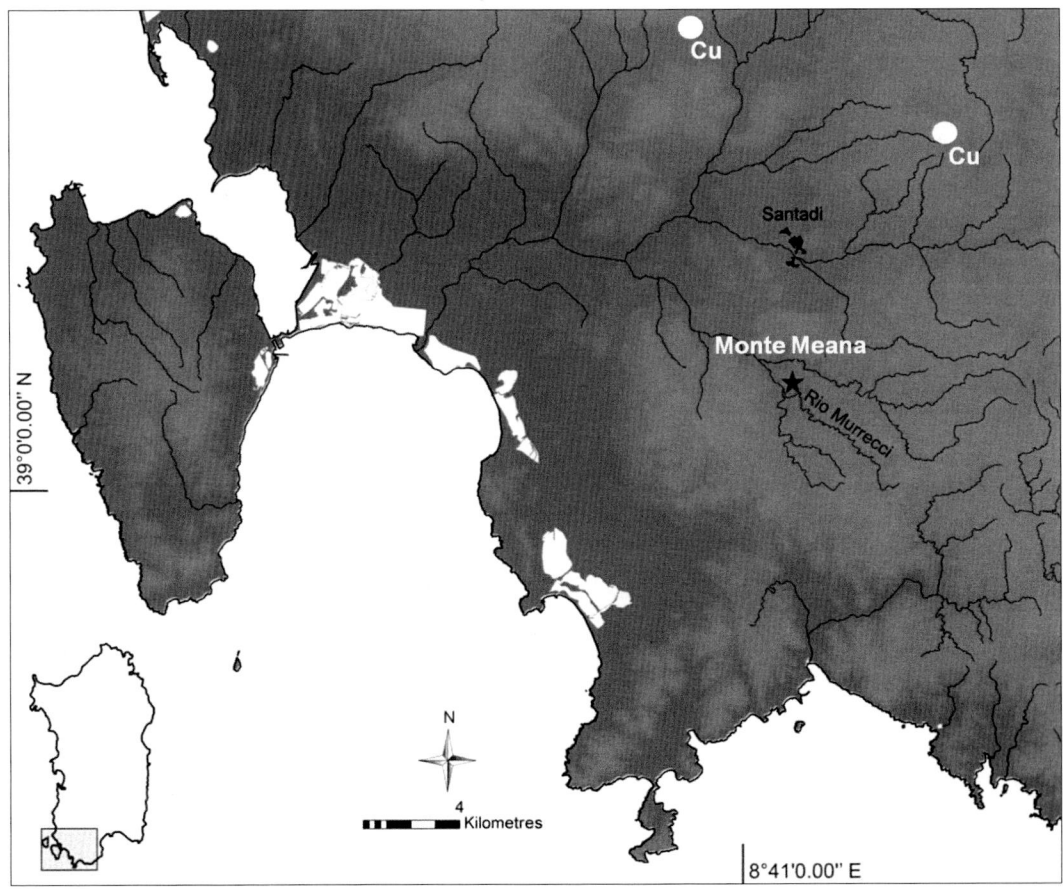

FIGURE 1. MAP OF SOUTH-WEST SARDINIA (ITALY) AND LOCATION OF THE MONTE MEANA CAVE AND CLOSE MINES OF COPPER (ELABORATED BY BUOSI ET AL. 2014).

iron oxides, fluorite and barite (Marcello *et al.* 2008). The cave of Monte Meana is located 4 km from Santadi, in the province of Carbonia-Iglesias. It is a karst cave hosted by Lower Cambrian carbonate rocks located at 236 m above the sea level. A small river (Riu Murecci) flows at the foot of the cave. Within 10 km from the cave, several minor copper ores occur in the areas of Monte Tamara and Rosas-Sa Marchesa mines (Buosi *et al.* 2014) (Fig. 1). In the 1960's the cave has been quarried for the extraction of onyx, leading to the destruction of most of the archaeological strata. Nevertheless, five recent excavation campaigns conducted by Giuseppa Tanda, Full Professor at the University of Cagliari, have identified some archaeological areas not affected by modern interventions (Paglietti 2010; Tanda *et al.* 2012; Buosi *et al.* 2014). One of these is located on the south side of the cave, an area of metallurgical activities (layer 27) characterized by a little fire place with several smelting slags, charcoals fragments and vitrified ceramic (Figg. 2, 3). Radiocarbon measurements on a

FIGURE 2. THE INTERIOR OF THE CAVE WITH THE INDICATION OF THE FINDING OF THE SLAGS AND THE DAGGER.

FIGURE 3. SLAGS AND DATED CHARCOAL FOUND AREA.

Site	Layer	Definition	Local phase	Lab. code	Material	14C date BP	δ13(‰)	Cal. BC 68.2%	Cal. BC 95.4%
Monte Meana cave	27	Smelting furnace	*Sa Turricula*	LTL6007A	charcoal	3463 ± 50	-24.6 ± 0.2	1878-1696	1909-1646
Sa Turricula Hut 2	2	fireplace	*Sa Turricula*	R-963α	charcoal	3460 ± 50	-24.5 ± 0.2	1878-1695	1901-1643

TABLE 1. 14C DATES OF THE MONTE MEANA CAVE'S SMELTING FURNACE AND SA TURRICULA DOMESTIC AREA. OXCAL V4.2.4 (BRONK RAMSEY, SCOTT, VAN DER PLICHT 2013); R:5: INTCAL 13 ATMOSPHERIC CURVE (REIMER *ET AL*. 2013).

charcoal fragment found amid the slags dated the smelting furnace between 1920 and 1660 BC (2σ) cal. BC, at the beginning of the Middle Bronze Age (Tab. 1). Close to this area we have found a leaf shaped metal dagger with two rivets typical of the Middle Bronze age of the local *Sa Turricula* phase (Fig. 4). Several daggers of this kind were found in some archaeological sites of Sardinia: from the dolmenic grave of Ena 'e Muros-Ossi-Sassari, from the hut 1 of Sa Turricula-Muros-Sassari, from the hypogeic tomb of Sant'Iroxi-Decimoputzu-Cagliari and from the *tomba di giganti* number 2 of Iloi-Sedilo-Oristano (Bagella 2003). In particular, the dagger discovered in the floor of the hut 1 of Sa Turricula village is supported by radiocarbon dating (Alessio *et al.* 1976 334) that confirmed the cultural attribution of the dagger of Monte Meana and the relationships with a local metallurgical activity (Tab. 1).

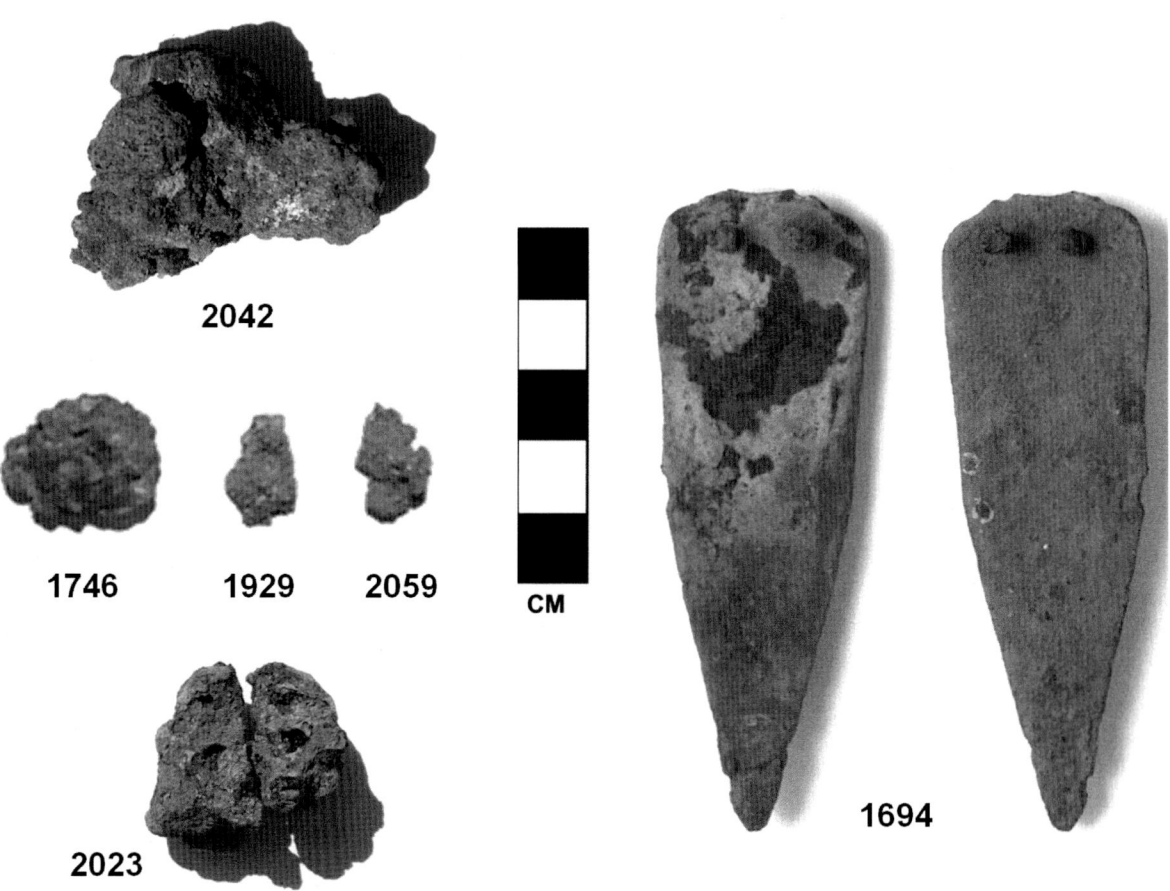

FIGURE 4. THE SLAGS AND THE DAGGER.

3. Metalworking processes in the Bronze Age

After mining, ore minerals were processed with removal of gangue (barren rock) by means of mechanical crushing and gravimetric separation; reduced to small fragments, the ore underwent to a stream of water that carried away the gangue and precipitate the heavier minerals on the bottom of the containers (Giardino 2010 55). Mineral processing was followed by the smelting phase. In the case of copper carbonates, metals were directly smelted from the ores for instance, inside a pit furnace (furnace bowl). The heating of carbonates with a wood or coal fire, leaded to their transformations into oxides and dioxides (e.g. $CuCO_3 \cdot Cu(OH)_2 \rightarrow 2\ CuO + CO_2 + H_2O$). The reduction from oxides to metal could be achieved in a fournace in which the combustion, in presence of forced air draught, produced high temperatures (1000°C-1200°C) and provided CO_2 as the main reducing agent (Yazawa 1974). However, togheter with the useful mineral certain amounts of gangue were introduced. This material was separated during the smelting process, forming the predominant component of slags. For an efficient separation, copper metal and slags needed to be molten. In this case, the metal mass precipitated on the furnace bottom due to its high specific gravity and low viscosity (Atzeni 2011 20).

Copper sulphides could undergo a previous process of open-air roasting (Goffer 2007 147-148), necessary to transform sulphides into oxides in order to remove a large part of volatile elements as S and As. This refinement was necessary to keep a low sulphur level into the metal, enough to not affect negatively its mechanical properties. Roasting did not produced real slags but black or dark gray oxidated copper compounds. At this point, the sulphides were smelted. This could happen within pits or ceramic kilns, whose presence in archaeological sites is usually suspected from fictile fragments with vitrified interior surfaces. In such containers, the oxygen necessary to raise the combustion temperature up to the smelting point of the metal could be blown through the use of blowpipes (Giardino 2010 56-60; Atzeni 2011 21). The waste of smelting was represented by extraction slags while the useful product was a relatively pure metal (95-97%, whit small amounts of other metals as iron and sulphur), called black copper or blister copper. It was molten a second time in a crucible (melting phase) where the new formed slags were skimmed from the surface of the molten metal mass that, finally, was poured into molds or matrices to make the artifacts (casting phase) (Atzeni 2011 24-25).

4. Material and methods

4.1. Archaeological samples and analytical techniques

The investigations here described were conducted on the dagger (sample 1694) and five slag samples (sample 1746, 1929, 2059, 2023, 2042), coming from the metallurgical fireplace found inside the cave of Monte Meana-Santadi (Fig. 3A, B). A preliminary investigation on the slags and the dagger was performed by pXRF (Buosi *et al.* 2014). In this work we present a more detailed study. The first analytical approach was autoptic, aimed at defining, in broad terms, the characteristics of the samples detectable at a visual level: recognition by the naked eye of minerals through their colors, assessment of the possible presence of alterations, presence of cratering, porosity and blistering. Subsequently, the same findings were subjected to instrumental chemical analyses. In particular, there has been a new set of non-destructive and non-invasive measurements by portable Energy Dispersive X-ray Fluorescence (pXRF) for qualitative analyses of the materials. Further, a sample of slag (2042) was investigated by the polarizing microscope on transmitted light (thin polished section) and reflected light (metallographic polished cross section); a small portion of the same sample underwent X-ray Powder Diffraction (PXRD) and was analysed by ICP-OES after acid digestion. For the dagger, a few mg of unaltered metal bulk were removed under the corroded layers of the blade, and investigated by ICP-OES.

4.2. Instruments and softwares

ED-XRF analyses have utilised the ASSING LITHOS 3000 spectrophotometer, through the following analytical conditions: acquisition time 600 s; voltage 25 kV; electric current 150 µA;

collimator diameter 5 mm; distance from the sample 10 mm. For the qualitative attribution of the ED-XRF elemental signals, the software component ASSING LITHOS has been used. For ICP-OES analyses, we have used the Perkin Elmer OPTIMA 7000 DV spectrometer. The ICP-OES elemental concentrations have been determined by WinLab32 management system. The Rigaku Geigerflex X-ray diffractometer has worked under the following experimental conditions: voltage 30 kV; electric current 30 mA; angular range from 4° to 70° 2ϑ; goniometer step 0.05 ϑ/s; acquisition time 33'. The assignment of the diffraction patterns has made using the software MDI/Jade5.0. The microscopy studies in transmitted and reflected polarized light have been conducted by a Zeiss AxioPlan polarizing microscope.

5. Results

5.1. Autoptic analyses

5.1.1. Slags

The slags are distinctly coloured: blue-green colors can be indicative of the presence of copper oxides and carbonates, while yellow-brown colors are probably due to the presence of 'limonitic' iron oxides/hydroxides. These occurrences may indicate the formation of scoriaceous materials in a strongly reducing environment (Atzeni 2011 22). The specific gravity is high. The materials include copper drops, coal fragments and mineral charge. The structure is poorly porous, glassy and, in contrast to what usually happens in the melting slags, is not fluidal nor iso-oriented. This latter character suggests that they are smelting slags and not melting ones, as these are usually very fluid and glassy (Atzeni 2011 25).

5.1.2. Dagger

The artifact presents lightly cratered surfaces. Therefore, in wide parts of the surfaces is visible a thick mineralized layer. Its green colour highlights the presence of copper in the artifact (see Atzeni *et al.* 2011 146).

5.2. pXRF Analyses

5.2.1. Slags

From the qualitative point of view, the composition of the five slags is substantially identical (Fig. 5A, B). The Cu peaks intensities are greater than the other ones, suggesting that slags have been originated from copper smelting. There is also an high signal intensity of Fe, together with peaks of Zn, As, Pb, Ca, S, Rb, Sr and Mn. The presence of sulphur in the slags is an indication that the primary ore used in the metallurgical process contained sulphides.

5.2.2. Dagger

The elemental composition of the dagger and its right rivet, is identical (Fig. 5C, D). The highest signal intensity is that of Cu, while slight intensities have been evidenced for the peaks of Fe, Zn and As, definitely lower than in the slags. This may indicate a quite efficient refining, with few impurities in the metal. The presence of Zn and As in the artifact may be come from the original composition of the mineral feed. In fact, most of these analytes are volatile in the stages of roasting, smelting and melting of the metal but they do not pass off completely as vapor during the various metallurgical processes. The As, furthermore, tends to bind with the metallic Cu originating Cu arsenates, also detectable in the finished products. Sometimes, the presence of As on the artifacts can be also due to the formation of intentional or spontaneous Cu-As alloys (Atzeni 2011 25-26). Mn peaks are also evident in the spectra; Mn quickly oxidizes and slags together with Fe, but sometimes not completely. Therefore, traces of it can be found in all metallurgical steps, although it decreases from ore to finished product (Atzeni 2011 25). Very small S, Ca, Rb and Sr peaks were also detected.

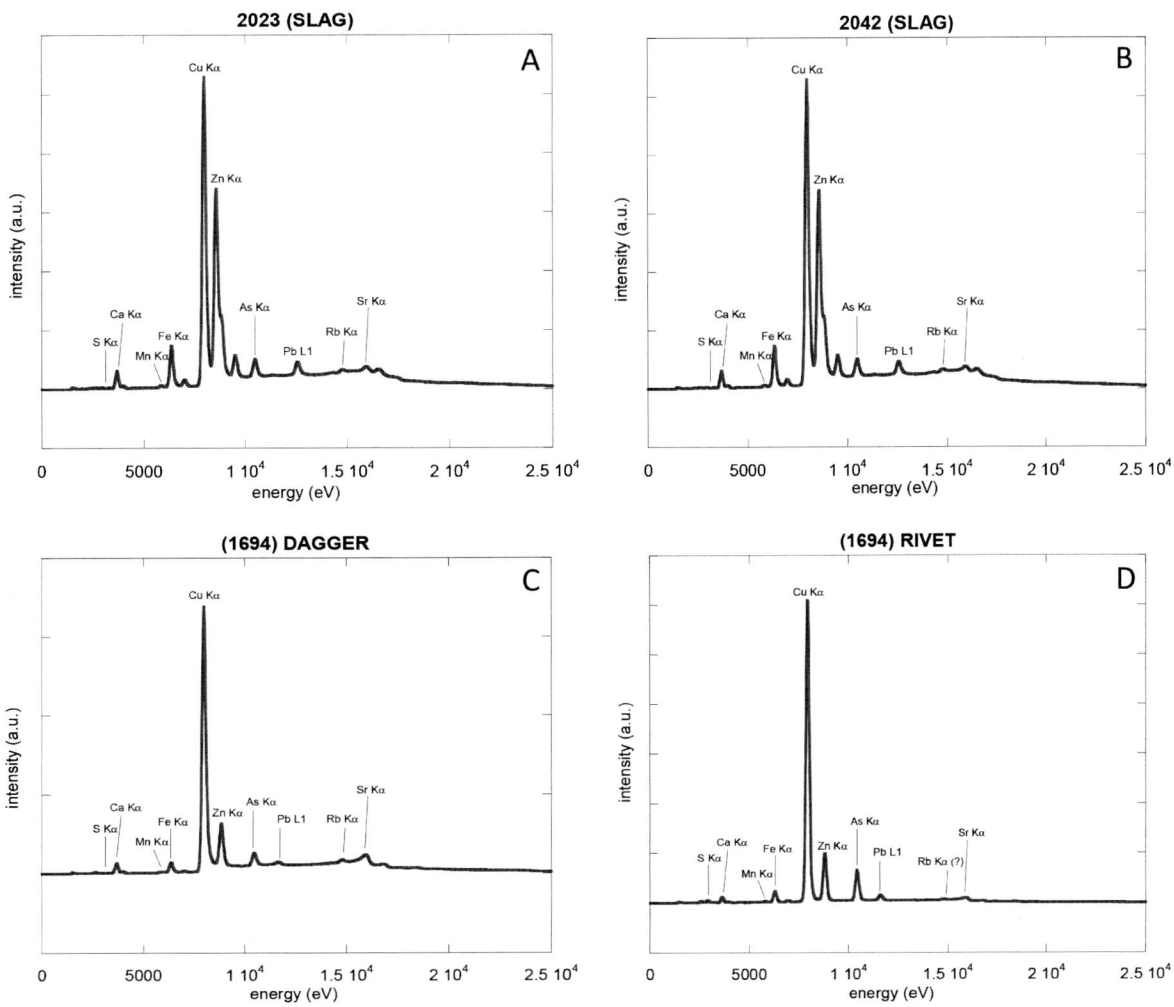

FIGURE 5. PXRF QUALITATIVE ELEMENTAL DATA OBTAINED ON THE METALLURGICAL SLAGS (A-B) AND THE DAGGER (C-D).

5.3. ICP-OES analyses

5.3.1. ICP-OES on the slags

The concentration of Cu in the sample 2042 (slag) is 7.44% (Tab. 2). High Fe concentration (8.40%) confirms that the slag derives from smelting processes rather than melting, that produces 'light slags' (Atzeni *et al.* 1986 153-154) generally containing low concentrations of Fe and little amounts of other metals (Atzeni 2011 25). Fe amounts in the slag can result from the original mineral feed; during reduction, Fe tends to bind with SiO_2, originating silicate minerals of iron (Atzeni 2011 22). Alternatively, a marked presence of Fe in the slag may also reflect the use of fluxing agents based on iron silicate during the reduction process (Giardino 2010 56). Pb concentration is 2.94%. Mn contents (0.05%) are related to the presence of mafic minerals. The small amounts of As (0.002%) and Sb (0.001%) in the slags are coherent with the high volatility of these elements during the metallurgical processes (Hauptmann 2007 28).

5.3.2. ICP-OES on the dagger

The quantitative chemical analyses on the sample 1694 (dagger) revealed Cu contents of 61.5% (Tab. 2). In the dagger Fe and Mn amounts are much lower than in the slags (0.14% and 0.006%,

2042 (SLAG)			1694 (DAGGER)		
Analyte	ppm	%	Analyte	ppm	%
Ni 231.604	2.4	0.00024	Ni 231.604	124.8	0.01248
Sb 206.836	12.4	0.00124	Sb 206.836	38	0.0038
Cu 324.752	74400	7.44	Cu 324.752	615000	61.50%
Cr 267.716	24	0.0024	Cr 267.716	28.4	0.00284
Se 196.026	3.6	0.00036	Se 196.026	0.8	0.00008
As 193.696	19.2	0.00192	As 193.696	0.8	0.00008
Ag 328.068	7.6	0.00076	Ag 328.068	2	0.0002
Be 313.107	0.4	0.00004	Be 313.107	0	0
Co 228.616	15.6	0.00156	Co 228.616	263.6	0.02636
Mn 257.610	512	0.0512	Mn 257.610	63.2	0.00632
Tl 190.801	2.4	0.00024	Tl 190.801	0.8	0.00008
Al 308.215	6708	0.6708	Al 308.215	2027.6	0.20276
Fe 239.562	83960	8.396	Fe 239.562	1406	0.1406
Cd 226.502	47.2	0.00472	Cd 226.502	32	0.0032
Pb 220.353	29440	2.944	Pb 220.353	27790	2.78
Zn 206.200	18640	1.864	Zn 206.200	1156	0.1156
Ca 317.933	10276	1.0276	Ca 317.933	10812	1.0812
U 409.014	1.6	0.00016	U 409.014	0.8	0.00008
Ba 233.527	2368.4	0.23684	Ba 233.527	32	0.0032
Cd 228.802	32.4	0.00324	Cd 228.802	10	0.001

TABLE 2. ANALITICAL CONTENTS (PPM AND %) FROM THE SLAG 2042 AND THE DAGGER 1694.

respectively): in the process of smelting, these analytes were held in large part from the slags (Atzeni 2011 25). The concentration of the Pb (2.78%) is high like in the slag. This metal is bounded with difficulty by the slags because of its high specific weight that leads it to precipitate on the bottom of the fusion (gravitational segregation). Pb is also practically immiscible in Cu (Atzeni *et al.*, 1986 150; Giardino 1987 204). As content in the dagger is under the instrumental detection limit (<0.0001%), thus less than in the slag. Sb and Bi, often found in the metalliferous mineralisation of Sardinia, are absent in the dagger of Monte Meana. The same evidences have been reported for the dagger B4 of the cave I Frommosa-Villanovatulo (NU) (Atzeni *et al.*, 2011 142), attributable to the Bonnanaro Bronze Age culture (Cincotti, Demurtas, Lo Schiavo 1998 160).

5.4. Microscopy

On polarizing microscope (samples prepared as polished thin sections and metallographic specimens for transmitted and reflected light examinations), sample 2042 (slag) reveals a widespread glassy matrix, in which are included small residues of gangue minerals, silicates, carbonates, coal fragments and widespread droplets of metal. The abundant presence of glass may be indicative of metallurgical processes reaching temperatures over 800°C (Fig. 6A). In transmitted light, both gangue minerals and newly-formed phases related to metallurgical processes have been detected. Gangue remnants are in most part represented by frequent quartz crystals and aggregates, usually fractured by heath; their presence, along with that of some rock fragment (shales), testify of low-effective mineral processing. Quartz-bearing gangues are known in many metalliferous mineralisation from southern Sardinia (Sulcis region). Similar quartz inclusions were noted in a cupric fragment derived from sulphide reduction found in the hut of 12 nuragic Genna Maria-Villanovaforru-Cagliari (Atzeni *et al.* 1986 149). Rare fragments of coal, incorporated into the scoriaceous mass during the operations of

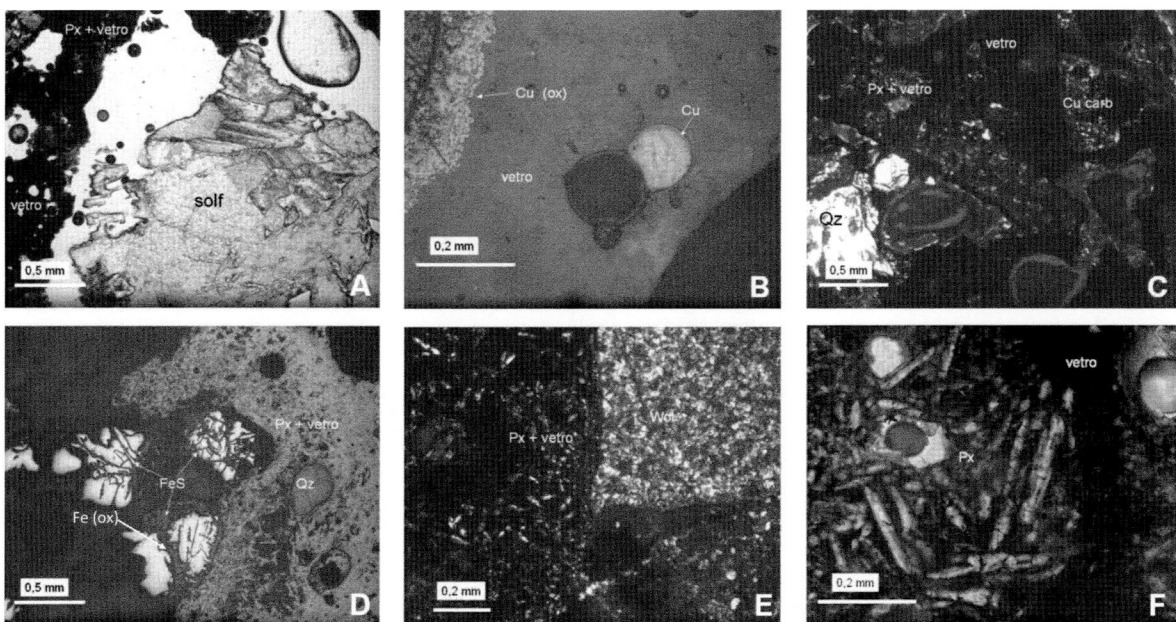

FIGURE 6. MICROSCOPIC FEATURES OF THE METALLURGICAL SLAG 2042. THIN SECTION (TRANSMITTED LIGHT): A) PYROXENE, SULFIDES AND GLASSY MATRIX (// NICOLS); C) MALACHITE, QUARTZ GANGUE, PYROXENE AND GLASS MATRIX (+ NICOLS); E) WOLLASTONITE (+ NICOLS); F) PIROXENE (+ NICOLS). METALLOGRAPHIC CROSS SECTION (REFLECTED LIGHT): B) METALLIC COPPER DROPS AND COPPER OXIDES; D) IRON SULPHIDES (PYRRHOTITE).

smelting, have also been observed. Newly-formed minerals observed in transmitted light are mostly represented by silicates, including abundant pyroxenes (augites) and wollastonite (Fig. 6E); the presence of this Ca-silicate may indicate pyrometallurgical processes operating around 600-700°C (Deer *et al.* 2006 23, fig. 2.4). Reflected light microscopy allowed to study opaque and metallic minerals. Immersed in the matrix, frequent drops of metallic copper, often covered by multi-layered oxides including cuprite (Cu_2O; Fig. 6B), are visible. Other drops are evidently carbonated, with formation of malachite and other carbonates of Cu (Fig. 6C). There are also distinguishable phases of iron minerals, in the form of sulphides, oxides and hydroxides. Ferrous sulphide is presented in frequent small aggregates; it shows the optical features of pyrrhotite (Fig. 6A, D). Its presence may confirm that the mineral feed used in reduction process may have consisted of mixed (Fe-Cu-Pb-Zn) sulphides, possibly coming from some small ores of the same area (as Monte Tamara-Narcao; Fig. 1; Marcello *et al.* 2008). Among the Fe oxidates, 'limonitic' ones (as goethite) are the most spread; magnetite has been also observed (Fig. 6D).

5.5. PXRD analyses

X-Ray Powder Diffraction was performed on selected portions of the 5 slag samples. PXRD patterns substantially confirmed the mineralogy evidenced from microscopy studies, with presence of quartz, wollastonite, pyroxenes (diopside, augite), feldspars (sanidine), Fe oxides/hydroxides (magnetite, gohetite) and amorphous (vitreous) matter. Among silicates, particular relevance has the probable detection of ferrous olivine (fayalite), whose presence indicates that was not exceeded the temperature of 1100°C, beyond which fayalite, especially under reducing conditions (see par. 5.1.1), decomposes to quartz and magnetite (Hauptmann 2007 193). Concerning the metallic minerals, Cu carbonates (malachite) and hydroxide chlorides (atacamite) were identified.

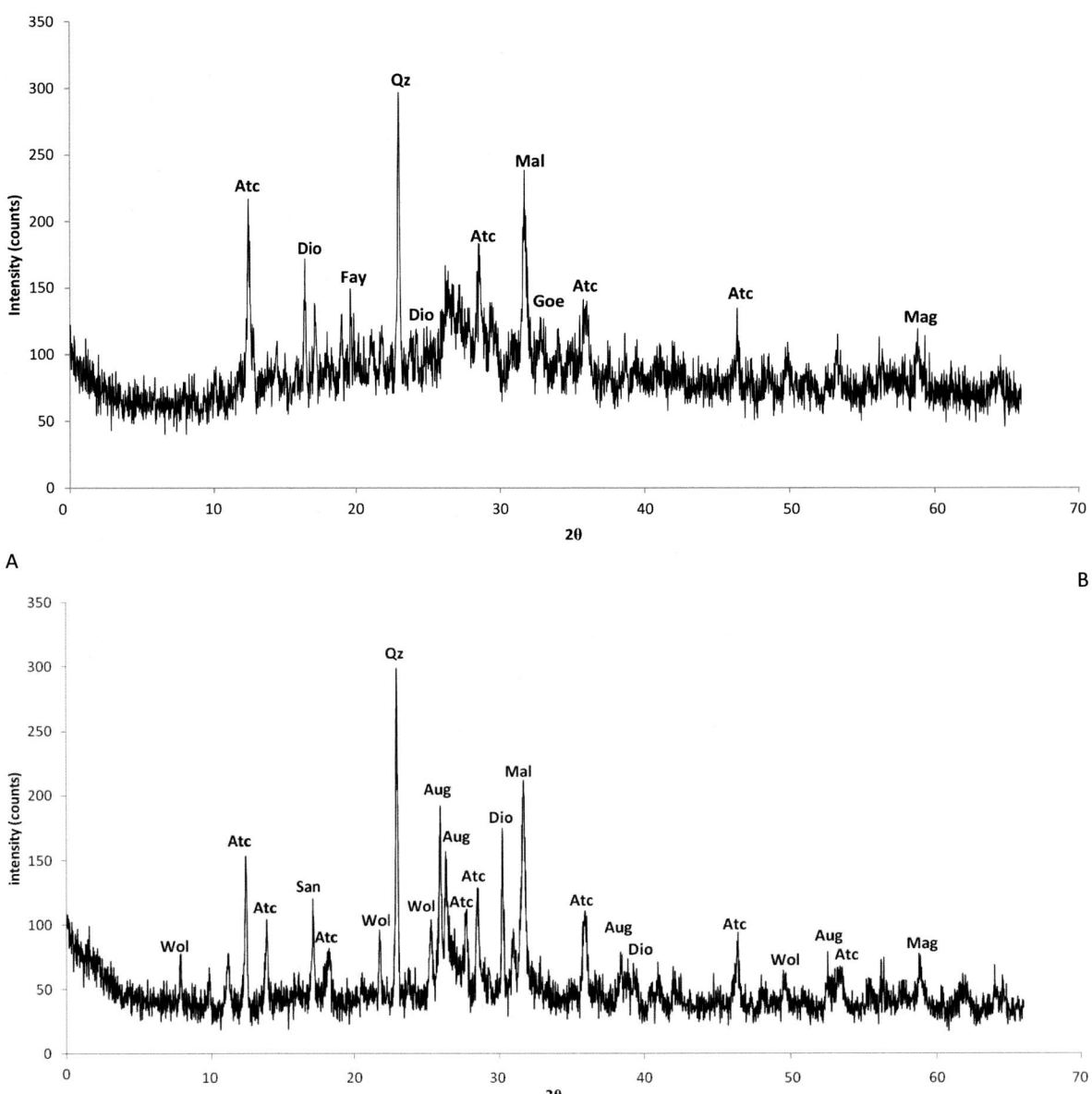

FIGURE 7. A, B. MAIN CRYSTALLOGRAPHIC PHASES OF THE SLAG 2042. QZ: QUARTZ; MAL: MALACHITE; AUG: AUGITE; ATC: ATACAMITE; DIO: DIOPSIDE; SAN: SANIDINE; WOL: WOLLASTONITE; FAY: FAYALITE; MAG: MAGNETITE; GOE: GOHETITE.

6. Discussion

The high signal intensity of Cu in the five slag samples' pXRF spectra, and the high concentration of the same metal in the ICP-OES measurements performed on the sample 2042, confirm the link of these waste products to copper metallurgy. The poorly fluid and glassy appearance of the slags indicates that they resulted from the smelting process. This is also confirmed by the high percentage of Fe and Mn detected for the slag sample 2042 by ICP-OES. Fe and Mn can be derived directly from the original mineral fill. Also, S (pXRF on five slags), As, Zn (pXRF on five slags and ICP on sample 2042) and Sb (ICP on sample 2042) represent residual elements coming from mineral charge that were not eliminated by metallurgical refining. Residues of gangue minerals and shales, identified by microscopy and PXRD, are compatible with the Paleozoic formations hosting the mixed sulphides deposits outcropping in the Sulcis. The three mineralogical thermometers (glass matrix, wollastonite and fayalite), recognized in the sample 2042, indicate that metallurgical temperatures never exceeded 1100°C.

Even in the dagger Cu is the predominant metal. The low amounts of Fe and Mn in this artifact, evidenced from both pXRF and ICP-OES analyses, can be an indication of good refining. The residual sulphur detected by pXRF suggests that the metallurgical processes can be involved sulphide minerals. Only traces of As and Zn are present in the artifact. This fact seems to exclude the possibility of an intentional Cu-As alloy, because percentages of As over 2% are requested for alloying (Pernicka et al. 1990, Hauptmann 2007 28). However, future analyses on the metalliferous ores of Sulcis closed to Monte Meana (especially Monte Tamara-Narcao) could be able to clarify if the presence of As in this artifact is due to raw materials or to purposefully alloying.

7. Conclusions

The multidisciplinary approach adopted in the study for the analysis of the metallurgical slags and the dagger from the Monte Meana cave, allowed to highlight the close compositional relationship between all the examined remains. It is very probable that the dagger was produced through a metallurgical process performed inside the cave. This metallurgical activity is typical of the Sardinian Early Middle Bronze cultural phase of *Sa Turricula*, as shown by radiometric dating obtained from the pyrometallurgic working area of Monte Meana and by the comparison with the metal daggers found in the Santadi site and in the *Sa Turricula* one. The *Sa Turricula* dagger allows some considerations on technological strategies in the production of similar copper artifacts: the analyses carried out on it, show an As content of 2% (Cincotti, Demurtas, Lo Schiavo 1998 159-164), which appears to differs from the low percentage found on the Monte Meana artifact. This difference can be interpreted as a sign of the impossibility to standardised the protohistoric Sardinian technological processes performed to obtain copper artifacts. To the contrary, it indicates different productive processes, probably influenced by the different employed copper minerals.

Acknowledgements

We are grateful especially to the prof. Giuseppa Tanda of University of Cagliari for encouraging this research. We would like to thank Antonello Pilloni and Raffaele Cani, president and administrator of Cantina Santadi respectively, for the research funding. A particular word of thanks also goes to Remo Forresu, the curator of the Archaeological Museum of Santadi, for his willingness.

References

Alessio, M.; Bella, F.; Improta, S.; Belluomini, G.; Calderoni, G.; Cortesi, C.; Turi, B. 1976. University of Rome carbon date XIV, *Radiocarbon* 18 (3), 321-349.

Atzeni, C. 2011. Alcuni aspetti della metallurgia antica. In U. Sanna, R. G. Valera, F. Lo Schiavo (eds.), *Archeometallurgia in Sardegna. Dalle origini al primo ferro*. Cagliari: DIGITA, 18-37.

Atzeni, C.; Massidda, L.; Sanna, U.; Virdis, P. F. 1986. Archeometallurgia nuragica nel territorio di Villanovaforri. In Atti del II Convegno di Studi *Un millennio di relazioni fra la Sardegna e i paesi del Mediterraneo*, Cagliari: Stef, 147-165.

Atzeni, C.; Massidda, L.; Sanna, U. 2011. I dati archeometrici. In Sanna, U.; Valera, R. G.; Lo Schiavo, F. (eds.), *Archeometallurgia in Sardegna. Dalle origini al primo ferro*. Cagliari: DIGITA, 134-221.

Bagella, S. 2003. Un pugnaletto dalla tomba di giganti 2 di Iloi (Sedilo, OR). In G.Tanda (ed.) La Tombe di Giganti 2 di Iloi (Sedilo OR), *Antichità Sarde* 4 (I-IV), 249-254.

Buosi, C.; Pittau, P.; Paglietti, G.; Scanu, G. G.; Serra, M.; Ucchesu, M.; Tanda, G. 2015. A Human Occupation Cave during the Bronze Age: Archaeological and Palynological Applications of a Case Study in Sardinia (Western Mediterranean). *Archaeometry* 57, 1, 212-231. DOI 10.1111/arcm.12132.

CINCOTTI, A.; DEMURTAS, G.; LO SCHIAVO, F. 1998. Copper arsenic in the prehistory of Sardinia. Archaeometric determinations, *Proceedings of The Fourth International Conference on the Beginning of the Use on Metals and Alloy (BUMA IV)*, Kunibiki Messe Matsue: Shimane, Japan, 159-164.

DEER, W. A, HOWIE, R. A.; ZUSSMAN, W. S. 2006. *Rock-Forming Minerals,* Vol. 4B. Framework Silicates-Silica Minerals, Feldspathoids and Zeolites. 2nd edition. London: Geological Society of London.

GIARDINO, C. 1987. Sfruttamento minerario e metallurgia nella Sardegna protostorica. In Balmuth, M. S. (ed.), *Studies in ancient Sardinia III. Nuragic Sardinia and the mycenean world.* BAR International Series 387, Oxford: Archaeopress, 189-219.

GIARDINO, C. 2010. *I metalli nel mondo antico: introduzione all'archeometallurgia*, Roma-Bari: Laterza.

GOFFER, Z. 2007. *Archaeological Chemistry*. 2nd edition. Hoboken: John Wiley.

HAUPTMANN, A. 2007. *The Archaeometallurgy of Copper. Evidence from Faynan, Jordan.* Berlin-Heidelberg-New York: Springer.

MARCELLO, A.; MAZZELLA, A.; NAITZA, S.; PRETTI, S.; TOCCO, S.; VALERA, P.; VALERA, R. 2008. *Carta metallogenica e delle Georisorse della Sardegna (Scala 1:250.000)*. Firenze: Litografia artistica Cartografica.

PAGLIETTI, G. 2010. Notiziario. Monte Meana (Santadi, Prov. di Carbonia-Iglesias). *Rivista di Scienze Preistoriche* 60, 393.

PERNICKA, E.; BEGEMANN, F.; SCHMITT-STRECKER, S, GRIMANIS, A. P. 1990. On the composition and provenance of metal artefacts from Poliochni on Lemnos. *Oxford Journal of Archaeology* 9, 3, 263-298.

REIMER, P. J.; BARD, E.; BAYLISS, A.; BECK, J. W.; BLACKWELL, P. G.; BRONK RAMSEY, C.; GROOTES, P. M.; GUILDERSON, T. P.; HAFLIDASON, H.; HAJDAS, I.; HATTŽ, C.; HEATON, T. J.; HOFFMANN, D. L.; HOGG, A. G.; HUGHEN, K. A.; KAISER, K. F.; KROMER, B.; MANNING, S. W.; NIU, M.; REIMER, R. W.; RICHARDS, D. A.; SCOTT, E. M.; SOUTHON, J. R.; STAFF, R. A.; TURNEY, C. S. M.; VAN DER PLICHT, J. 2013. IntCal13 and Marine13 Radiocarbon Age Calibration Curves 0-50,000 Years cal BP. *Radiocarbon* 55, 4, 1869-1887.

SANNA, U.; VALERA, R.; LO SCHIAVO, F. (eds.) 2011. *Archeometallurgia in Sardegna: dalle origini al primo ferro.* Cagliari: DIGITA.

TANDA, G.; BASCIU, V.; PAGLIETTI, G.; PEÑA CHOCARRO, L.; UCCHESU, M.; ZEDDA, M. 2012. *Grotta di Monte Meana (Santadi, Carbonia-Iglesias), campagne di scavo 2008-2009. Notizia preliminare.* In La Preistoria e la Protostoria della Sardegna. Atti della XLIV riunione scientifica dell'Istituto Italiano di Preistoria e Protostoria, III, 877-884.

YAZAWA, A. 1974. Thermodynamic considerations of copper smelting. *Canadian Metallurgical Quaterly* 13, 3, 443-453.

Bronze Age silver artifacts from Romania – an archaeo-metallurgical study

Bogdan CONSTANTINESCU, Daniela CRISTEA-STAN
National Institute for Nuclear Physics and Engineering, Bucharest, Romania

Anca-Diana POPESCU
'Vasile Parvan' Institute of Archaeology, Bucharest, Romania

Abstract

Bronze Age silver artifacts were found mainly in Extra-Carpathian region of Romania, despite Inter-Carpathian region (Transylvania) is famous for its rich in silver (until 30%) native gold. The most spectacular aspect of these Bronze Age artifacts is the predominant presence of 'exotic' alloys as auriferous silver and high-content copper silver alloy. Our archaeo-metallurgical study was performed using X-Ray Fluorescence (XRF) non-destructive elemental analysis technique. The first artifacts studied were hair rings discovered in graves belonging to the early period of EBA (the second half of the fourth millennium BC – the first half of the third millennium BC) in Southern Romania, the most interesting item being a gilded silver spiral ring from Ariceștii Rahtivani. We continued with two cases of silver weapons: a dagger found at Poduri, Central Moldavia, made from a strange silver-copper alloy and the auriferous silver axes from Perșinari. Because the axes are broken, it was possible to investigate their bulk structure. The microscope examination revealed a mixture of silver alloys nuggets also including few gold nuggets, suggesting an incomplete melting. Auriferous silver was also identified in a metallic disc of Vulchitrun type found in Călărași. A comparison with other Bronze Age artifacts realized from similar 'exotic' alloys is discussed. The similarities with artifacts found in Eastern Mediterranean – Middle East area (auriferous silver) and with Kozarac-type axes found in former Yugoslavia, now in Axel Guttmann collection (high-content copper silver alloy) are evident. Despite it is not possible yet to distinguish between natural and anthropic alloys, the provenance of our artifacts from Eastern Mediterranean area, including Anatolia and possibly Caucasus, is a credible hypothesis.

Key-words: *Bronze Age, Lower Danube area, auriferous silver, silver-copper alloy, gilded silver, X-Ray Fluorescence*

Résumé

Des artefacts d'argent de l'Âge du Bronze ont été trouvés principalement dans la région extra-Carpates de la Roumanie, malgré la région Inter-Carpates (Transylvanie) est célèbre pour sa richesse en argent (jusqu'à 30%) de l'or natif. L'aspect le plus spectaculaire de ces artefacts de l'Âge du Bronze est la présence prédominante d'alliages 'exotiques' comme l'argent aurifère et l'alliage d'argent en haute teneur de cuivre. Notre étude archéo-métallurgique a été réalisée à l'aide de la technique d'analyse non-destructive élémentaire de X-Ray Fluorescence (XRF). Les premiers objets étudiés étaient des anneaux de cheveux découverts dans des tombes appartenant à la première période de l'EBA (entre la deuxième moitié du quatrième millénaire a. J.C. et la première moitié du troisième millénaire a.J.C.) en Roumanie du Sud, l'élément le plus intéressant était un anneau en spirale en argent doré de Ariceștii Rahtivani. Nous avons continué avec deux cases d'armes d'argent: un poignard trouvé à Poduri, dans la Moldavie centrale, fabriqué à partir d'un alliage argent-cuivre étrange et les axes d'argent aurifère de Perșinari. Soit que les axes sont rompus, il a été possible d'étudier leur structure de masse. L'examen au microscope a révélé un mélange d'alliages de pépites d'argent incluant aussi quelques pépites d'or, ce qui suggère une fusion incomplète. L'argent aurifère a également été identifié dans un disque métallique de type Vulchitrun trouvé dans Călărași. Une comparaison avec d'autres objets de l'Âge du Bronze réalisés à partir d'alliages similaires 'exotiques' est discutée. Les similitudes avec les artefacts trouvés dans la Méditerranée orientale – région du Moyen-Orient (argent aurifère) et avec axes du type Kozarac trouvés dans l'ex-Yougoslavie, maintenant dans la collection Axel Guttmann (alliage de cuivre à haute teneur en argent) sont évidents. Malgré qu'il ne soit pas encore possible de faire la distinction entre les alliages naturels et anthropiques, la provenance de nos artefacts de Méditerranée orientale, y compris l'Anatolie et peut-être du Caucase, est une hypothèse crédible.

Mots-clés: *Âge du Bronze, région du Bas Danube, argent aurifère, alliage argent-cuivre, argent doré, Fluorescence Ray X*

Introduction

The earliest silver objects appeared in Southeastern Europe during the Eneolithic/Chalcolithic period, more precisely between 4500-3500 BC. They are mostly jewellery items, such as pendants, rings, beads and bracelets. Among the most famous early discoveries one could mention Alepotrypa Cave – Southern Peloponnese, Eileithyia Cave – Amnissos, Crete island, Štramberk – Czech Republic and Tiszalúc-Sarkad – Hungary (Maran 2000, 185-187; Makkay 1976, 287-288; Patay, Szathmári 2001, 5-13). During the second half of the fourth millennium and the first half of the third millennium BC the variety and quantity of silver objects in Southeastern Europe, Caucasus and Near East increased. We can talk about a whole range of types of jewellery (headbands, bracelets, pendants, hair-rings, beads, pins), weapons (daggers, shaft-hole axes, spearheads) and vessels, the largest number coming from funerary contexts – burials (Primas 1995, 80-88; Hansen 2014). Starting with the end of the fourth millennium BC we have more and more evidences concerning the smelting of silver from lead ores through cupellation from Aegean and Near East areas (Gale and Stos-Gale 1981, 176-192; Pernicka 1995, 58). Impressive through their aspect, variety and multitude are the silver objects discovered inside the burial mounds of Maikop culture, dated to 3800/3600-3000 BC, in the area of Kuban (Chernykh 1992, 67-83; Rezepkin 2000; Hansen 2014). Elements of Maikop culture spread through the southern region of Caucasus, as shown by recent finds discovered at Soyuq Bulaq (Azerbaidjan) (Courcier *et al.* 2008, 21-34). In the barrows no. 1 and 4 from this site were found some beads and rings made of silver and auriferous silver. These two barrows were assigned to the first half of the fourth millennium BC. A large amount of remarkable silver objects was also found in sites from Anatolia, such as Arslantepe, Troy, Alacahöyük, Eskiyapar, mainly dated to the third millennium BC (Frangipane *et al.* 2001; Tolstikov, Treister 1996; Koşay 1955; Koşay 1951; Özgüç, Temızer 1993). The precious metal used for making jewellery and vessels in Cyclades islands during the third millennium BC was mainly silver, perhaps due to its availability (a source of silver was found on the Siphnos island and another one was located in close proximity to the Cyclades, at Laurion). The Cretan silver production – characterized by a relative large number of silver daggers (six in total) – must be also mentioned (Renfrew 1967; Primas 1991, 184).

In the Middle and Lower Danube area, the most items made of silver were found in graves, mainly attributed to the Yamnaya culture (late fourth to mid-third millennium BC). In most cases they were hair-rings (Motzoi-Chicideanu, Olteanu 2000, 28-32, 55-57). Very spectacular silver artifacts were found in the former Yugoslavia and Romania: the silver shaft-hole axes from Mala Gruda and Stari Jancovci, those from Axel Guttmann's collection, the shaft-hole axes from Perşinari hoard and the dagger from Poduri (Primas 1996; Balen, Mihelić 2007; Hansen 2001; Vulpe 1997; Munteanu, Dumitroaia 2010). As time-evolution, in the Middle and Lower Danube area the number of silver artefacts dramatically decreased starting from the second half of the third millennium BC, together with an important increasing presence of various gold adornments. For the first half of the second millennium BC there are less and less silver artefacts both from Southeastern Europe and Anatolia. A revival of the silver metallurgy occurred only with the second half of the same millennium in Mycenaean Greece, while the silver objects in the Lower Danube area remained still scarce.

Experimental

The analyses were performed with an Oxford Instruments portable spectrometer X-MET 3000TX+, were the exciting X-ray beam is generated by a Rh anode tube. The measurement spot size is about 30 mm². The spectrometer has a Hewlett-Packard (HP) iPAQ personal data assistant (PDA) for software management and data storage (Constantinescu *et al.* 2012, 21).

We studied a large number of Bronze Age silver items found in Southern Romania: 33 Early Bronze Age (EBA) hair rings discovered in graves at Ariceştii Rahtivani, Ploieşti-Triaj (both from Prahova county), Zimnicea (Teleorman county), Pleniţa and Verbiţa (Dolj county), 32 beads from an EBA cemetery at Zimnicea, a hafting-plate dagger from Poduri (Bacău county), at least four broken shaft-

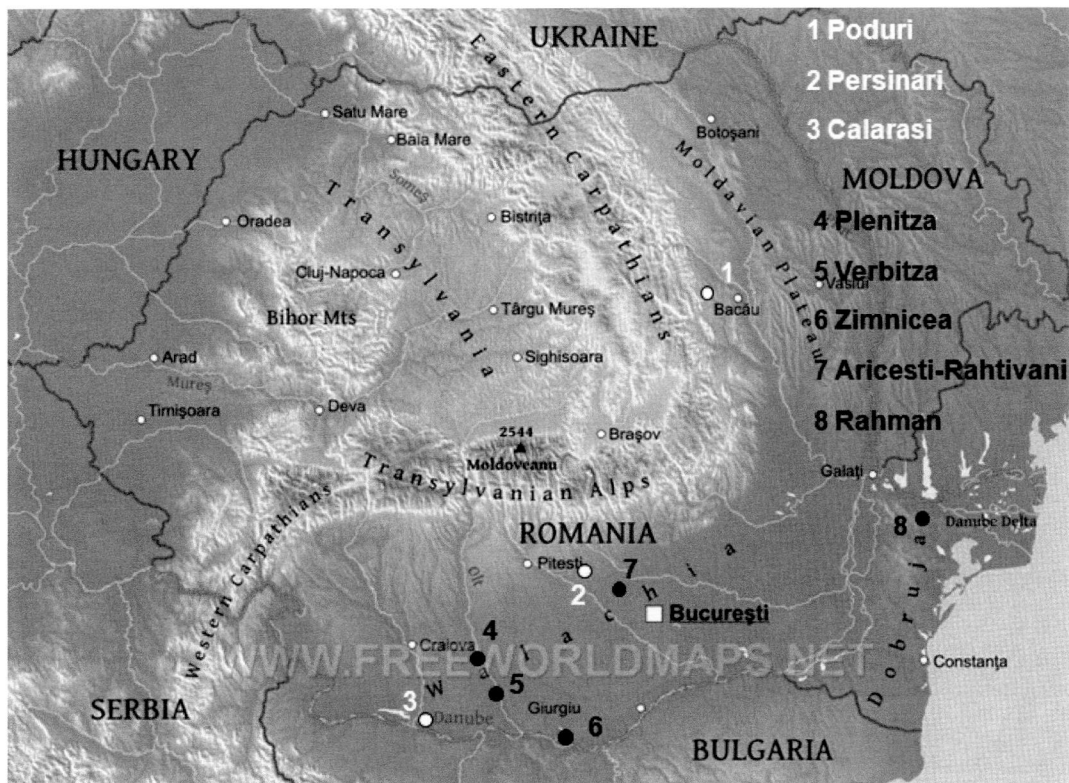

FIGURE 1. MAP OF SILVER ARTIFACTS PROVENANCE SITES.

hole axes from Perşinari hoard (Dâmboviţa county) and a Vulchitrun-type disc accidentally found some 40 years ago at Călăraşi (Dolj county) – see Figure 1.

Silver hair rings

The hair rings were discovered in graves belonging to the early period of Early Bronze Age -EBA (the second half of the fourth millennium BC – the first half of the third millennium BC). They can be classified in three categories: simple rings (round shaped, made from a wire with a constant thickness), multi-spiral rings (made by twisting a wire or a bar), crescent-shaped rings with a thickened median area and thinner ends (Zimnicea-type – see Motzoi-Chicideanu, Olteanu 2000, 28, Popescu 2010, 166). The first two categories of rings – in gold, silver and copper – are often found in funerary inventories from the North Pontic (Black Sea) area – Maikop, Late Tripolye/Usatovo and Yamnaya cultures (Motzoi-Chicideanu, Olteanu 2000, 28-30; Gej 2000, 159-162; Ivanova 2007). Such rings can be also found in Anatolia – e.g. the spiral rings from Arslantepe 'royal tomb' and from Troy (Frangipane *et al.* 2001, 117, 119, fig. 19/6-9, 12-17; Tolstikov, Treister 1996, 191, no. 252). In the Middle and Lower Danube area, the presence of these rings is connected to the spreading of Yamnaya culture funerary practices. Crescent rings – in silver and gold – are found on both banks of Danube (Romania and Bulgaria). We must mention that similar gold crescent rings were discovered at Ampoiţa (Alba county, Central Romania) in a tumulus grave belonging to the Livezile group (Ciugudean 1996, 33, 127-128, fig. 31/8-9), in some graves from Leukas Greek island (Early Helladic II-III period) (Primas 1995, 84-85) and in the principal grave of Velika Gruda tumulus (Montenegro, on the Adriatic coast), dated to 2800-2700 BC (Primas 1996, 77-79). Because these rings were found mainly in the skull region, their use as hair rings (directly worn on hair locks or sewn on a textile hair cover) is generally accepted.

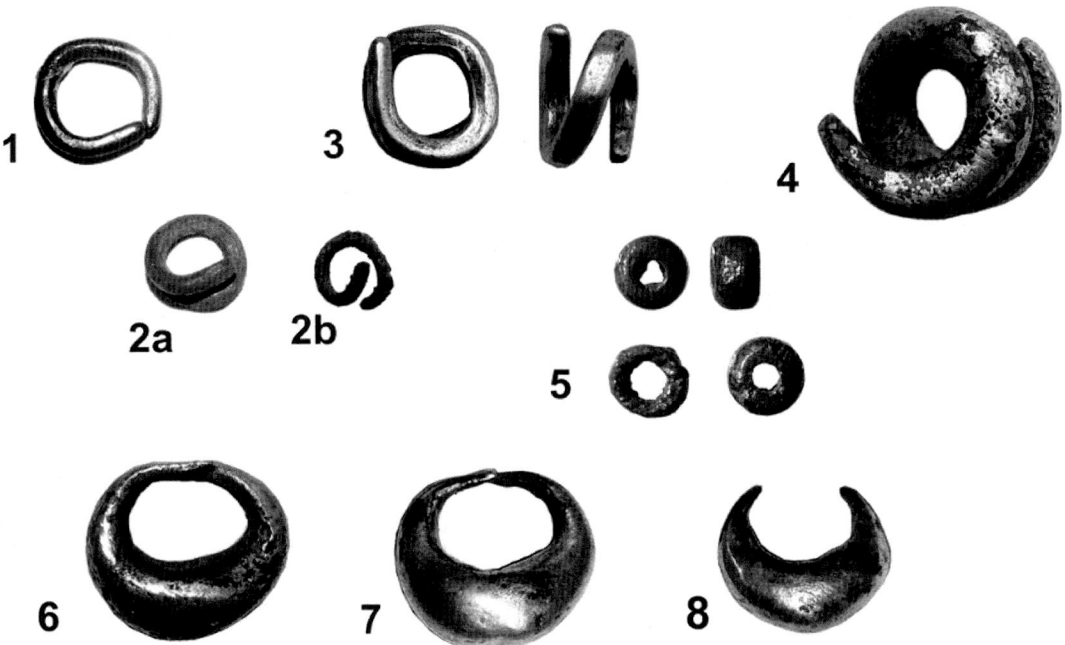

FIGURE 2. SILVER HAIR RINGS AND BEADS: 1. VERBIȚA; 2A-B. PLENIȚA;
3-6. ZIMNICEA; 7-8. ARICEȘTII RAHTIVANI.

Our analyses – practically surface ones (approx. 50 microns in depth), sometimes on partially cleaned areas – revealed different silver (alloy) compositions. Some hair rings have a very high content in silver and only traces of gold and copper; it is the case of a spiral-ring from Zimnicea grave no. 11 (Alexandrescu 1974): Ag=98.1%, Au=0.4%, Cu=0.5%, Pb=0.05%, Fe=0.8% (iron was very probably adsorbed from the soil – see Giumlia-Mair, Lucchini 2005, 407). Bromine – detected in most of analyzed rings – is a similar case with iron but related to corrosion process (Wanhill 2005). A similar composition has two spiral-rings from Plenița grave no. 1 (SCIV 1952, 164) – see Figure 2: Ag=96.1%, Au=0.7%, Cu=0.3%, Pb=0.1%, Fe=1.6%, Br traces and Ag=97.4%, Au=0.6%, Cu=0.5%, Pb=0.1%, Fe=0.5%, Br traces, respectively. However, there are also hair rings with a relevant copper content (higher in crescent as in spiral rings). It is the case of five crescent rings from Zimnicea grave no. 9 – see Figure 2; Ag=91.6–96.6%, Cu=1.8-6.8%, while the most of spiral rings from Zimnicea cemetery have only Cu=0.2–0.6%.

From the variation of Ag K_α ray/Ag K_β ray intensities ratio, on and far from the gilded area (Chiojdeanu et al. 2011, 690), a 30 microns thickness for the gold foil was estimated. The gilding procedure – mechanical adhesion with or without organic adhesives – can't be identified non-destructively. The oldest gilded silver items known until now are considered the nails with gilded heads discovered in the Eye-Temple at Tell Brak, Syria, with a debatable dating that has been push back to the first part of the fourth millennium BC (Mallowan 1947, 32, pl. IV/2; Oates et al. 2007, 596-597). From the second half of the fourth millennium BC, the gilding technique had spread, being often used in Syria-Mesopotamia region, Caucasus, Anatolia, Egypt – e.g. for the third millennium BC

A high copper content was also measured for two crescent rings – see Figure 2, items no. 7 and 8 – from Ariceștii Rahtivani tumulus grave no. 3 (Frînculeasa 2007, 185 –187; Frînculeasa et al. 2013, 24-25, 41): Ag=94.7%, Au=0.7%, Cu=3.8%, Pb=0.1%, Fe=0.7%, Br traces and Ag=94.6%, Au=0.7%, Cu=3.1%, Pb=0.1%, Fe=0.95, Br traces, respectively. A similar case is the round ring

	Ag	Cu	Au	Pb	Hair ring shape
Aricesti-374	94.6	3.1	0.7	0.1	crescent shaped
Aricesti-373	94.7	3.8	0.3	0.1	crescent shaped
Zimnicea-i2	91.7	6.8	0.4	0.09	crescent shaped
Zimnicea-i5	91.9	4.3	1.5	0.05	crescent shaped
Zimnicea-i1	94.9	3.2	0.3	0.1	crescent shaped
Zimnicea-i3	91.6	6.4	0.8	0.03	crescent shaped
Zimnicea-i4	96.6	1.8	0.2	0.03	crescent shaped
Verbita	94.6	1.5	2.3	0.2	round
Aricesti-1	90.4	6.6	0.1	0.02	spiral
Aricesti-2	93.8	4.2	0.1	0.02	spiral
Zimnicea-i10	96.6	1.3	0.25	0.1	spiral
Zimnicea-i12	93.4	0.6	0.2	0.1	spiral
Zimnicea-i15	98.1	0.5	0.4	0.05	spiral
Zimnicea-i13	96.9	0.8	0.4	0.02	spiral
Zimnicea-i11	93.81	0.3	0.2	0.2	spiral
Zimnicea-i8	90	0.1	0.15	0	spiral
Plenita1	96.1	0.3	0.7	0.1	spiral
Plenita 2	97.4	0.5	0.6	0.1	spiral

FIGURE 3. THE COMPOSITION OF THE ANALYZED SILVER HAIR RINGS.

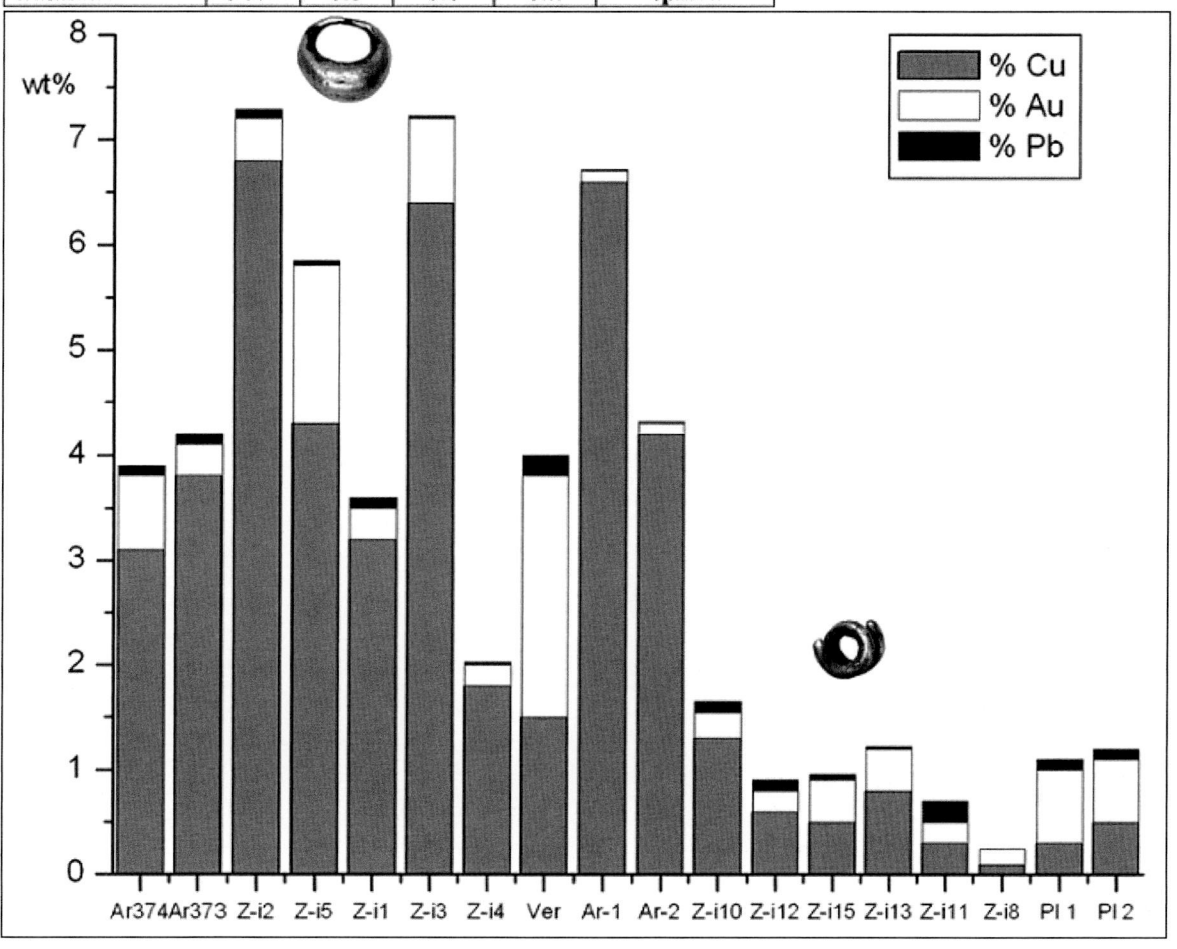

found in grave M1 from the second tumulus in Verbița (Berciu, Roman 1984, 16, fig. 1/3) – see Figure 2: Ag=94.6%, Au=2.3%, Cu=1.5%, Pb=0.2%, Fe=1%, Br traces; the high content in gold could suggests a rare geological silver source (in Serbia?). The explanation of relatively high copper content is the necessity of an increased hardness for the rings.

The most interesting analyzed silver artifact is the spiral ring found in Aricestii Rahtivani tumulus grave no. 1, near by the skull (Frînculeasa 2007, 185-187) – see Figure 4. It is made from a 2.5-2.8 mm thick silver wire covered with a thin gold foil relatively well preserved. The silver 'bulk' has the composition: Ag=95.8%, Au=1.7% (a probable influence of the gilding), Cu=1.2%, Fe=0.6%, Br traces. adornments from Karataş-Semayük (Mellink 1969, 323) and Ur (Plenderleith 1934, 295) graves and for the anthropomorphic figurines found in the Alacahöyük (Yalçın, Yalçın 2013) magnificent burials. The Aricestii Rahtivani spiral hair ring can be considered at the moment the earliest gilded silver artifact from Southeastern or even all Europe.

A special case is the presence of 32 small silver round beads – together with the five above mentioned crescent rings – in Zimnicea grave no. 9. The elemental analysis performed on their un-cleaned surface suggests a relative homogeneous composition: Ag=94-98.4%, Au=0.1-0.9%, Cu=0.2-0.7%, Pb=0.1-0.4%, different from the high copper content crescent rings from the same grave (beads don't need an increased hardness).

Only few prehistoric silver objects from Middle and Lower Danube area were compositionally analyzed and published until today. So, the small spiral ring for Rahman (Romania) tumulus grave no. 2 (Ailincăi *et al.* 2014, 78) and the two spiral rings from Sárrétudvari – 'Őrhalom' (Eastern Hungary) tumulus graves no. 4 and 7 (Dani 2011, 29-30, 42) have a high content in gold: 4.82% and 8.7%, 11.3%, respectively (one 'Hungarian' ring has also a high copper presence: 14.9%). The spiral ring from Tarnak – 'Ninovska Mogila' (Bulgaria) tumulus (Torbov 1994, 17) has a strange composition: Ag=85.55%, Sn=13.2%, Au=0.2%, Pb=1.03%, traces of As, Bi, Sb, Zn (probably a poly-metallic geological surface deposit now exhausted as silver provenance). In Bulgaria were also discovered seven spiral rings in Smyadovo cemetery (Chohadzhiev, Mihaylova 2014, 40), one of them being from a silver alloy with 3.21% copper, similar with our above mentioned crescent rings. The compositional differences between all these silver rings can be explained by the use of different

FIGURE 4. ARICEȘTII RAHTIVANI GILDED SPIRAL RING.

silver geological deposits (different silver minerals, not only argentiferous galena – Pb(Ag)S, the most exploited during all times).

Silver weapons

A spectacular case is the weapons made of precious metals, discovered in Eastern and Southern Romania, dating mainly between the fourth and the second millennia BC. For example, at Poduri (Bacău county) was found a dagger with a trapeze-shaped hafting plate and three rivets, very well preserved (Munteanu, Dumitroaia 2010) – see Figure 5. The 44.5 g item is 11.6 cm long, 4.5 cm broad (maximum). Before cleaning, the dagger aspect was relatively green and the archaeologists considered it as a bronze or copper item. Unfortunately, the archaeological context of the artifact had been destroyed by a modern pit, so its dating must be based only on typological analogies for such kind of weapons. There are two hypotheses until now: EBA or Middle Bronze Age (MBA) and Cucuteni-Tripolye phase B (middle of the fourth millennium BC) (Munteanu, Dumitroaia 2010, 133, 140-141; Popescu 2013, 74). Our XRF analyses indicated the dagger and its rivets are from a silver-copper alloy (Constantinescu *et al.* 2010) – see Table 1.

Similar high copper content (more than 20%) silver alloys artifacts are found on a large area – Southern and Southeastern Europe, Anatolia, Caucasus, Mesopotamia, Egypt (Horejs *et al.* 2010, 27-28). Mainly are weapons found in funerary contexts, dated to the fourth to the second millennium BC (Primas 1991; Hansen 2001). Relatively closed to Romania are four Kozarac-type silver-copper axes (the first half of the third millennium BC) from Axel Guttmann collection (Hansen 2001, 13-28, 269), very probably discovered somewhere in former Yugoslavia (copper content is from 43 to 67%). More important are the 28 objects (diadems, bracelets, hair rings, a dagger) found in the 'royal tomb' of Arslantepe – dated to the beginning of the third millennium BC. They are made from copper-silver alloys, having a bright-silvery aspect

FIGURE 5. THE SILVER-COPPER DAGGER FROM PODURI (AFTER MUNTEANU, DUMITROAIA 2010).

Area	Blade	Rivet 1	Rivet 2	Rivet 3
Ag %	65.7	55.3	65.4	71.1
Cu %	31.9	41.5	31.9	26.5
Au %	0.5	0.5	0.6	0.7
Fe %	0.4	0.5	0.6	0.5
As %	0.08	0.16	0.36	0.15
Pb %	0.02	0.04	0.04	0.02

TABLE 1. ELEMENTAL COMPOSITION OF PODURI DAGGER ALLOY.

(Frangipane *et al.* 2001, 105-139; Hauptmann *et al.* 2002, 47). Other similar artifact is the spearhead from Uruk-Warka (Iraq), dated to the end of the fourth millennium BC: copper 65-70% and silver 26-28% (Lutz *et al.* 1996, 132-136). From the third millennium BC we can mention the dagger found in the Gamma grave at Kumasa (Crete): Ag=71.04%, Cu=27.47%, Sn=0.78% (Primas 1991, 184) and the dagger found in a grave at San Biagio della Valle (Northern Italy) having Ag=33.1% (Heyd 2013, 35). We can conclude our Poduri dagger is not a singular silver-copper artifact but could be one of the earliest if its dating to the middle of the fourth millennium BC is accepted.

Our most relevant case of gold and silver weapons is the famous Perşinari hoard. It consists in a short gold sword (Au=88.5%, Ag=9%, Cu=2.5%), 12 gold daggers or halberds (Au=55-65%, Ag=30-36%, Cu=5-9%) and probable four broken (by people who discovered them) auriferous silver shaft-hole axes – see Figures 6 and 7. Alexandru Vulpe considered the hoard related to the Tei culture and dated

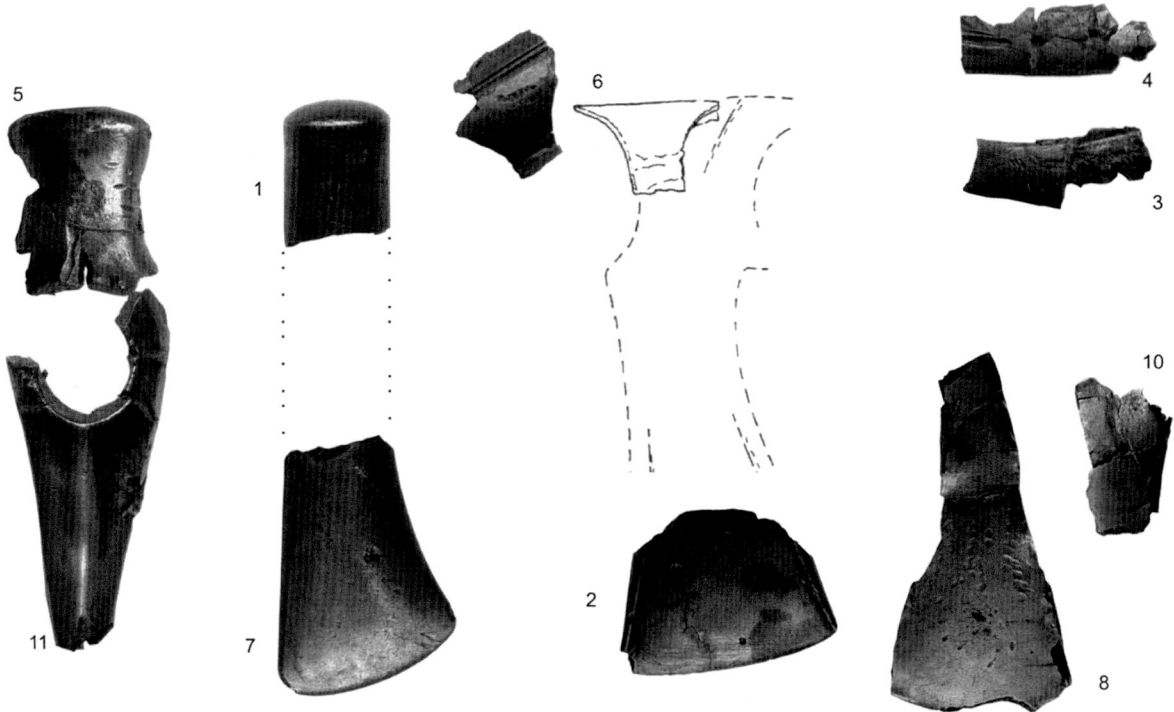

FIGURE 6. PERŞINARI SILVER SHAFT-HOLE AXES.

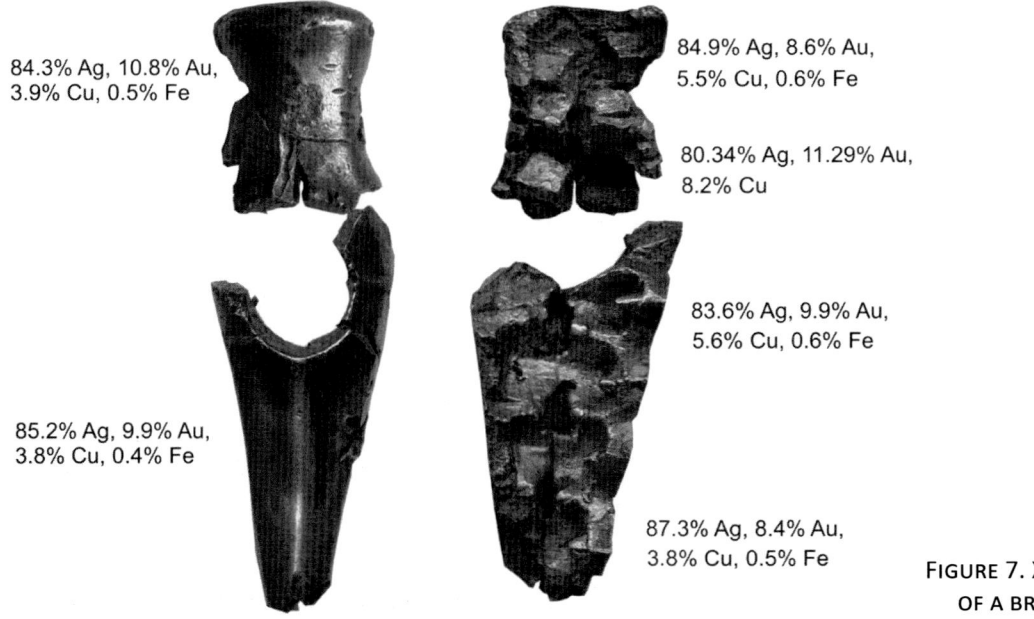

FIGURE 7. XRF ANALYSES OF A BROKEN AXE.

its burial from the end of the third millennium or from the beginning of the second millennium BC (Vulpe 1997, 276-277).

We analyzed the axes (practically the existing fragments) both on their external surface and on their 'internal' -broken areas: Au=9.9%-15.4% (external) and 7.1-12.6% (internal), Cu=1.8%-5.9% (external) and 2.5-9.2% (internal), Ag=78–88% (external) and 78-90% (internal). No lead was found. A very spectacular finding is the identification of few gold nuggets (see Figure 8) 'embedded' in the silver structure (Au=60-72%, Ag=21-23%), suggesting the ancient 'metallurgists' used electrum nuggets with very different gold/silver ratios, not completely melted due to the relatively low heating temperature in the smelting furnace (technical problems?).

Bronze Age auriferous (Au more than 15%) silver artifacts were found on a large area, from Carpathians region to Mesopotamia and Egypt. The closest similar to Perşinari objects are Stari Jancovci axes (Balen, Mihelić 2007, 105)– dated to the middle of the third millennium BC: Ag=71.61%, Au=15.76%, Cu=9.87%, Pb=2.08%, Fe=0.68% (XRF analysis). In the famous Ur cemetery (Mesopotamia – approx. 2600-2200 BC), an auriferous silver spearhead was found: Ag=59.37%, Au=30.30%, Cu=10.35% (Plenderleith 1934, 294). A ring with a similar composition was discovered in a grave belonging to the Resuloğlu cemetery (North-central Anatolia), dated to the second half of the third millennium BC: Ag=50%, Au=24%, Cu=25% (Zimmermann *et al.* 2009).

Auriferous silver was used and more 'recently' (the second half of the second millennium BC) to obtain beautiful artifacts. Such an object is the Vulchitrun-type disc (see Figure 9) with a central umbo accidentally found some 40 years ago in Călăraşi – Southern Romania (Bondoc 2003-2005). Seven similar discs – but in gold (two of them have silver-spirals decoration) belong to the famous Vulchitrun hoard (Bonev 1995; Zaykov *et al.* 2010). Two similar silver discs are exposed in a Bulgarian private collection (Marazov 2011, 20-21). All these discs were dated to the Late Bronze Age (LBA) and likely manufactured by craftsmen specialized in Mycenaean metallurgy (for Mycenaean artifacts see Demakopoulou *et al.* 1995). Most probably these discs belong to precious ritual sets (e.g. lids to cover vessels used for libations). The results of our analyses on different parts of Călăraşi disc are:
- silver foil: Ag=72%, Au=24%, Cu=4%;
- gold foil: Au=86.4%, Ag=13%, Cu=0.5%, traces of tin and iron;
- bronze bulk: Cu=75%, Sn=21%, Ag=3%, As=1%, traces of lead and iron

The gold is a native alluvial one, probably from Balkans riverbeds. The bronze is a typical Bronze Age alloy. As for silver-copper alloys, for auriferous silver it is not clear if it can be considered an anthropic (metallurgical) or natural (geological) product.

FIGURE 8. GOLD NUGGET.

FIGURE 9. VULCHITRUN-TYPE DISC FOUND IN CĂLĂRAŞI.

Conclusions

Our analyses revealed two 'exotic' types of silver alloys: a combination of silver with copper (Ag-Cu) and an alloy of silver with gold and copper (Ag-Au-Cu). Both native silver and the one obtained through cupellation do not have more than 1% Cu (Gale, Stos-Gale 1981, 114; Philip, Rehren 1996, 139). So, one can consider the presence of higher percentages of copper in gold and silver – the case of our Ag-Cu alloy – might be the consequence of an intentionally obtained alloy, with copper added to increase the hardness of the metal (Gale, Stos-Gale 1981, 114; Ogden 1993, 40; Philip, Rehren 1996, 136; Rehren *et al.* 1996, 7). However, the use as silver geological source of a poly-metallic surface deposit, today exhausted (e.g. from Caucasus area), can't be excluded.

An even more controversial issue is the origin of the auriferous silver (an alloy where gold is present in a higher percentage than silver). The possibility of an intentional alloy – resulting from the mixing of metals during recycling operations – was seen by certain researchers as more probable than that of its origin in a geological ore (Philip, Rehren 1996 140; Rehren *et al.* 1996, 6-7). The discovery of gold and silver ores in southern Caucasus indicates a possible potential source of auriferous silver that might have been used during the fourth to the second millennia BC, but, of course it remains still to be determined if those could have been the ores used for the discovered auriferous silver artifacts (Courcier *et al.* 2008, 31).

For the Middle and Lower Danube area we have no proofs regarding either the exploitation of silver ores or the cupellation during prehistory. There is to be considered though the possibility that some of the artifacts found there were locally manufactured, using silver brought in as ingots or even finished products.

The presence of spiral hair rings in the Middle and Lower Danube area is the consequence of the diffusion from the North-Pontic region, or from the Caucasus through the North-Pontic area (Kristiansen 2014), of a complex set of funerary practices (e.g. from Yamnaya culture) and innovations in metallurgy and land transportation by the wheeled-wagon, that took place starting with the fourth millennium BC (Primas 2007; Hansen 2010, Hansen 2013; Hansen 2014; Heyd 2013). It is thus very possible that these hair rings were in fact 'foreign' goods in the Danube area. In what the crescent-shaped ones are concerned, the situation is quite different. They only appeared in the Carpathian-Danube area, obviously suggesting a local production of this type of artifacts (see also Maran 2007, 9). The silver came probably from elsewhere, since, as we mentioned, a local prehistoric exploitation of silver ores has not yet been proved.

A similar case is that of the Poduri dagger, very much alike the Cucuteni ones. The metal used for its manufacturing (a silver-copper alloy) originated probably in the Caucasian or the Anatolian areas. Other artifacts locally made but using imported silver were the shaft-hole axe from the 'princely' tomb of Mala Gruda and the shaft-hole axes from Axel Guttmann collection (Primas 1996, 105-107; Hansen 2001). They are nothing but the silver transpositions of the Kozarac type of shaft-hole axes, a type that occurred during the third millennium BC in the area of the Sava river (most of them made of copper). Moreover, the Mala Gruda axe displays a particular feature – the faceting of its surface – that connects it even more with the Balkan area (Vulpe 2001, 422).

There is a rather high probability that the Perşinari shaft-hole axes were not made locally, since the shape of two of them (the cylindrical butt type occurring in the Caucasus and the North-Pontic areas during the second half of the fourth millennium and the beginning of the third millennium BC, but reaching Central Europe through trade), the composition of the metal (auriferous silver) and the manufacturing technique (the lost-wax process used mostly in Kuban, Caucasus, Levant and Mesopotamia) suggest an Eastern origin.

In what the Vulchitrun discs are concerned, they only occur in the Lower Danube area (Northern Bulgaria and Southern Romania). Still, their ornamentation technique, the complex way of interweaving gold and silver is specific to the Mycenaean metallurgy. The discussion referring to the area/workshop where such discs were produced remains open.

Acknowledgements

Funding from the Romanian National Scientific Research Agency ANCS grant PN-II-ID-PCE-2011-3-0078 is gratefully acknowledged.

We are thankful as well to our archaeologists and geologists collaborators for providing samples for the analysis and for valuable discussions.

References

AILINCĂI, S.-C.; MIHAIL, F.; CAROZZA, L.; CONSTANTINESCU, M.; SOFICARU, A.; MICU, C. 2014. Une découverte funéraire du début de l'Age de Bronze en Dobroudja (Sud-est de Roumanie). Le tumulus de Rahman (com. Casimcea, dep. Tulcea), *Prilozi. Instituta za arheologiju u Zagrebu*, 31, 73-87.

ALEXANDRESCU, A. D. 1974. La nécropole du bronze ancien de Zimnicea (dép. de Teleorman), *Dacia – Revue d'Archéologie et d'Histoire Ancienne, Nouvelle Série (Dacia N.S.)*, 18, 79-93.

BALEN, J.; MIHELIĆ, S. 2007. *Silver axes from Stari Jankovci and the problem of finds of precious metals during the Early Bronze Age in continental Croatia*, in I. Galanaki, H. Tomas, Y. Galanakis, R. Laffineur (eds.), *Between the Aegean and Baltic Seas. Prehistory across borders*, Proceedings of the International Conference Bronze and Early Iron Age Interconnections and Contemporary Developments between the Aegean and the Regions of the Balkan Peninsula, Central and Northern Europe, University of Zagreb, 11-14 April 2005, Aegaeum 27, 105-113.

BERCIU, D.; ROMAN, P. 1984. Mormintele tumulare de la Verbița (jud. Dolj), *Thraco-Dacica* 5/1-2, 15-21.

BONDOC, D. 2003-2005. Un disc de tip Vălcitrăn descoperit la Călărași (jud. Dolj), *Studii și cercetări de istorie veche și arheologie (SCIVA)* 54-56, 279-289.

BONEV, A. 1995. *The Gold Treasure from the Vulchitrun Village (Pleven District) and the Problems of Cultural Contacts in Southeast Europe in the Second Half of the Second Millenium BC*, în D. W. Bailey, I. Panayotov (eds.), *Prehistoric Bulgaria*, Madison, 277-289.

CHERNYKH, E. N. 1992. *Ancient metallurgy in the USSR. The Early Metal Age*, Cambridge.

CHIOJDEANU, C.; CRISTEA STAN, D.; CONSTANTINESCU, B. 2001. Gold and Silver Coating Characterization Using an X-Ray Fluorescence Based Method – The Case of Archaeological Artefacts, *Romanian Reports in Physics* 63, 3, 685-692.

CHOHADZHIEV, S.; MIHAYLOVA, N. 2014. *Smyadovo – Prehistoric cemetery (2005-2008)*, Sofia.

CIUGUDEAN, H. 1996. *Epoca timpurie a bronzului în centrul și sud-vestul Transilvaniei*, Bibliotheca Thracologica 13, București.

CONSTANTINESCU, B.; CONSTANTIN, F.; PĂUNA, C.; POPESCU, A. D.; STAN, D. 2010. Considerații privind proveniența pumnalului de la Poduri plecând de la datele sale compoziționale, *Studii și cercetări de istorie veche și arheologie (SCIVA)* 61/1-2, 143-148.

CONSTANTINESCU, B.; CRISTEA-STAN, D.; VASILESCU, A.; SIMON, R.; CECCATO, D. 2012. Archaeometallurgical Characterization of Ancient Gold Artifacts from Romanian Museums Using XRF, Micro-PIXE and Micro-SR-XRF Methods, *Proceedings of the Romanian Academy, Series A*, 13(1), p. 19-26.

COURCIER, A.; GASANOVA, A.; HAUPTMANN, A. 2008. Ancient metallurgy in the Caucasus during the Chalcolithic and Early Bronze Age: recent results from excavations in Western Azerbaidjan, *Metalla* 15/1, 21-34.

DANI, J. 2011. Research of Pit-Grave culture kurgans in Hungary in the last three decades, in Á. Pető, A. Barczi (eds.), Kurgan studies. An environmental and archaeological multiproxy study of burial mounds in the Eurasian steppe zone, *BAR International Series* 2238, Oxford, 25-69.

DEMAKOPOULOU, K.; MANGOU, E.; JONES, R. E.; PHOTOS-JONES, E. 1995. Mycenaean Black Inlaid Metalware in the National Archaeological Museum, Athens: A Technical Examination, *The Annual of the British School at Athens* 90, 137-153.

FRANGIPANE, M.; DI NOCERA, G. M.; HAUPTMANN, A.; MORBIDELLI, P.; PALMIERI, A.; SADORI, L.; SCHULTZ, M.; SCHMIDT-SCHULTZ, T. 2001. New Symbols of a New Power in a 'Royal' Tomb from 3000 BC Arslantepe, Malatya (Turkey), *Palèorient* 27/2, 2001, 105-139.

FRÎNCULEASA, A. 2007. Contribuții privind mormintele Jamnaja din Muntenia. Cercetări arheologice la Aricestii-Rahtivani- jud. Prahova, *Tyragetia* 1/1, 181-193.

FRÎNCULEASA, A.; PREDA, B.; NEGREA, O.; SOFICARU, A.-D. 2013. Bronze Age Tumulary Graves recently Investigated in Northern Wallachia, *Dacia. Revue d'Archéologie et d'Histoire Ancienne, Nouvelle Série (Dacia N.S.)* 57, 23-63.

GALE, N. H.; STOS-GALE, Z. 1981. Cycladic Lead and Silver Metallurgy, *The Annual of the British School at Athens* 76, 169-224.

GEJ, A. N. 2000. *Novotitorovskaja kul'tura*, Moskva.

GIUMLIA-MAIR, A.; LUCCHINI, E. 2005. Surface analyses on modern and ancient copper based fakes, *Surface Engineering* 21, 5-6, 406-410.

HANSEN, S. 2001. *Waffen aus Gold und Silber während des 3 und frühen 2 Jahrtausends v.Chr. in Europa und Vorderasien*, in H. Born, S. Hansen (Hrsg.), *Helme und Waffen Alteuropas*, Mainz, 2001, 11-59.

HANSEN, S. 2010. *Communication and exchange between the Northern Caucasus and Central Europe in the fourth millennium BC*, in S. Hansen, A. Hauptmann, I. Motzenbäcker, E. Pernicka (eds.), *Von Majkop bis Trialeti. Gewinnung und Verbreitung von Metallen und Obsidian in Kaukasien im 4.-2. Jt. v. Chr.;* Bonn, 297-316.

HANSEN, S. 2013. *Innovative Metals: Copper, Gold and Silver in the Black Sea Region and the Carpathian Basin During the 5th and 4th Millennium BC*, in S. Burmeister, S. Hansen, M. Kunst, N. Müller-Scheeßell (eds.), *Metal Matters. Innovative Technologies and Social Change in Prehistory and Antiquity*, Leidorf, 2013, 137-167.

HANSEN, S. 2014. *Gold and silver in the Maikop Culture*, in H. Meller, R. Risch, E. Pernicka (eds.), *Metalle der Macht – Frühes Gold und Silber / Metals of power – Early gold and silver*, Halle (Saale), 389-410.

HAUPTMANN, A.; SCHMIDT-STRECKER, S.; BEGEMANN, F.; PALMIERI, A. 2002. Chemical Composition and Lead Isotopy of Metal Objects from the 'Royal' Tomb and Other Related Finds at Arslantepe, Eastern Anatolia, *Paléorient* 28/2, 43-70.

HEYD, V. 2013. *Europe at the Dawn of the Bronze Age*, in V. Heyd, G. Kulcsár, V. Szeverényi (eds.), *Transitions to the Bronze Age. Interregional Interaction and Socio-Cultural Change in the Third Millennium BC Carpathian Basin and Neighbouring Regions*, Budapest, 9-66.

HOREJS, B.; MEHOFER, M.; PERNICKA, E. 2010. Metallhandwerker im frühen 3. Jt. v. Chr. – Neue Ergebnisse vom Çukuriçi Höyük, *Istanbuler Mitteilungen* 60, 7-37.

IVANOVA, S. V. 2007. 'Serebrjanyj vek' severo-zapadnogo Prichernomorja, http://www.nbuv.gov.ua/Portal/Soc_Gum/Mtdza/2007_7/ivanova.pdf

KOŞAY, H. Z. 1944. *Ausgrabungen von Alaca Höyük*, Ankara.

KOSAY, H. Z. 1951. *Les fouilles d'Alaca Höyük entreprises par la Societe d'Histoire Turque. Rapport preliminaire sur les travaux en 1937-1939*, Ankara.

KRISTIANSEN, K. 2014. *Towards a new European Prehistory. The decline of the Neolithic and the Rise of the Bronze Age*, Keynote Conference UISPP XVII 2014.

LUTZ, J.; HELWING, B.; PERNICKA, E.; HAUPTMANN, H. 1996. Die Zusamensetzung einiger Metallfunde aus Uruk-Warka, *Baghdader Mitteilungen* 27, 117-139.

MAKKAY, J. 1976. Problems concerning Copper Age chronology in the Carpathian Basin. Copper Age gold pendants and discs in Central and South-East Europe, *Acta Archaeologica Hungarica* 28/3-4, 251-300.

MALLOWAN, M. E. L. 1947. Excavations at Brak and Chagar Bazar, *Iraq* 9, 1-87.

MARAN, J. 2000. *Das Ägäische Chalkolithikum und das erste Silber in Europa*, în C. Işik (Hrsg.), *Studien zur Religion und Kultur Kleinasiens und des ägäischen Bereiches*,

Festschrift für Baki Öğün zum 75. Geburtstag, Asia Minor Studien 39, Bonn, 179-193.

MARAN, J. 2007. *Seaborne Contacts Between The Aegean, The Balkans and The Central Mediterranean in the 3rd Millennium BC: The Unfolding of the Mediterranean World*, in I. Galanaki, H. Tomas, Y. Galanakis, R. Laffineur (eds.), *Between the Aegean and Baltic Seas. Prehistory across borders*, Proceedings of the International Conference Bronze and Early Iron Age Interconnections and Contemporary Developments between the Aegean and the Regions of the Balkan Peninsula, Central and Northern Europe, University of Zagreb, 11-14 April 2005, Aegaeum 27, 3-21.

MARAZOV, I. 2011. *Thrace and the Ancient World. Vassil Bojkov Collection*, Thrace Foundation.

MELLINK, M. J. 1969. Excavations at Karataş-Semayük in Lycia, 1968, *American Journal of Archaeology* 73/3, 319-331.

MOTZOI-CHICIDEANU, I.; OLTEANU, GH. 2000. Un mormânt în cistă din piatră descoperit la Văleni-Dâmbovița, *Studii și cercetări de istorie veche și arheologie (SCIVA)* 51/1-2, 3-70.

MUNTEANU, R.; DUMITROAIA, GH. 2010. Un pumnal din epoca bronzului descoperit la Poduri (jud. Bacău), *Studii și cercetări de istorie veche și arheologie (SCIVA)* 61/1-2, 133-141.

OATES, J.; MCMAHON, A.; KARSGAARD, P.; AL QUNTAR, S.; UR, J. 2007. Early Mesopotamian urbanism: a new view from the north, *Antiquity* 81/313, 585-600.

OGDEN, J. 1993. *Aesthetic and technical considerations regarding the colour and texture of ancient goldwork*, in S. La Niece, P. Craddock (eds.), *Metal Plating and Patination. Cultural Technical and Historical Developments*, Oxford.

ÖZGÜÇ, T.; TEMIZER, R. 1993. *The Eskıyapar Treasure*, N. Özgüç'e Armağan (ed.), *Aspects of Art and Iconography: Anatolia and its Neighbors*, Ankara, 613-628.

PATAY, P.; SZATHMÁRI, I. 2001. Über einem seltenen urzeitlichen silbernen Blechanhänger aus dem Karpatenbecken, *Communicationes Archaeologicae Hungariae*, 5-13.

PERNICKA, E. 1995. Gewinnung und Verbreitung der Metalle in prähistorischer Zeit, *Jahrbuch des Römisch-Germanischen Zentralmuseums* 37/1, (1990) 1995, 21-129.

PHILIP, G.; REHREN, T. 1996. Fourth millennium BC silver from Tell Esh-Shuna, Jordan: archaeometallurgical investigation and some thoughts on ceramic skeuomorphs, *Oxford Journal of Archaeology* 15/2, 129-150.

PLENDERLEITH, H. J. *Metals and Metal Technique*, in C. L. Woolley, *Ur Excavations: The Royal Cemetery. A Report on the Predynastic and Sargonid Graves Excavated between 1926 and 1931*, vol. II, London, 284-298.

POPESCU, A.-D. 2010. Silver artefacts of the third and second millennia BC at the Lower and Middle Danube, *Transylvanian Review* 19, Suppl. 5/1, 2010, 163-182.

POPESCU, A.-D. 2013. *Cele mai timpurii obiecte de argint din Europa*, in S.-C. Ailincăi, A. Țârlea, C. Micu (eds.), *Din preistoria Dunării de Jos. 50 de ani de la începutul cercetărilor arheologice la Babadag (1962-2012)*, Brăila, 67-88.

PRIMAS, M. 1991. Waffen aus Edelmetall, *Jahrbuch des Römisch-Germanischen Zentralmuseums* 35, 161-185.

PRIMAS, M. 1995. *Gold and silver during 3rd Mill. cal. B.C.;* in G. Morteani, J. P. Northover (eds.), *Prehistoric Gold in Europe. Mines, Metallurgy and Manufacture*, Dordrecht, 77-93.

PRIMAS, M. 1996. Velika Gruda I. Hügelgräber des frühen 3. Jahrtausends v. Chr. im Adriagebiet – Velika Gruda, Mala Gruda und ihr Kontext, *Universitätsforschungen zur prähistorischen Archäologie* 32, Bonn.

PRIMAS, M. 2007. Innovationstransfer vor 5000 Jahren. Knotenpunkte an Land- und Wassewegen zwischen Vorderasien und Europa, *Eurasia Antiqua* 13, 1-19.

REHREN, T.; HESS, K.; PHILIP, G. 1996. Auriferous Silver in Western Asia: Ore or Alloy?, *Historical Metallurgy* 30/1, 1996, 1-10.

RENFREW, C. 1967. Cycladic Metallurgy and the Aegean Early Bronze Age, *American Journal of Archaeology* 71/1, 1-20.

REZEPKIN, A. D. 200. Das frühbronzezeitliche Gräberfeld von Klady und die Majkop-Kultur in Nordwestkaukasien, *Archäologie in Eurasien* 10, Rahden/Westf.

SCIV, 1952. Șantierul Verbicioara, *Studii și cercetări de istorie veche (SCIV)* 3, 141-189.

TOLSTIKOV, V.; TREISTER, M. 1996. *The Gold of Troy. Searching for Homer's Fabled City*, London.

TORBOV, N. 1994. Rezultati ot arheologiecheskoto prouchvane na Ninovskata Mogila pri Tarnak, Beloslatinsko, *Izvestija na muzeite v severnozapadna Bălgarija* 22, 11-21.

VULPE, A. 1997. Tezaurul de la Perşinari. O nouă prezentare, *Cultură şi Civilizaţie la Dunărea de Jos* 15, 265-301.

VULPE, A. 2001. *Consideration upon the Beginning and the Evolution of the Early Bronze Age in Romania*, in R. M. Boehmer, J. Maran (eds.), *Archäologie zwischen Asien und Europa*, Festschrift für Harald Hauptmann, Rahden/Westf.; 419-426.

WANHILL, R. J. H. 2005. Embrittlement of ancient silver, *Journal of Failure Analysis and Prevention* 5/1, 41.

YALÇIN, Ü.; GÖNÜL YALÇIN, H. 2013. Reassessing anthropomorphic metal figurines of Alacahöyük, Anatolia, *Near Eastern Archaeology* 76/1, 38-49.

ZAYKOV, V.; GERGOVA, D.; KHVOROV, P.; BONEV, P. 2010. Archaeometric studies of Thracian golden objects from The National Archaeological Museum in Sofia, *Interdisciplinary Studies* XXII-XXIII, 75-80.

ZIMMERMANN, T.; YILDIRIM, T.; ÖZEN, L.; ZARARSIZ, A. 2009. 'All that glitters is not gold, nor all that sparkles silver'- fresh archaeometrical data for Central Anatolian Early Bronze Age metalwork, *Antiquity* 83/321, Project Gallery.

http://www.antiquity.ac.uk/projgall/zimmerman321/

Prehistoric gold metallurgy in Transylvania – an archaeometrical study

Daniela CRISTEA-STAN and Bogdan CONSTANTINESCU
National Institute for Nuclear Physics and Engineering, Bucharest, Romania

Abstract

Transylvania is one of the richest in gold European region. Consequently, many gold artifacts were discovered here, dated from Late Neolithic, Bronze Age and Iron Age periods. To clarify the metallurgical techniques used by our ancestors a compositional study on relevant gold artifacts from each period was realized. We used X-Ray Fluorescence, a non-destructive elemental analysis method performed 'in situ', directly on artifacts exposed in some representative Romanian Archaeological Museums. For Late Neolithic we analyzed small beads from Pestera Ungureasca (Cheile Turzii) and for Bronze Age artifacts (hair rings, phalerae, bracelets) from Smig, Cauas, Sacuieni, Pecica, Cacova and Sibiu. Their gold is alluvial – a mixture of small nuggets and dust soldered together by local heating and hammering in one final object. A similar primitive metallurgy was also used in the case of 13 Dacian gold spiraled bracelets (1st Century BC) found in Sarmizegetusa, Dacian capital situated in Central Transylvania. The relative in-homogeneity of the ingots used for the manufacture of the Dacian bracelets could be caused by the fact that the technique implied incomplete melting of a mixture of gold dust and nuggets (not reaching the high melting point of gold), without perfect homogenization. The primitive sintering of the gold concentrates (simultaneously with hammering and non-uniform or insufficient heating) into ingots is expected to preserve impurities like isolated mineral grains and micro-inclusions. Using micro-PIXE (Proton Induced X-ray Emission) we identified tin (from cassiterite), copper and iron (from chalcopyrite) micro-inclusions, proving the above mentioned primitive metallurgical procedure. Our conclusion is that in Transylvania rich in gold, from Late Neolithic to Dacian period, during more than 2000 years, practically the same relatively primitive metallurgy of alluvial gold was used to produce the spectacular artifacts exhibited now in Romanian Museums.

Key-words: *Bronze Age, Dacian bracelets, alluvial gold, primitive metallurgy, X-Ray Fluorescence, Transylvania*

Résumé

La Transylvanie est l'une des régions européennes plus riches en or. Par conséquent, de nombreux objets en or ont été découverts ici, datés du Néolithique, l'Âge du Bronze et de l'Âge du Fer. Afin de clarifier les techniques métallurgiques utilisées par nos ancêtres, a été réalisée une étude de la composition des objets en or de chaque période. Nous avons utilisé la Fluorescence de Rayons X, une méthode d'analyse élémentaire non-destructive réalisée 'in situ', directement sur les objets exposés dans certains musées archéologiques roumains représentatifs. Pour le Néolithique, nous avons analysé les petites perles de Pestera Ungureasca (Cheile Turzii) et pour les artefacts de l'Âge du Bronze les anneaux de cheveux, des phalerae, et des bracelets de Smog, Cauas, Sacuieni, Pecica, Cacova et Sibiu. Leur or est alluviale – un mélange de petites pépites et poussières soudées par chauffage local et martelage dans un objet final. Une métallurgie primitive similaire a également été utilisée dans le cas de 13 bracelets en spirale d'or Daces (1er siècle a. J.C.) trouvés dans Sarmizegetusa, la capitale Dace située en Transylvanie centrale. La relative homogénéité des lingots utilisés pour la fabrication des bracelets Daces pourrait être causé par le fait que la technique implique la fusion incomplète d'un mélange de poudre d'or et des pépites (pas d'atteindre le point de fusion élevé de l'or), sans homogénéisation parfaite. L'agglomération primitive des concentrés d'or (simultanément avec martelage et un chauffage non-uniforme ou insuffisant en lingots) est prévue pour conserver des impuretés telles que des grains minéraux isolés et des micro-inclusions. Avec l'utilisation du micro-PIXE (Proton Induced X-ray Emission) nous avons identifié micro-inclusions de l'étain (de cassiterite), du cuivre et du fer (de chalcopyrite), ce qui prouve la procédure métallurgique primitive indiqué ci-dessus. Notre conclusion est que, en Transylvanie riche en or, du Néolithique à la période Dace, pendant plus de 2000 ans, a été utilisé pratiquement la même métallurgie relativement primitive de l'or alluvial pour produire les artefacts spectaculaires exposés maintenant dans les musées Roumains.

Mots-clés: *Âge de Bronze, brassards (bracelets?) Daces, or alluvial, métallurgie primitive, Fluorescence de Rayons X, Transylvanie*

Transylvania is one of the richest in gold European region. Most gold deposits and occurrences (Fig. 1) are in the Apuseni Mountains (Rosia Montana, Musariu, Valea Morii) and in the Baia Mare district (Cavnic-Roata) of East Carpathians (Udubasa *et al.* 2002, 73-82; 52-60). Gold was first identified by humans since prehistory as nuggets, which shone in riverbeds which stemmed from areas rich in gold deposits. This is the case for many Transylvanian rivers – alluvial gold sources from ancient times until present – Valea Tebei, Valea Ariesului, Lipova, Valea Pianului, Fizesti, Sebes, Rahau, Valea Oltului (Cristea 2012, 131-148).

Gold was used for decorative objects for persons with a special status in society, worn especially at various ceremonies, but also included in the funeral ritual. Many gold artifacts were discovered in Transylvania (Fig. 2), dated from Late Neolithic, Bronze Age, Iron Age and classical Dacian periods

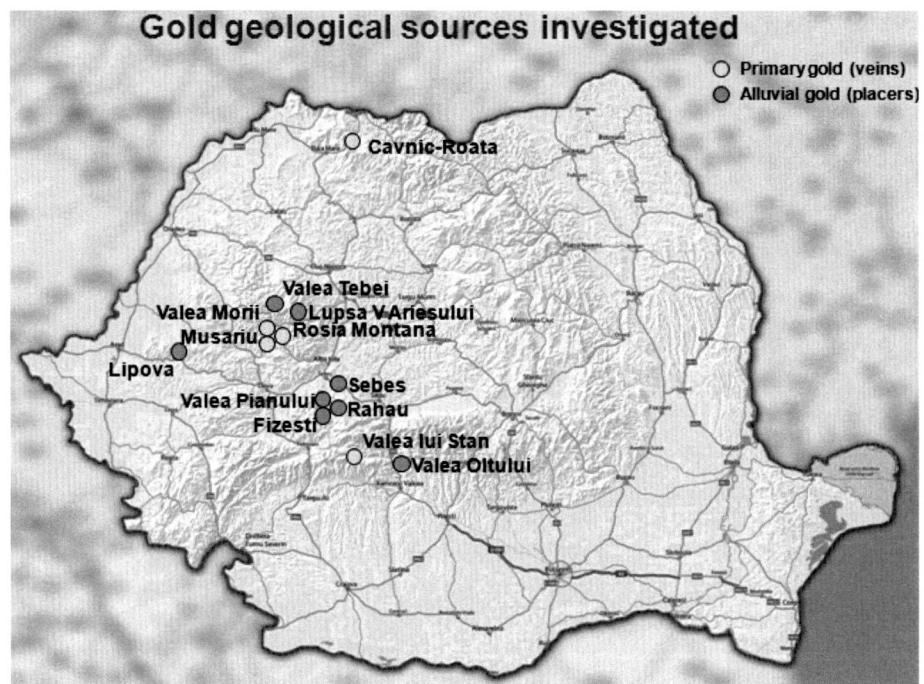

FIGURE 1. MAP OF GOLD GEOLOGICAL SOURCES INVESTIGATED BY OUR GROUP (CRISTEA 2012).

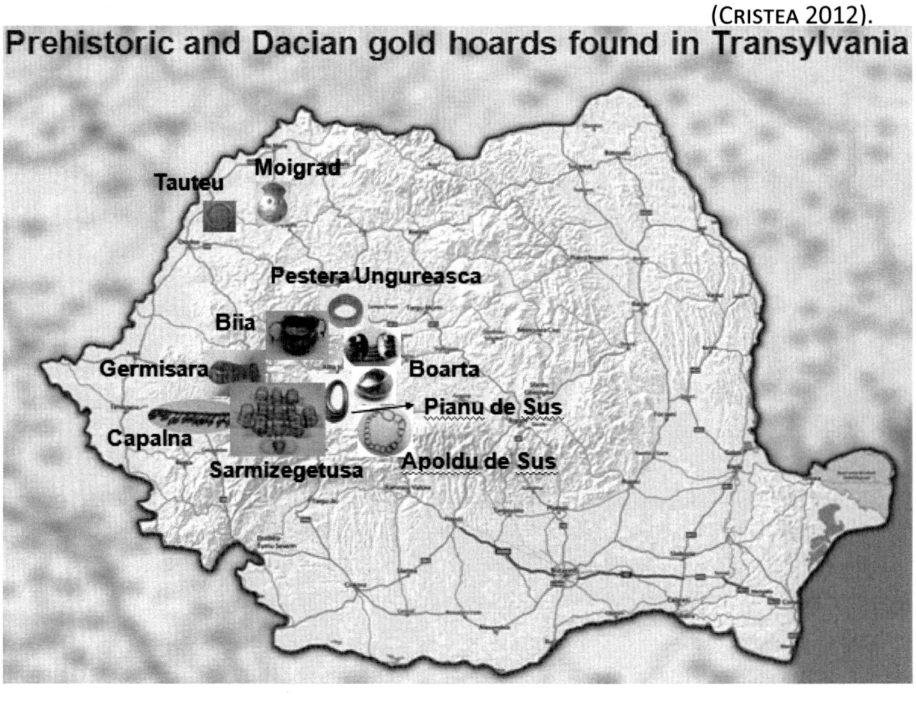

FIGURE 2. MAP OF ARCHAEOLOGICAL GOLD ARTIFACTS INVESTIGATED BY OUR GROUP (CONSTANTINESCU ET AL.; 2010; CONSTANTINESCU ET AL. 2012A; CONSTANTINESCU ET AL. 2012B; CONSTANTINESCU ET AL. 2012C).

(Exhibition Catalogue 2013, 48-115). As seen in Figure 1 and 2, the maps of archaeological hoards and of gold geological deposits are very similar, suggesting the local use of Transylvanian gold.

To clarify the metallurgical techniques used by our ancestors a compositional study on relevant gold artifacts from each period was realized. We used X-Ray Fluorescence – a non-destructive elemental analysis method performed 'in situ' – directly on artifacts exposed in some representative Romanian museums as: National History Museum of Romania, Bucharest (the main hoards are exposed in its treasure room), National History Museum of Transylvania, Cluj-Napoca, 'Unirii' Alba Iulia Museum. The analyses were performed with an Oxford Instruments portable spectrometer X-MET 3000TX+, were the exciting X-ray beam is generated by a Rh anode tube. The measurement spot size is about 30 mm^2. The spectrometer has a Hewlett-Packard (HP) iPAQ personal data assistant (PDA) for software management and data storage (Constantinescu *et al.* 2012a, 21).

From Late Neolithic we analyzed some small beads (under 4 mm diameter) at different stages of processing – finished or unfinished – found in the site of Pestera Ungureasca – Cheile Turzii (Lazarovici, 2012, 2), near Aries river – known for alluvial gold mining by more than twenty centuries – approx. 50 km away from the Apuseni Mountains. We identified the use of small gold nuggets, some of them cold hammered and others partially heated and hammered. The mean gold composition – Au=91.4%, Ag=7.7%, Cu=0.2%, Fe=0.8% – is practically identical with present alluvial gold composition from Aries river.

From Bronze Age we analyzed artifacts like hair rings (lock rings), phalerae, bracelets discovered in site as Smig, Cauas, Sacuieni, Pecica, Cacova, Tauteu (Fig. 3, Table 1). A synthesis of prehistoric Transylvanian gold objects now belonging not only to Romanian museums but also to Budapest and Viena museums can be found in (Popescu, 1956, 158-212).

FIGURE 3. GOLD BRONZE AGE ARTIFACTS FROM SMIG, BIIA, CAUAS, SACUIENI, PECICA-ROVINE, CACOVA.

Object	Mass (g)	Cu (%)	Ag (%)	Sn (%)	Au (%)	Others %
SMIG						
Phalera	4,50	0,15	22,2	n.m.	77,6	
Disc		0,57	19,2	n.m.	80,2	
Bracelet	32,50	0,52	13,4	n.m.	86,0	
Hair ring 1	4,65	0,15	5,0	n.m.	94,8	
Hair ring 2	5,70	0,09	24,5	n.d.	75,4	
BIIA						
Cup	144,00	0,48	15,1	0,03	84,3	Sb 0,015
CAUAS						
Bracelet 1	136,35	0,46	12,4	0,085	87,0	
Bracelet 2	137,00	0,47	13,1	0,05	86,3	
Bracelet fragment	34,50	0,48	13,4	0,08	86,0	
SACUIENI						
Phalera 1	27,95	0,06	25,5	n.d.	74,4	
Phalera 2	26,70	1,00	25,8	0,12	73,6	Sb 0,015
PECICA-ROVINE						
Disc	0,21	0,15	26,3	n.m.	73,5	
CACOVA (AIUD)						
Hair ring	29,18	0,31	10,8	0,03	88,8	
Hair ring spiraled	4,75	0,23	19,7	n.m.	80,0	
Ring anchor	4,40	0,42	23,2	n.m.	76,4	
TAUTEU						
Ring	7,20	1,01	6,0	0,016	92,9	

n.m. – not measured; n.d. – not detected

TABLE 1. ELEMENTAL COMPOSITION OF ARTIFACTS FROM SMIG, CAUAS, SACUIENI, PECICA, CACOVA, TAUTEU.

The presence of tin indicates the alluvial origin of the gold (Schlosser, 2009, 409-504). Antimony traces could come from surface gold veins (antimony and tellurium are chemical fingerprints for Apuseni Mountains – Udubasa *et al.* 2002, 73-82).

Cauas items are practically from the same gold source (a big nugget?). Smig items have different gold sources – probably small nuggets (a small gold ingot – now lost – was discovered in Smig hoard).

Surprising results were obtained when we measured separate areas in each artifact: their composition was sometimes significantly different, most probably due to the use of different nuggets by the ancient 'jeweler'. We illustrate with two hair rings from Cacova (Aiud) and Sibiu (Fig. 4 and Table 2).

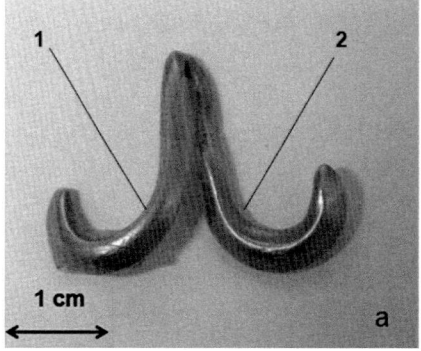 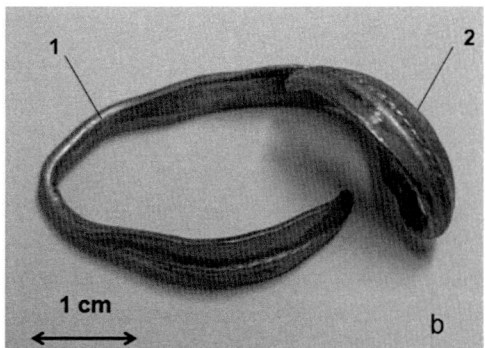

FIGURE 4. HAIR RINGS (LOCK RINGS) FROM: A. CACOVA (AIUD) AND B. SIBIU (1, 2 – MEASURED AREAS).

Object	Au %	Ag%	Cu%	Fe%
Hair ring Cacova 1	74	23.4	0.4	0.7
Hair ring Cacova 2	68.7	29.3	0.2	1.2
Hair ring Sibiu 1	71	27.6	0.2	0.5
Hair ring Sibiu 2	61.8	36.6	0.1	0.9

TABLE 2. ELEMENTAL COMPOSITION OF ARTIFACTS FROM CACOVA (AIUD) AND SIBIU.

For both artifacts the use of two different nuggets is the explanation of the differences between their two halves, which were 'sold' by local heating and hammering.

To clearly put in evidence the presence of tin (main fingerprint for alluvial gold) we analyzed by micro-SR-XRF (Synchrotron Radiation induced X-Ray Fluorescence – the most powerful XRF analytical technique) at BESSY Synchrotron–Berlin (Vasilescu, *et al.*; 2011, 368) micro-fragments (approx. 200 microns diameter) from Tauteu hoard rings (Fig. 5) – see the spectrum from figure 6.

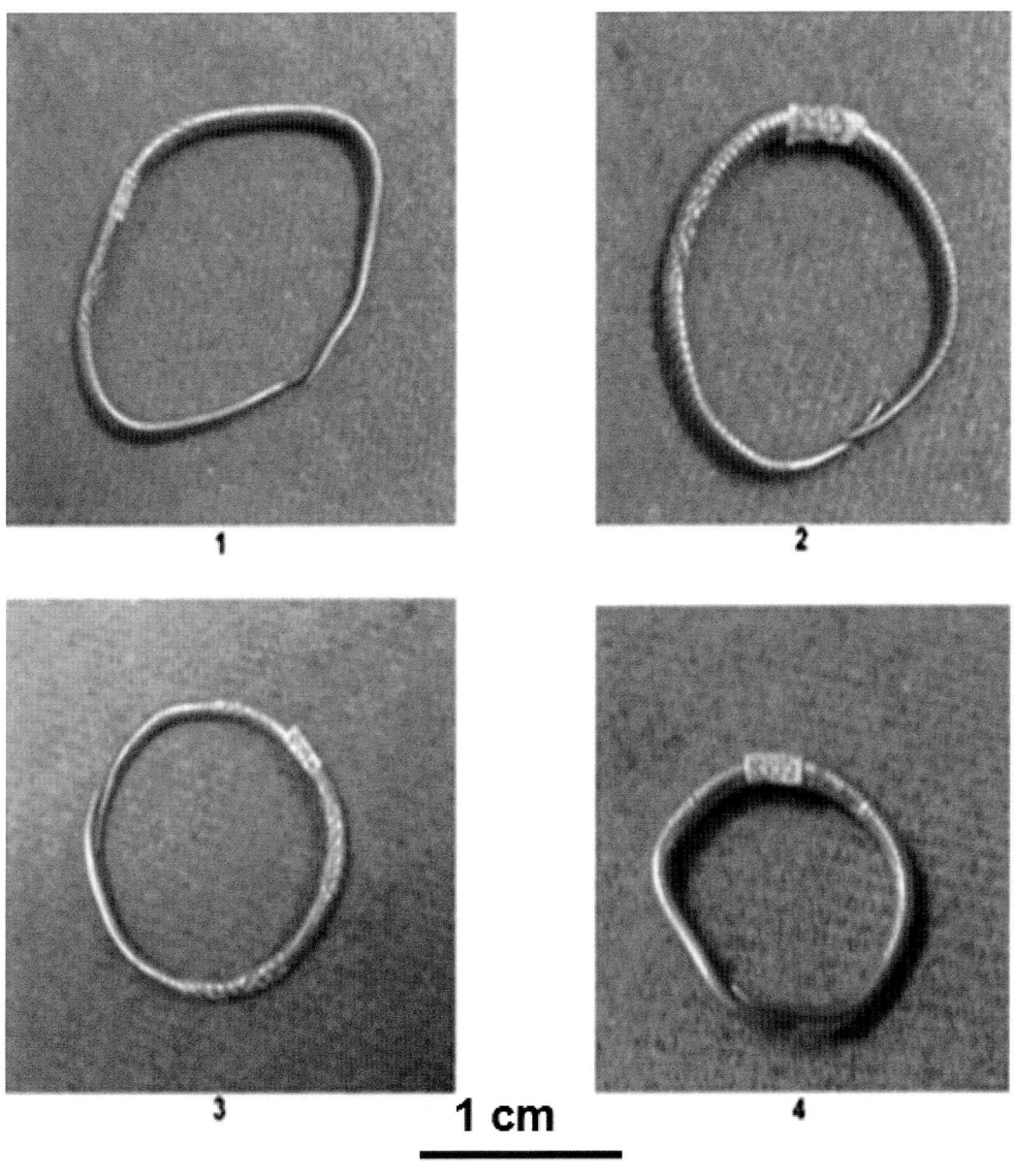

FIGURE 5. TAUTEU HOARD.

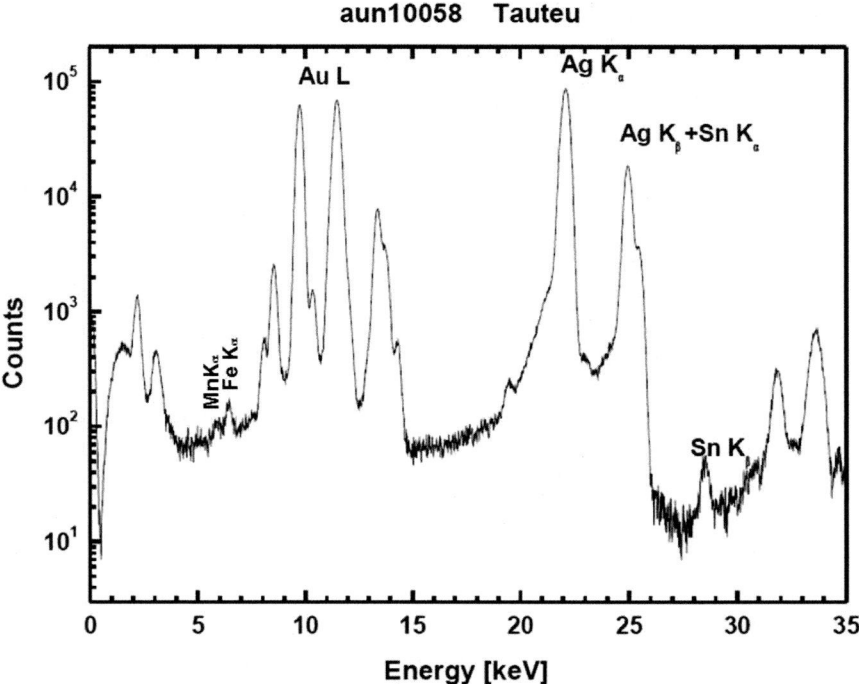

FIGURE 6. TAUTEU RING 1 – MICRO-SR-XRF SPECTRUM.

From Iron Age a spectacular example is a bracelet found at Boarta, near Valea Pianului – the best known ancient area of gold placers from Transylvania. In the visual inspection of this bracelet, we noticed two different types of gold (one white and the other yellow), XRF results showing different elemental compositional patterns: Au=55%, Ag=44%, Cu=2.6% (white aspect) and Au=79%, Ag=19%, Cu=1%, Sn=traces (yellow aspect). Most probably, different nuggets were put together, hammered and partially heated to obtain their 'welding' (Constantinescu *et al.* 2012b, 2077-2078).

In conclusion, the prehistoric gold artifacts from Transylvania were manufactured in a quite primitive manner. They are inhomogeneous due to the incomplete melting of different nuggets, partially heated and hammered, put together to obtain the requested artifact.

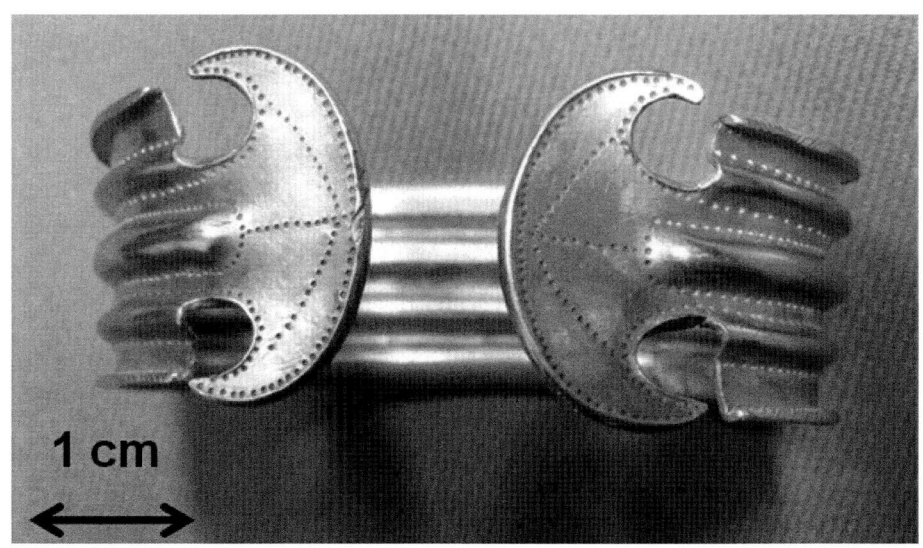

FIGURE 7. GOLD BRACELET BOARTA.

A spectacular confirmation of the continuation of this primitive metallurgy in Transylvania is the case of 13 Dacian (1st Century BC – 1st Century AD) gold spiraled bracelets (Fig. 8) found in the sanctuaries area of Sarmizegetusa, Dacian capital, situated in Central Transylvania (Constantinescu *et al.* 2012a, 19; Constantinescu *et al.* 2010, 1030).

Between 1999 and 2001 five hoards containing at least 24 gold spiral bracelets (armbands) together with gold staters (approx. 8.3 g weight) of posthumous Lysimachus type and a big hoard containing approx. 2000 Dacian gold staters type Koson with and without monogram were discovered by illegal treasure hunters in different spots in

FIGURE 8. A SPIRALED GOLD DACIAN BRACELET.

the area of Sarmizegetusa Regia Dacian fortress in the Orăştie Mountains (UNESCO World Heritage List site) and illegally exported to international black market. The bracelets are spiraled (5-7 spirals), weighting 800 to 1200 g each. They are 10 to 12 cm diameter, being adorned with stylized palm leafs and with zoomorphic protomae at both ends. The bracelets were probably insignia of power, if one take into account their dimensions and the context of their discovery.

According to international legislation, to recover the hoards from abroad (USA, Germany, France – where they were discovered by police). Romanian authorities presented evidences the provenance of artifacts is a Romanian territory. One of the most powerful argument during the international recuperation of Dacian artifacts was the provenance of artifacts' gold from Romanian geological deposits: Golden Quadrilateral where Romans, after Dacia's conquest in 106 A.D. exploited the mine of Rosia Montana – famous for its well-preserved until now mining galleries, Valea Pianului placer, Baia-Mare and Banat.

To demonstrate the gold of the 13 bracelets recovered until now (2007-2011) has Transylvanian origin we performed the first compositional analysis in our laboratory and in some cases in the rooms of National History Museum of Romania using XRF method – see Table 3. We also investigated geological gold samples from Transylvanian deposits illustrated in Fig. 1 A.

The results (see Table 3) revealed each bracelet was made from a different ingot, the gold concentration – from 78% to 93% – practically covering a major part of Transylvanian native gold concentration for primary (veins) – low values – and for alluvial – high values. A very important result was the relevant traces of tin (between 60 and 1500 – ppm) found in 10 bracelets, tin being a principal indicator of panned (alluvial origin) gold, which is consistent with the fact that prehistoric gold was mainly of alluvial origin. Copper concentration was also different from bracelet to bracelet and significantly higher (between 0.3 and 2.1%) than the Cu content in Transylvanian native gold which is less than 0.1%.

Bracelet no.	Weight (g)	Au (wt%)	Ag (wt%)	Cu (wt%)	Sn (mg/kg^{-1}) ppm
1	982.2	89.8	9.5	0.6	200
2	1076.72	78.2	20.3	1.5	<60
3	1115.31	82.4	16.2	1.4	360
4	927.98	91.5	8.1	0.4	125
5	764.95	92.8	6.9	0.3	<MDL*
6	1062.55	92	7.1	0.9	230
7	1196.03	92.9	6.3	0.7	<MDL*
8	1136.06	85	12.8	2.1	1500
9	682.3	87.1	12.2	0.6	120
10	1047	88.7	10.3	0.9	425
11	825	86.1	12.6	0.7	400
12	884.37	83.5	14.3	1	500
13	933.4	84.8	14.6	0.6	<MDL*

* MDL – Minimum Detection Limits

TABLE 3. DACIAN BRACELETS COMPOSITION
(1 PPM = 1MG/KG = 10^{-6} = 10^{-4}%).

For a more detailed study, we also performed micro-analyses using micro-SR-XRF at BESSY Synchrotron – Berlin, focusing on the detection of trace elements and on the micro-homogeneity of the artifacts (Constantinescu *et al.* 2012c, 397-398). The archaeological micro-samples were tiny fragments taken in the least destructive manner possible from parts of the objects with little relevance as to their shape and decoration. The results not only confirmed different composition from bracelet to bracelet but also revealed different composition from head A to head B at the same bracelet. The micro-SR-XRF compositional data form basically two groups centered at 83 and 91% Au concentration (Fig. 9). The higher Au concentration peak corresponds to alluvial gold – most probably from Valea Pianului which is closed to Sarmizegetusa (see maps in Fig. 1) and the lower one is probably due to a mix of alluvial with surface vein gold – probably from Valea Morii. The micro-SR-XRF investigation also revealed that on a micrometer scale the bracelets contain remains of imperfect smelting and inclusions (small areas with different composition from the surroundings) – for example micro-grains of pyrite (iron sulfide – FeS) and cassiterite (tin oxide – SnO_2).

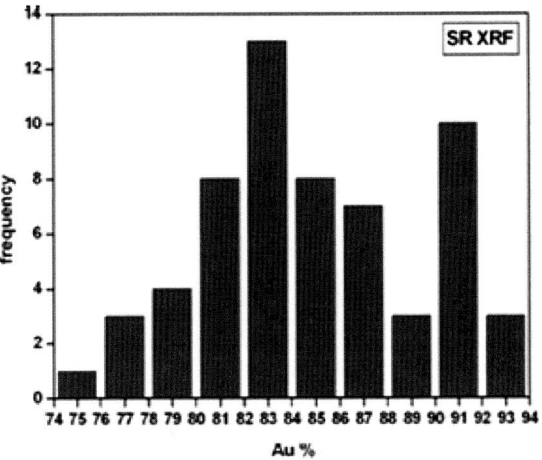

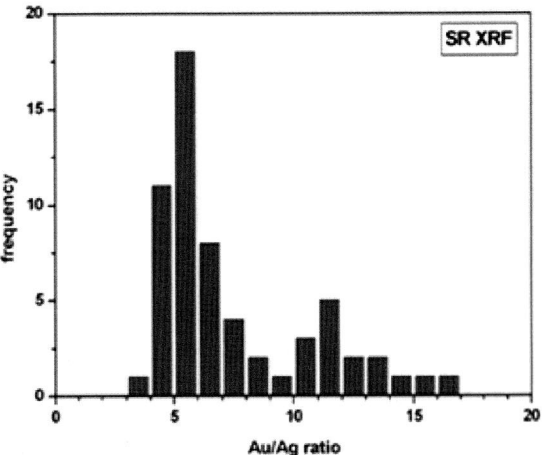

FIGURE 9. FREQUENCY DISTRIBUTION FOR THE AU/AG RATIO AND THE AU CONTENT [%] IN DACIAN BRACELETS.

Dacian Koson with monogram

Dacian Koson without monogram

FIGURE 10. GOLD DACIAN KOSON STATERS.

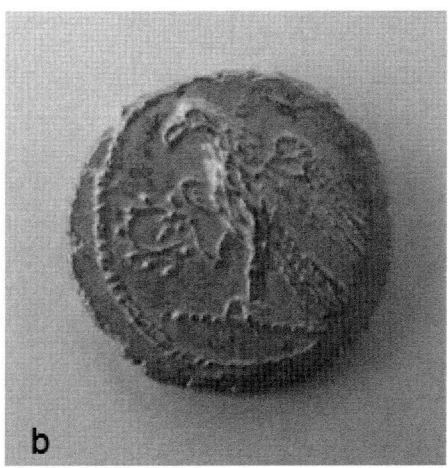

We also investigated some Koson Dacian staters, having Roman images – three lictors on averse and an eagle with Greek inscription 'Koson' on obverse, coins with and without the monogram BR, probably from Brutus – Figure 10 (Cojocaru *et al.* 2000, 185-190). The micro-SR-XRF analyses were performed on micro-samples (less than 300 microns diameter) obtained from the coins edge, with 2-3 measurements on different areas for each micro-sample.

The results are presented in Tables 4 and 5.

The Koson staters with monogram have a high-title (Au: 94.41% – 99.21%) and are rather homogeneous, with a reduced content of copper (0.10% – 0.30%) and tin (0 – 67 ppm). On the contrary, the Koson staters without monogram have a higher content of silver (8.31% – 15.99%) and copper (0.96% – 2.90%), and a significant presence of tin (149 – 1066 ppm), coupled with an evident in-homogeneity in all metallic elements, but especially in tin, copper and iron.

Evidently, the two categories of Koson staters were minted with two different metallurgical 'recipes', and, consequently, represent two types of gold 'alloy': the use of refined gold (advanced – real – metallurgy) for the Koson staters with monogram and the use of native (mainly alluvial) gold in a primitive metallurgy for the Koson staters without monogram.

Sample	Measurement	Au %	Ag %	Cu %	Fe %	Sn ppm
KM 23	1	95.66	4.026	0.25	0.056	10
KM 23	2	95.24	4.43	0.27	0.045	15
KM 53	1	94.49	5.19	0.25	0.05	37
KM 53	2	94.41	5.20	0.28	0.09	10
KM 10	1	96.98	2.76	0.18	0.07	10
KM 10	2	96.71	2.80	0.15	0.34	–
KM 8	1	95.12	4.50	0.30	0.06	19
KM 8	2	94.83	4.84	0.27	0.04	31
KM 719	1	99.21	0.64	0.10	0.03	62
KM 719	2	99.17	0.67	0.11	0.04	35
KM 321	1	98.42	1.28	0.16	0.06	67
KM 321	2	98.47	1.32	0.15	0.04	48
KM 321	3	98.41	1.38	0.15	0.05	42

KM = Koson with monogram

TABLE 4. ELEMENTAL CONCENTRATION VARIATIONS IN KOSON STATERS WITH MONOGRAM
(1 PPM = 1MG/KG = 10^{-6} = 10^{-4}%).

Sample	Measurement	Au %	Ag %	Cu %	Fe %	Sn ppm
K73	1	82.15	15.14	2.44	0.22	522
K73	2	81.99	15.53	2.25	0.17	496
K73	3	81.80	15.99	2.90	0.20	1066
K 135	1	83.06	14.41	2.29	0.17	532
K 135	2	84.09	13.68	2.08	0.106	426
K 118*	1	87.49	8.69	1.49	2.31	149
K 118	2	85.52	12.18	1.60	0.67	291
K 54	1	88.57	9.71	1.49	0.19	365
K 54	2	85.59	12.39	1.49	0.41	1036
K 131	1	87.99	10.72	0.98	0.26	338
K 131	2	87.27	11.41	1.04	0.24	361
K 132	1	88.09	10.92	0.18	0.75	553
K 132	2	90.55	8.31	0.96	0.14	268
K 40	1	89.01	9.07	1.75	0.13	388
K 40	2	86.82	11.29	1.71	0.09	772
K 38	1	88.78	9.93	0.92	0.31	439
K 38	2	88.08	10.33	1.48	0.06	412
K 65	2	86.14	12.71	1.07	0.034	428
K 92	1	85.81	12.10	1.93	0.09	677
K 92	2	85.61	12.66	1.31	0.38	309
K 43	1	86.97	11.24	1.63	0.053	1031
K 43	2	87.10	11.09	1.69	0.055	667

K = Koson without monogram; * – pyrite micro-inclusion

TABLE 5. ELEMENTAL CONCENTRATION VARIATIONS IN KOSON STATERS WITHOUT MONOGRAM
(1 PPM = 1MG/KG = 10^{-6} = 10^{-4}%).

A most trustful hypothesis is that the Koson staters with monogram – the original coins – were minted somewhere in the neighboring Roman provinces (in the Balkans) from refined (for coins) and/or jewelry gold and the Koson staters without monogram are 'Barbarian' copies made in Dacia (Transylvania) from native gold using a primitive metallurgy incapable to completely melt the small pieces of alluvial gold.

The main conclusions of our compositional studies on Transylvanian prehistoric archaeological gold are:
- Strong in-homogeneity in composition for the same artifact, indicating a primitive metallurgy process: relatively low temperature (lower than the melting point of Au) and hammering during heating to obtain an ingot through sintering;
- Large variations of Au concentration from 50% to 93%;
- Traces of tin observed in practically all items;
- Small traces of antimony observed in some artifacts;
- Copper concentration higher than in Transylvanian native gold.

Our compositional analyses on geological gold samples explained the main characteristics of Romanian archaeological gold, supporting its local (Transylvanian) provenance. So, if we compare gold/silver ratios for both archaeological and geological gold sample analyzed by us it is clear their similarity (Cristea, 2012, 149-158).

Tin traces found in the artifacts were explained as a consequence of the presence of some fine grains of cassiterite contained in the alluvial gold, the corresponding tin being not removed at the first melting of gold.

Copper concentration found in the artifacts higher than in Transylvanian native gold is related to the presence of accompanying colored minerals in gold dust and nuggets – e.g.; chalcopyrite ($CuFeS_2$), 'fool's gold' and pyrite (FeS) – due to the probable confusion made by Dacian 'miners' and to the primitive processing of the raw material.

Synthesizing, the relative in-homogeneity of the ingots used for the manufacture of the Dacian bracelets could be caused by the fact that the technique implied incomplete melting of a mixture of gold dust and nuggets (not reaching the high melting point of gold), without perfect homogenization. The primitive sintering of the gold concentrates (simultaneous hammering and non-uniform or insufficient heating) into ingots is expected to preserve impurities like isolated mineral grains and micro-inclusions. Using micro-SR-XRF, we identified tin (from cassiterite), copper and iron (from chalcopyrite) micro-inclusions, proving the above mentioned primitive metallurgical procedure.

In conclusion, in Transylvania rich in gold, from Late Neolithic to Dacian period during more than 2000 years practically the same relatively primitive metallurgy of alluvial gold was used to produce the spectacular artifacts exhibited now in Romanian Museums.

Acknowledgements

Funding from the Romanian National Scientific Research Agency ANCS grant PN-II-ID-PCE-2011-3-0078 is gratefully acknowledged.

Many thanks go as well to the BESSY Synchrotron staff for technical support. We are thankful as well to our archaeologists and geologists collaborators for providing samples for analysis and for valuable discussions.

References

Cojocaru, V.; Constantinescu, B.; Stefanescu, I.; Petolescu, C. M. 2000. EDXRF and PAA Analyses of Dacian Gold Coins of 'Koson' Type, *Journal of Radio-analytical and Nuclear Chemistry*, 246, 1, p. 185-190.

Constantinescu, B.; Oblerlaender-Tarnoveanu, E.; Bugoi R.; Cojocaru, V.; Radtke, M. 2010. The Sarmizegetusa bracelets, *Antiquity* 84 (2010), p. 1028-1042.

Constantinescu, B.; Cristea-Stan, D.; Vasilescu, A.; Simon, R.; Ceccato, D. 2012a. Archaeometallurgical Characterization of Ancient Gold Artifacts from Romanian Museums

Using XRF, Micro-PIXE and Micro-SR-XRF Methods, *Proceedings of the Romanian Academy, Series A*, 13(1), p. 19-26.

CONSTANTINESCU, B.; VASILESCU, A.; STAN, D.; RADTKE, M.; REINHOLZ, U.; BUZANICH, G.; CECCATO, D. and OBERLAENDER-TARNOVEANU, E. 2012b. Studies on archaeological gold items found in Romanian territory using X-Ray-based analytical spectrometry, *Journal of Analytical Atomic Spectrometry*, Vol. 27. No. 12, p. 2076-2081.

CONSTANTINESCU, B.; VASILESCU, A.; RADTKE, M.; REINHOLTZ, U.; PACHECO, C.; PICHION, L.; OBERLAENDER-TARNOVEANU, E. 2012c. SR SRF and micro-PIXE studies on ancient metallurgy of thirteen Dacian gold bracelets. *Applied Physics A*, 109, p. 395-402.

CRISTEA, D. 2012. *Gold geological sources for Romanian archaeological gold objects*, PhD Thesis, Bucharest University, p. 1-171 (in Romanian unpublished).

EXHIBITION CATALOGUE 2013. *Ancient gold and silver of Romania*, National History Museum of Romania, Bucharest, p. 1-700 (in Romanian).

LAZAROVICI, C.-M.; CONSTANTINESCU, B.; LAZAROVICI, G. 2012. About the analyses of gold artifacts from the jewellery workshop at Cheile Turzii / Peștera Caprelor-Peștera Ungurească, *Apulum*, XLIX (1), p. 1-12 (in Romanian).

POPESCU, D. *Gold processing in Transylvania before Roman conquest*, in Archaeological research in Transylvania, Editura Academiei Republicii Populare Romane, 1956, p. 158-212 (in Romanian).

SCHLOSSER, S.; KOVACS, R.; PERNICKA, E.; GUNTHER, D.; TELLENBACH, M. 2009, *Fingerprints in Gold*, in Reindel, M.; Wagner, G. A. (eds.) *New Technologies for Archaeology*, Springer-Verlag Berlin Heidelberg, p. 409-504.

UDUBASA, G. *Mineralogical Regions of Romania* in *Minerals of the Carpathians*, edited by Sandor Szakall, Granit, Prague, 2002 p. 52-84.

VASILESCU, A.; CONSTANTINESCU, B.; BUGOI, R. 2011. Micro-SR-XRF studies of gold provenance in archaeology, *Romanian Journal in Physics,* 56, 3-4, p. 366-372.

Passage of technologies – an archaeometric case study of iron artifacts of a Scythian Age grave from the Carpathian Basin

B. Török
Institute of Metallurgical and Foundry Engineerings, University of Miskolc,
3515 Miskolc-Egyetemváros, Hungary
bela.torok@uni-miskolc.hu

A. Gyucha
Center for National Heritage Protection at the Hungarian National Museum, Hungary

Á. Kovács, P. Barkóczy
Department of Physical Metallurgy and Metalforming, University of Miskolc, Hungary

Gy. Gulyás
Ásatárs Cultural, Archaeological Servicing and Commercial Ltd, Hungary

Abstract

The members of the Archaeometallurgical Research Group of University of Miskolc (ARGUM) conducted a complex archaeometric investigation on some Scythian Age iron weapons from the Scythian Period of the Carpathian Basin. The analyses are unique with regards to the period. The artifacts were unearthed from a possible burial context during the preventive excavations at Bátmonostor-Szurdok in the southern part of the Danube-Tisza Interfluve. The analyses were carried out at the Laboratory for Complex Image and Structure Analyses at the Institute of Materials Science at the University of Miskolc using computer-operated optical microscopy, scanning electron microscopy with energy dispersive x-ray spectrometry, and micro-hardness testing. The investigations aimed at answering two major questions: 1) Were the objects made of one or multiple types of raw materials? 2) Can similarities be revealed with regards to the technology of production, forging and the possible heat treatment of the artifacts?

Based on material structure and inclusion composition, the artifacts can be classified into two distinct groups in terms of quality of material and supposed manufacturing technology. The various analyses conducted on the artifacts imply that the burial assemblage may reflect shared cultural traditions and commercial activities between different regions of Scythian Culture of the Great Hungarian Plain and Transdanubian Hallstatt Culture

Key-words: *archaeometry, Middle Iron Age, iron weapons, optical microscopy, SEM-EDX, hardness test, forging technology*

Résumé

Les membres du Group de Recherche Archeometallurgique de l'Université de Miskolc (ARGUM) ont mené une investigation archéométrique complexe sur certaines armes Scythes de l'âge du Fer à partir de la Période Scythe du bassin des Carpates. Les analyses sont uniques en ce qui concerne la période. Les artefacts ont été découverts dans un contexte funéraire possible lors des fouilles préventives à Bátmonostor-Szurdok dans la partie sud du Danube-Tisza interfluve. Les analyses ont été effectuées au Laboratoire de l'Image Complexe et de Analyse Structurelle à l'Institut des Sciences des Matériaux à l'Université de Miskolc en utilisant la microscopie optique commandée par ordinateur, la microscopie électronique à balayage avec dispersion d'énergie pour spectrométrie à rayons X, et les tests de micro-dureté. Les recherches visant répondre à deux grandes questions: 1) les objets ont été produits en un ou plusieurs types de matières premières? 2) Peuvent être révélés des similitudes en ce qui concerne la technologie de la production, le forgeage et le traitement thermique possible des artefacts?

Sur la base de structure de la matière et de la composition de l'inclusion, les artefacts peuvent être classés en deux groupes distincts en termes de qualité des matériaux et de la technologie de fabrication supposée. Les différentes analyses menées sur les artefacts impliquent que l'assemblage funéraire peut refléter les traditions culturelles partagées et des activités commerciales entre les différentes régions de la Culture Scythe de la Grande Plaine hongroise et la Culture d'Hallstatt transdanubienne.

Mots-clés: *Archeometrie, Moyen Âge du Fer, armes de fer, microscopie optique, SEM-EDX, test de dureté, technologie de forgeage*

Introduction – the excavation and the finds

During the Middle Iron Age the southern part of the Carpathian Basin was the contact zone for several major cultural groups of fundamentally different origins and traditions. The Great Hungarian Plain was characterized by the westernmost occurrence of the Scythian style material culture, while the easternmost Hallstatt groups occupied Northern Transdanubia. Moreover, southern Transdanubia and the Drava – Sava Interfluve likely were inhabited by Illyrian and Venetic tribes. Examining the nature and direction of contacts between these contemporary cultural units in the aforementioned regions, this paper presents the results of typological and archaeometric analyses on Middle Iron Age iron artifacts from a grave excavated in the southern part of the Danube-Tisza Interfluve on the eastern bank of the Danube as a case study. The area is considered to be part of the Alföld group of the Great Hungarian Plain during the period however the site is located ca. 100 km apart from the nearest Alföld group sites.

During the preventive excavations associated with the construction of the Croatian-Hungarian gas pipeline a unique feature was discovered at Bátmonostor-Szurdok in 2009. The archaeological works were conducted by the Field Service of Hungarian Cultural Heritage Protection in a 1470 m long and 5 m wide section of the site and revealed 454 features from multiple periods. In the northern section of the excavated part of the site a rectangular feature with rounded corners, measuring 270 cm by 260 cm, oriented on cardinal axes was unearthed. The depth of the steep-walled feature ranged between 80 and 88 cm from the surface after the removal of the plowzone, and ca. 180-188 cm from the current surface.

Although human remains were not observed, the feature might be associated with mortuary ritual. Traces of burning on the artifacts that could be related to the funerary ritual were not observed. Graves lacking human remains with no or few artifacts are often interpreted as symbolic burials, and are numerous in the Middle Iron Age cemeteries of the Plain and the surrounding regions. Other burials or settlement features dating to the Middle Iron Age were not revealed during the excavations of the Bátmonostor site.

The typochronological analysis allows to date the assemblage to a considerably wide chronological framework from the second half of the 6th to the turn of the 5th and 4th centuries BC which corresponds to the HaD2-3–LTA in the Carpathian Basin (Friedrich 1999; Trachsel 2004). The radiocarbon dating of a tube sample from the grave confirms this chronology. The grave construction and the vast majority of findings, including the ceramic vessel, the antler tubes, the bronze arrowhead and most of the iron artifacts, fit well in the Scythian Period of the Great Hungarian Plain (Kemenczei 2005; Kemenczei 2009).

The iron artifacts (an acinaces, robust adze-axe, slender adze-axe, long axe, shaft hole axe, trunnion axe, two spearheads and a sheath) found in the Bátmonostor-Szurdok burial feature represent nearly the full spectrum of weaponry for the Scythian Age Alföld group. Although the typological analysis suggests that several objects, namely the shaft-hole axe, the probable long axe and the trunnion axe, are rare or unknown types during the Middle Iron Age of the Plain, they are found in cemeteries of neighboring areas, particularly in the Transdanubian Hallstatt Culture (Mithay 1980, 62, Fig. 9. 4; Figler 2010, 43, Table 11. 1.; Horváth 1969, 112, Fig. 6. 8; 115, Fig. 10. 1; 124, Fig. 23. 1, 5).

Examination and disscussion

A variety of archaeometric analyses were carried out on the iron artifacts of the assemblage. Six objects proved to be suitable for the analyses, namely the probable long axe, the trunnion axe, the shaft-hole axe, the robust adze-axe, the larger spearhead and its sheath (Fig. 1). The rest of iron artifacts were too corroded to be examined. These investigations are unprecedented on Middle Iron Age metal assemblages from the Carpathian Basin.

The researchers of ARGUM utilized computer-operated optical microscopy (OM), scanning electron microscopy with energy dispersive x-ray spectrometry (SEM-EDX), and micro-hardness testing (HV1). The cross-sections of examinable iron artifacts have been etched in 2% nital solution.

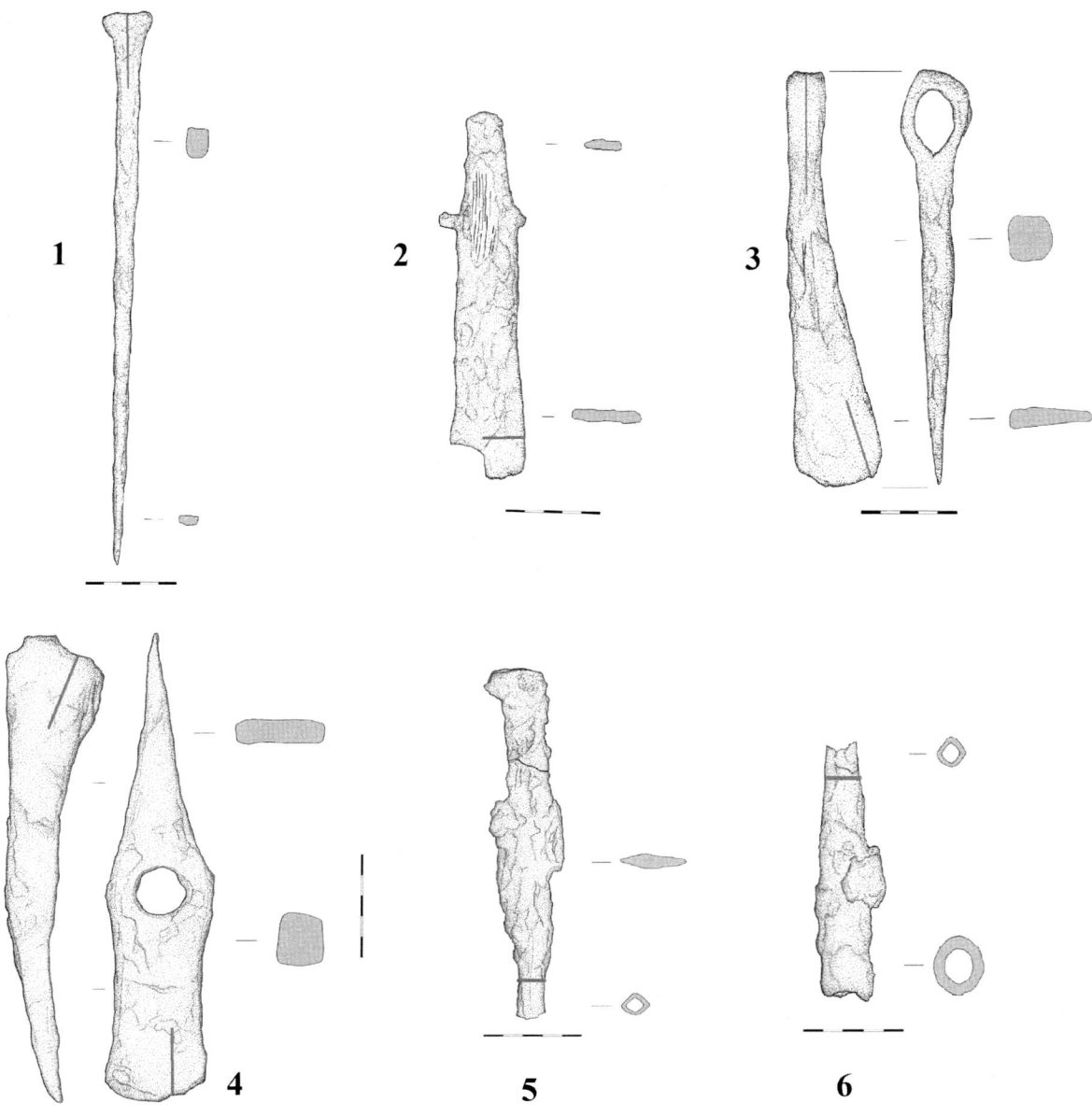

FIGURE 1. THE EXAMINED IRON ARTIFACTS – LONG AXE (1), TRUNNION AXE (2), SHAFT-HOLE AXE (3), ADZE-AXE (4), SPEARHEAD (5) AND SHEATH (6), THE STUDIED CROSS-SECTIONS ARE MARKED.

Long axe

Net like ferrite could be found around the pearlite grains near the surface of the long axe. To see the whole microstructure this net like ferrite could be formed when an iron sheet with low carbon content was forged between two iron sheets with high carbon content. The carbon diffused to the sheet with low carbon content from the others with high carbon content in the temperature of the heating and warm forging. This phenomena caused also to increase the fraction of pearlite towards the surface of the axe. Additionally needle like ferrite also could be discovered, which imply an accelerated cooling.

During the SEM examination was discovered that the carbon content of the material decreased toward the middle regions of the axe from its surface. Near the surface approx. 0.8% carbon content during in the middle region only 0.3% carbon content was measured. The microstructure contains a lot of pearlite with a small amount of ferrite near the surface and in the middle fine ferrite grains and a small fraction of pearlite can be seen. This was mainly discovered in the head and the stem of the axe (Fig. 2).

Fig. 3 shows inclusions which are ordered regularly in rows. The chemical composition implied Ca-Fe-silicate with high phosphorus content: O: 19.20%; Fe: 17.87%; Si: 15.759%; Ca: 28.99%; Mn: 7.25%; Al: 4.28%; K: 1.98%, Mg: 0.55%; P: 2.01%; C: 2.11%.

Trunnion axe

On the optical micrographs it can be seen the fine grained pearlite and the pearlite with net like ferrite next to each other. Probably this type of microstructure formed by intensive deformation during the edge preparation.

The SEM examination also revealed ferrite-pearlite as a main part of the microstructure. Fig. 4 shows that the ferrite has a Widmanstätten nature. This means that ferrite needles growth from the

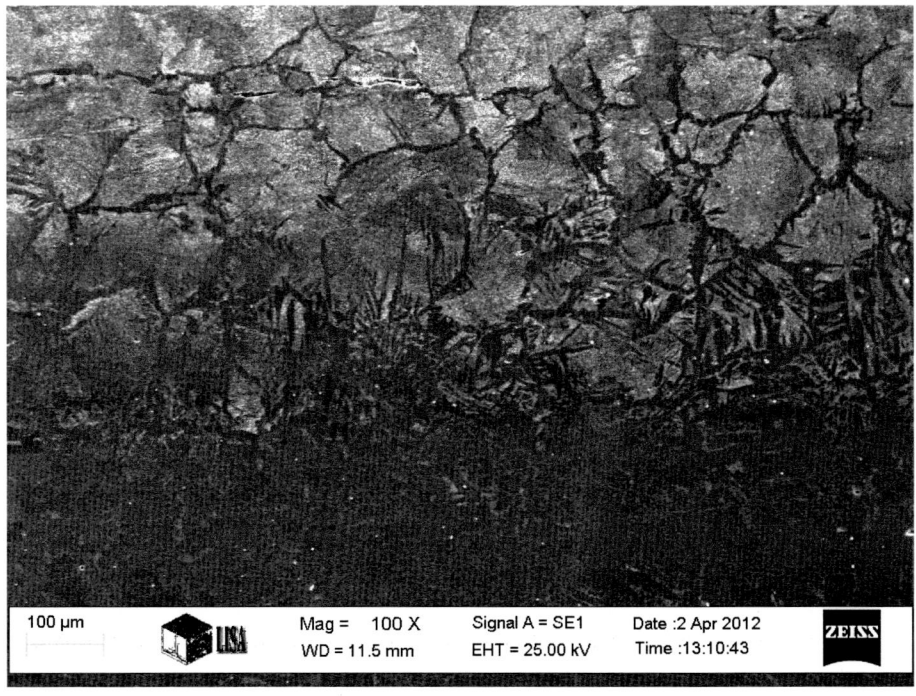

FIGURE 2. SEM MICROGRAPH OF THE LONG AXE – NEAR THE SURFACE OF ITS STEM.

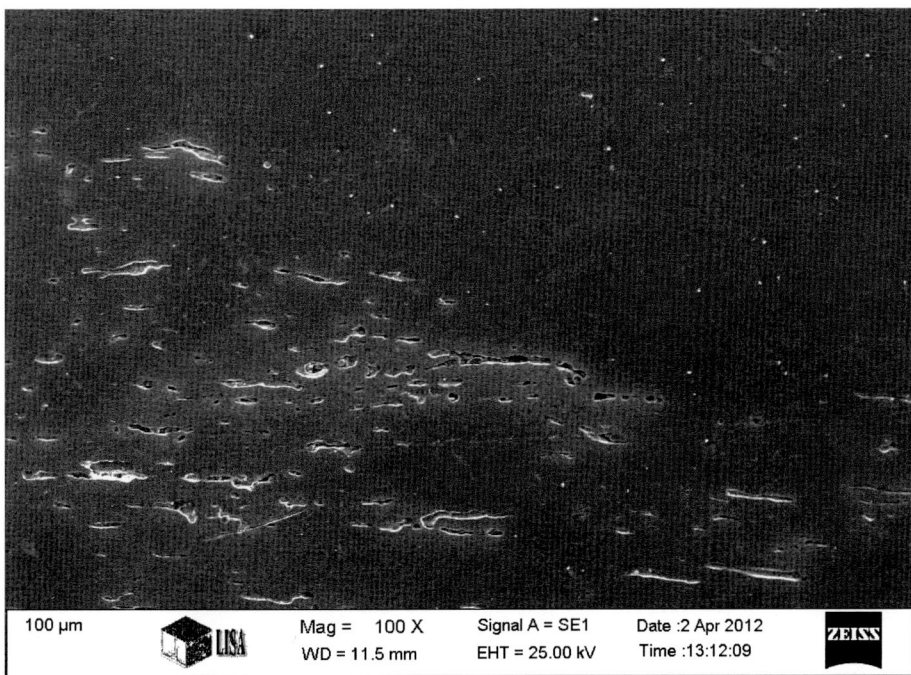

FIGURE 3. P-RICH SLAG INCLUSIONS IN THE INNER AREA OF THE LONG AXE ARRANGED IN THE DIRECTION OF FORMATION.

FIGURE 4. WIDMANSTÄTTEN-FERRITE ON A SEM MICROGRAPH OF THE TRUNNION AXE.

net like ferrite – which forms primarily from the austenite grains – to the austenite grains before the pearlite appears during cooling of the material. This caused by a not so much faster cooling as occur during cooling on air, but slower that cooling cause bainite formation. The volume fraction of pearlite increase towards the surface of the axe and the cementite structure much more finer. This may be caused by the intensive forging applied more times. The base material was iron with approx. 0.8% or slightly lower carbon content.

Homogeneously dispersed slag inclusions could be discovered in the material. One of them analyzed by SEM-EDX. The element composition was: O: 23.14%; Fe: 29.32%; Si: 24.29%; Ca: 7.76%; Mn: 7.98%; Al: 2.60%; K: 2.39%, Mg: 0.82%; P: 1.71%. This basically showed fayalite type slag ($2FeO \cdot SiO_2$) which is general in the slag of the bloomery furnaces (Török 2010).

Shaft-hole axe

Two samples were taken from this axe, one from the cross section of the shaft-hole and one from the blade. The section, which perpendicular to the edge was examined on the sample taken from the edge. Fig. 5 shows the section of the shaft-hole in 50x optical magnification.

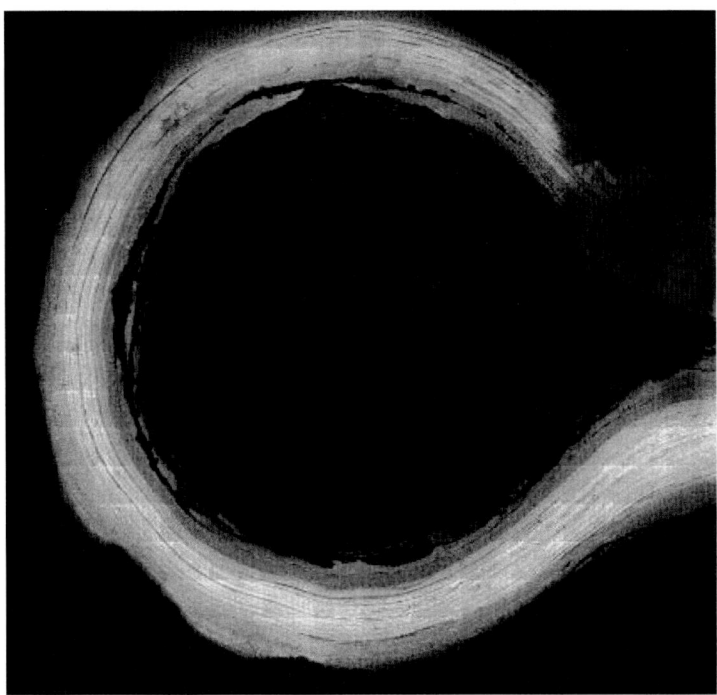

FIGURE 5. OM MICROGRAPH OF THE LOOP OF THE SHAFT-HOLE AXE.

It can be seen on the micrograph above, that the shaft-hole had a layered structure with 6 to 9 layer with different thickness. The boundaries between the layers were diffuse. This means that more sheets were forged together to form the raw rod. This rod was bent to form the hole, and the edge hammered on the other side of it. The remaining of this layered structure could be discovered on the examined section of the edge too. There was a large difference between the microstructure of the material in the surface or the middle of the axe. On both sides of the axe there was pearlite with a thin ferritic net. This means a relatively high carbon content (C=0.8%). In the inner region ferrite-pearlite (C=0.3-0.5%) and wide ferrite bands were observed. The transition between the two type of band was continuous. In the band of ferrite-pearlite needle like Widmanstätten ferite could be discovered consecutively.

In the middle region of the axe bands with large grain size exist, which are connected by bands with much more finer grains. This fine grained bands showed the boundaries of the sheets, which were forged together. This is also proved by the inclusions found in this bands (Fig. 6).

The flattened inclusions also formed layered structure and followed the shape of the loop of shaft hole. The inclusions had a very high iron content. To see the chemical composition of the inclusions, one constituent of the inclusions was iron-silicate (fayalite). Beside the fayalite it could be found iron-oxide which probably comes from high temperature corrosion. As it was described above, the material of the axe was produced by forging sheets with different carbon contents together. These inclusions might be the remaining of oxide skin formed on the temperature of warm forging. The phosphorus content of the inclusions is also high. A common elemental composition was: C: 2.40%,

FIGURE 6. PEARLITIC-FERRITIC LAYERS IN ALTERNATING SERIES WITH INCLUSION IN THE INNER AREA OF THE LOOP OF THE SHAFT-HOLE AXE.

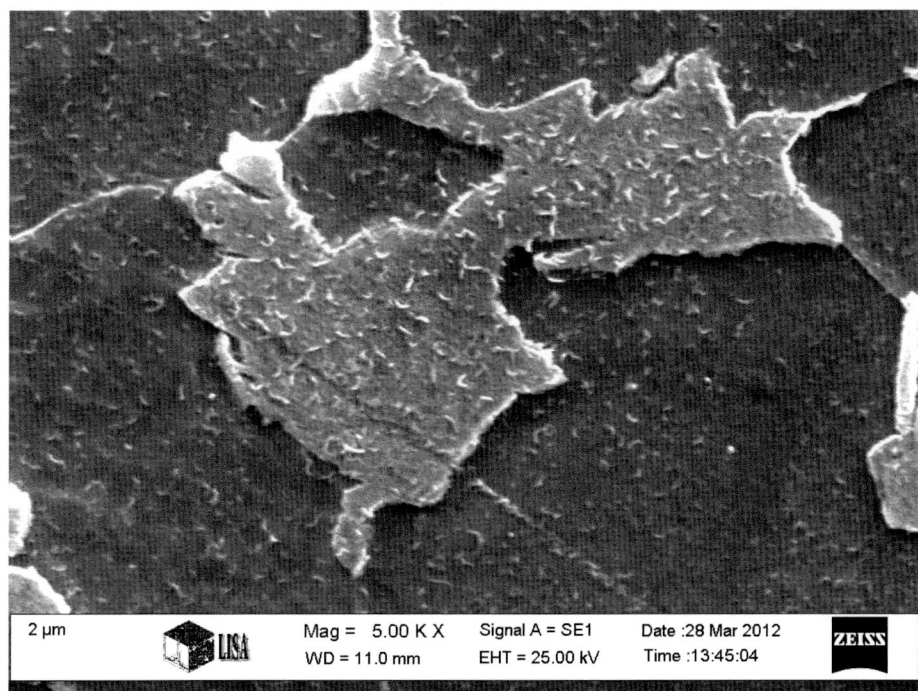

FIGURE 7. FRACTURED CEMENTITE OF THE EDGE OF THE SHAFT-HOLE AXE.

O: 28.88%, Fe: 40.97%, Si: 13.82%, Ca: 4.25%, Mn: 3.11%, Al: 1.89%, K: 1.80%, Mg: 0.54%, P: 2.34%.

The sample cut from the blade also had a layered structure but it contained a lower number of layers. The fine grained bands occupied much more volume near the blade in contrast to the shaft-hole. This presumably come from the more intensive deformation applied in the preparation of the blade.

The microstructure of the sample cut from the strongly corroded blade contained mainly ferrite and pearlite near the blade. Near the edge of the blade the cementite was strongly fractured in the pearlite. This shows that the blade was forged in more steps (Fig. 7). The microstructure contained lower amount of pearlite toward to the middle of the material. The carbon content was relatively low (0.4%) contrast to the other examined artifacts.

Inclusions could be found almost everywhere in the structure. The placement of these was uniform. Near the shaft hole the inclusions contained mainly iron-silicate as the analyzed one above.

The hardness of the material was tested in both samples. The values show a low spread despite the fact that the material built up from layers. The average hardness of the samples was 216HV1.

Adze axe

Also two samples were taken from this axe. Samples cut from the two perpendicular blades (see Fig. 1). The samples were signed by the position of their blade to the shaft hole. One signed 'perpendicular', the other signed 'parallel'.

The microstructure of the samples differs from each other, mainly in the inner volumes of the sample. In the case of the perpendicular blade the pearlitic material of the axe and the microstructure of the blade were separated by a wide band of ferrite-pearlite. In this band fine needle like Widmanstätten ferrite could be found together with the net like ferrite around the pearlite islands (Fig. 8). The hardness of this band not differs from the hardness of the other areas. This part of the axe probably was heated up more times than others. Hence the decarburization had stronger effect. So simply it could be said that this discovered additional ferrite forms during the heating cycles in the production process. The fine grained pearlite formed probably due to the heavy deformation applied in the forging of the blade.

The inclusions in this axe could be shown in the surface region contrast to the other axes where inclusions commonly could be discovered in the middle of the artifacts. It can be found deformable CaMnSi-based inclusions (chemical composition: O: 29.57%, Fe: 2.61%, Si: 17.33%, Ca: 46.83%, Mn: 0.51%, Al: 1.91%, K: 0.27%, Mg: 0.64%, Ti: 0.33%) as well as transition type not deformable Ca silicate based slag inclusions with higher Fe content (chemical composition: O: 31.03%, Fe: 19.14%,

FIGURE 8. PEARLITE AND NET LIKE FERRITE (WIDMANNSTÄTTEN-STYLE IN SOME PLACES) ON SEM MICROGRAPH OF THE EDGE PERPENDICULAR TO THE HOLE OF THE ADZE AXE.

Si: 25.31%, Ca: 11.30%, Mn: 3.09%, Al: 5.13%, K: 1.67%, Mg: 2.93%, Ti: 0.40%). The carbon content of the iron was approx. 0.8% but it was decreased toward the shaft hole to the value between 0.7-0.8%.

In the blade parallel to the shaft hole the mentioned band with lower carbon content could not discovered. The main different aspect of this microstructure, that it contained secondary-cementite beside to the pearlite (Fig. 9). The carbon content of the blade is enough high (approx. 1.2%) but it slightly decreased toward the shaft hole also in this case. The distribution of the inclusions in this section was more homogeneous, than the other sample and mainly contained deformable complex inclusions of Al-Ca-Mn silicate. It could not be controlled the extent of the decarburization due to the corrosion, but it was stated, that the two part of the material got different heat effect during the processing.

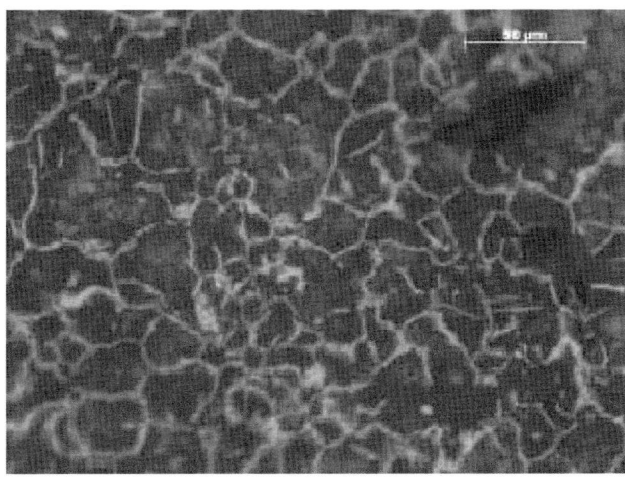

FIGURE 9. PEARLITE AND SECONDARY CEMENTITE ON AN OM MICROGRAPH OF THE EDGE-RING PARALLEL TO THE HOLE OF THE ADZE AXE.

In the results of the hardness measurement the changes of the microstructure towards the shaft hole also appeared, but valuable difference only between the blades and the wide pearlitic inner parts could be measured. The extent of this difference was a bit greater in the case of the parallel blade. The hardness values of the perpendicular blade were: HV1(edge): 327; HV1(inner): 255; and the parallel blade were HV1(edge): 384; HV1(inner): 228. This axe has a greatest hardness from the examined ones.

Spearhead and sheath

A heterogeneous microstructure was found in the optical microscopic investigation of the spearhead. An area can be identified which contained mainly ferrite-pearlite beside the almost fully pearlitic matrix. There was not a big difference in the carbon content of the two parts. To see the other metallic parts, this difference comes from the inhomogeneity. The basic structure built up coarse ferrite and pearlite grains (Fig. 10). The carbon content of the spearhead was approx. 0.6%.

The slag inclusions situated homogeneously in the inner regions of the sample. The inclusions had a relatively high manganese, aluminum and titanium content. The chemical composition of one of these was: O: 26.07%; Fe: 9.47%; Si: 33.30%; Ca: 7.34%; Mn: 7.55%; Al: 9.43%; K: 5.36%; Mg: 0.75%; Ti: 0.73%. During the analysis barium also could be detected, but in such a small content that the EDX equipment could not give a value of it.

The sheath microstructure contained mostly pearlite. In higher magnification it could be discovered small ferrite grains in not a valuable number. The structure is the pearlite was fine. The sheath got lower corrosive effects than the spearhead, so we could examine the whole cross section which contains mostly laminar pearlite with small amount of ferrite grains.

The carbon content of the metallic material was approx. 0.6%. The inner part of the sample relatively large inclusions could be found with a homogeneous distribution. The inclusions had extremely high Ca content. Mainly based on Al-Ca silicate and in this sample the barium content can be evaluated

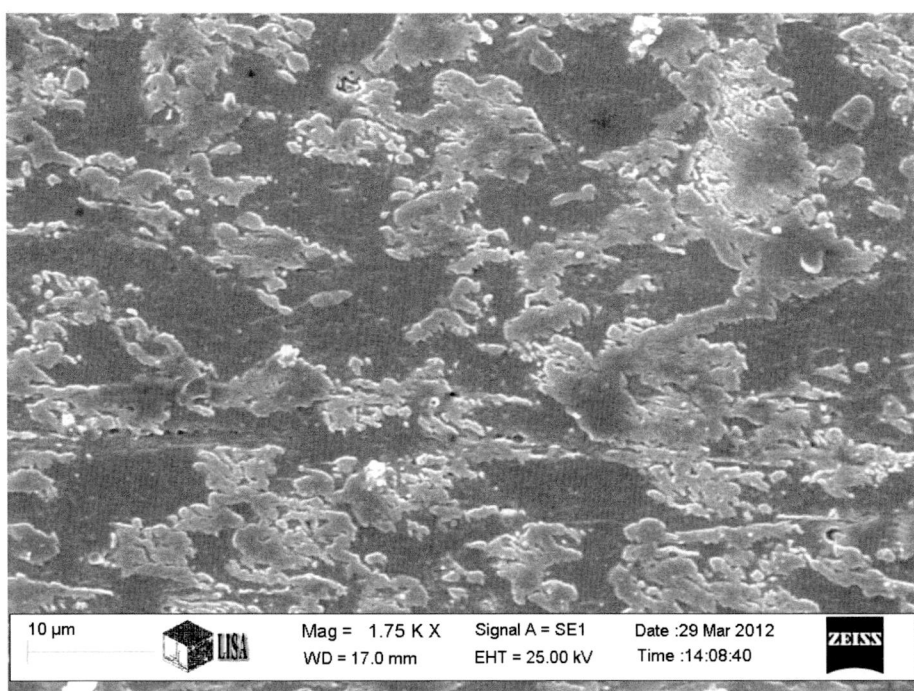

FIGURE 10. SEM MICROGRAPH OF THE SPEARHEAD.

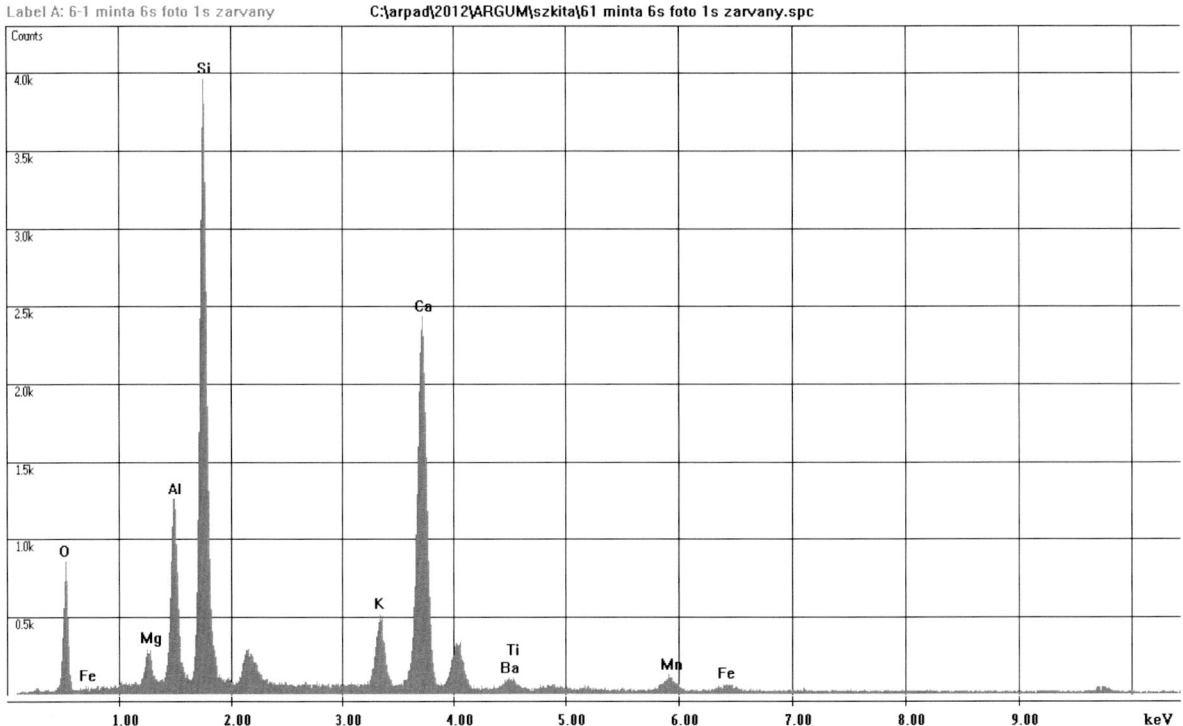

FIGURE 11. ELEMENT SPECTRUM OF A SLAG INCLUSION OF THE SHEATH.

(Fig. 11). The chemical composition of an inclusion was: O: 25.10%; Fe: 0.86%; Si: 30.59%; Ca: 24.41%; Mn: 1.91%; Al: 9.14%; K: 4.04%; Mg: 1.98%; Ti: 0.54%; Ba: 1.43%.

The average of the hardness tests in the pearlitic part of the spearhead was 192HV1. The hardness of the sheath's pearlitic material was 291HV1.

Conclusions

All of the examined artifacts were strongly corroded and made from unalloyed bloomery iron. The microstructures contained mainly ferrite-perlite in an inhomogeneous distribution. The carbon distribution in the iron was also inhomogeneous in all cases. The average carbon content in most cases was approx. 0.6%, but in some parts of the adze axe higher carbon content was detected. The trunnion axe was an exception, mainly its inner regions, where the carbon content was smaller. The examined artifacts had higher carbon content than the earlier examined artifacts (knives, pins, split, chain, etc.) from the migration period (Török et al. 2014) and iron artifacts (knife, hanger, awls, etc.) from Celtic period (Török et al. 2012)

To answer the first question the examination of the slag inclusions gives a lot of information. It can be found numerous articles in the archaeometric literature, which deal with analysis and classification of slag inclusions in metallic materials (Blakelock et al. 2009, Buchwald-Wivel 1998, Dillmann-L'Héritier 2007). It has no knowledge such an examination of artifacts from Scythians. Inclusions with extremely high Ca content and low Fe content could be found in the trunnion axe and the adze axe. This type of inclusions is not all that common in the large amount of Celtic iron artifacts found in Middle- and Middle-East Europe (Switzerland and Czech republic) (Buchwald 2005), and in no case of Celtic and Avar age iron artifacts from Hungary examined by the authors earlier (Török et al. 2012, Török et al. 2014). Nevertheless the phosphorus content also can be seen the main indicator to the raw material, which is a 'metallurgical heritage' from the ore.

Based on material structure and compositions of slag inclusions, the artifacts can be classified into two distinct groups in terms of quality of material and supposed manufacturing technology. The trunnion axe, the shaft-hole axe and the long axe were produced by forging by means of multiple reheating, as evidenced by layers containing different amounts of carbon. The artifacts of the other group were individually made from a piece of single bloom.

The blades of the adze-axe may be considered to be the hardest material among the relatively soft ferritic-perlitic structures of the samples. Grouping of the examined artifacts is also supported by the compositions of slag inclusions with special regard to different phosphorus contents.

The various analyses conducted on the artifacts imply that the burial assemblage may reflect shared cultural traditions between different regions. While the grave construction and the vast majority of ceramic, antler, bronze and iron findings revealed from the burial fit well in the Scythian Period of the Great Hungarian Plain and indicate that the individual was a member of the community of Alföld group, the quantity of grave-goods and several iron weapon types (long axe, shaft-hole axe and trunnion axe) bear resemblance to the Transdanubian Hallstatt Culture. The other analyzed objects were the products of a probable Scythian workshop located on the Great Hungarian Plain.

The archaeometric investigations clearly indicate technological choices that might also have derived from different practices. The individual with whom the Bátmonostor-Szurdok feature is associated was a high-ranked person with significant economic and political power. The isolated position of the burial might be related to commercial activities between the communities of the southern part of the Carpathian Basin, and may be associated with a trading outpost that controlled the flow of commodities across the Danube during the 6-5th centuries BC.

References

BLAKELOCK, E.; MARTINÓN-TORRES, M.; VELDHUIJZEN, H. A. & YOUNG, T. 2009. Slag inclusions in iron objects and the quest for provenance: an experiment and a case study. Journal of Archaeological Science 36 1745-1757.

BUCHWALD, V. F.; WIVEL, H. 1998. Slag analysis as a method for characterization and provenancing of ancient iron objects. Materials Characterization 40 Elsevier Science Inc. New York 73-96.

BUCHWALD, V. F. 2005. Celtic Europe and Noric Steel In: Buchwald, V. F.; Iron and steel in ancient times. Historisk-filosofiske Skrifter 29, 113-124.

DILLMANN, P.; L'HÉRITIER, M. 2007. Slag inclusion analyses for studying ferrous alloys employed in French medieval buildings: supply of materials and diffusion of smelting processes. Journal of Archaeological Science 34 1810-1823.

FIGLER, A. 2010. Hallstattkori halomsírok Nagybarátin. – Hallstatt Age Tumuli in Nagybaráti (Győrújbarát). Arrabona 48(2) (2010) 7-48.

FRIEDRICH, M. 1999. Der Aufbau von regionalen Eichen-Jahrringchronologien des letzten vorchristlichen Jahrtausends und ihre Bedeutung für die absoluten Daten der Hallstattzeit aus Süd- und Ostdeutschland. In: Jerem, E.; Poroszlai, I. (eds.): Archaeology of the Bronze and Iron Age: Experimental Archaeology, Environmental Archaeology, Archaeological Parks. Budapest 1999, 271-284.

HORVÁTH, A. 1969. A vaszari és somlóvásárhelyi Hallstatt-kori halomsírok. – Hügelgräber aus der Hallstattzeit nächst Somlóvásárhely és Vaszar. VMMÉ 8 (1969) 109-134.

KEMENCZEI, T. 2005. Zu den östlichen Beziehungen der skythenzeitlichen Alföld-Gruppe. CommArchHung 2005, 177-211.

KEMENCZEI, T. 2009. Studien zu den Denkmälern skytisch Geprägter Alföld Gruppe. Inventaria Praehistorica Hungariae XII. Budapest 2009. 35-50.

MITHAY, S. 1980. A vaszari koravaskori temető és telephely. – Gräberfeld und Siedlung von Vaszar aus der Früheisenzeit. ArchÉrt 107 (1980) 53-78.

TÖRÖK, B. 2010. Crystallization of Iron Slags Found in Early Medieval Bloomery Furnaces, Materials Science Forum 649, 455-460.

TÖRÖK, B.; KOVÁCS, Á.; BARKÓCZY, P. & KRISTÁLY, F. 2012. Complex Archaeometrical Examination of Iron Tools and Slag from a Celtic Settlement in the Carpathian Basin; Proceedings of the 39th International Symposium for Archaeometry, Leuven (2012) p. 125-134.

TÖRÖK, B.; KOVÁCS, Á. & GALLINA, Zs. 2014. Iron metallurgy of the Pannonian Avars of the 7th – 9th century based on excavations and material examinations. Proceedings of 3rd International Conference of Archaeometallurgy in Europe, Bochum (2011), Anschitt, in press.

TRACHSEL, M. 2004. Untersuchungen zur relativen und absoluten Chronologie der Hallstattzeit. Universitätsforschungen zur prähistorischen Archäologie 104, Bonn.

An indigenous pottery production strategy in the late Early Bronze Age site of Mursia, Pantelleria, Italy. Perspectives on social complexity and indigenous interaction patterns

Matteo CANTISANI

M3C Ph.D student, School of Archaeology and Ancienti History, University of Leicester

Abstract

A first analysis on the pottery production from Mursia was carried on in the 60s by Tozzi, followed by other typological studies aimed to understand both chronological development of the settlement dynamics and Rodì-Tindari-Vallelunga (RTV) morpho-stylistic patterns. Archaeometric analysis on some samples from the site have been carried on only recently to infer differences in technology in between RTV and Castelluccio productions. It is worth to note the absence of specific studies addressed to the comprehension of social organization of production first, as preliminary step towards a better understanding of material patterns of technological changes in between different communities. The results presented in this paper show first the existence of well-defined 'islander' pottery production. It seems to own specific technological features and, as spatial analysis results showed, it is related to a dynamic and articulated social context development.

Key-words: *Pantelleria, Bronze Age Sicily, materiality, pottery technology, interaction, social complexity*

Résumé

Une première analyse sur la production de la poterie de Mursia a été réalisée dans les années 60 par Tozzi, suivie par d'autres études typologiques visant à comprendre le développement chronologique de la dynamique de peuplement et) les patrons morpho-stylistique Rodì-Tindari-Vallelunga (RTV). L'analyse archéométrique sur certains échantillons provenant du site ont été réalisées seulement récemment, pour déduire les différences technologiques entre les productions RTV et Castelluccio. Il vaut la peine de noter l'absence d'études spécifiques adressées à la compréhension de l'organisation sociale de la production d'abord, comme première étape vers une meilleure compréhension des tendances matérielles des changements technologiques entre les différentes communautés. Les résultats présentés dans le présent document montrent d'abord l'existence de une bien défini production 'îlien' de la poterie. Il semble posséder des caractéristiques technologiques spécifiques et, comme les résultats d'analyse spatiale ont montré, elle est liée à un développement dynamique et un articulé contexte social.

Mots-clés: *Pantelleria, Âge du Bronze Sicilien, matérialité, technologie de la poterie, interaction, complexité social*

1. Introduction

1.1. On the study of the archaeological evidences and of the material culture of Mursia (Pantelleria, Sicily)

The first morpho-typological study on the pottery from the settlement dates back to the end of the '60s (Tozzi, 1968, p. 332). Between 1966 and 1971 the *Comitato per le ricerche archeologiche e storiche a Pantelleria*, organised four campaigns of excavation in the prehistoric settlement; the first two took place in 1966 and 1967 and the others in 1971, both directed by Carlo Tozzi of the Università di Pisa. The excavated area is now organised in four sectors (Figure 1). Three of them (A-B-C) investigated between 1966 and 1971, while the fourth one at the beginning of 2000.

In the first two campaigns the A and B areas were investigated. They were respectively set on the promontory itself and of the first terrace that overlooks the modern perimetral road that cuts into

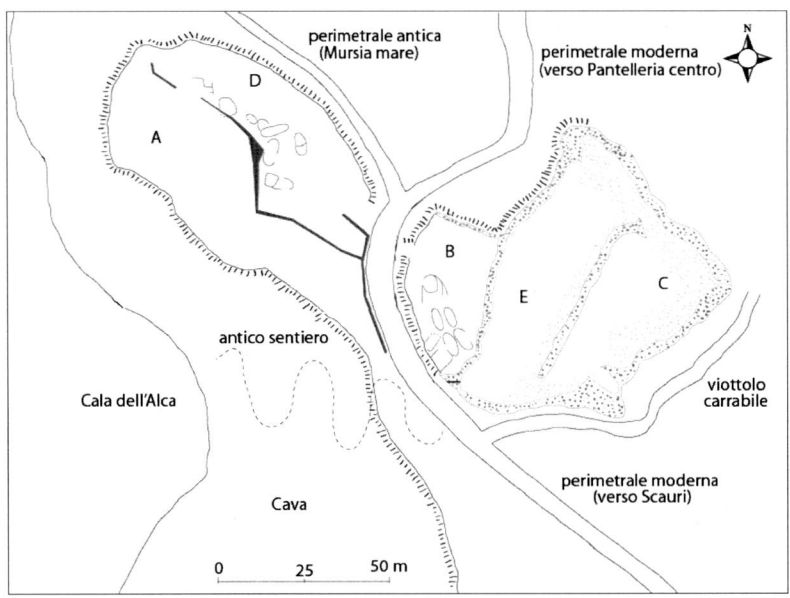

FIGURE 1. PLANIMETRY AND EXCAVATION AREAS (GRAPHIC FROM ARDESIA ET AL. 2006, RIELABORATED BY THE AUTHOR).

two parts the settlement. In 1971 the new area C was opened. It was set on the highest Terrace of the settlement, just near the East internal side of the fortification. On the whole four campaigns of excavations (1966-1971) 11 huts were investigated: 6 in the A area, 2 in the B area and 3 in the C area.

In these circumstances, the analysis of the pottery forms found in the context helped to '... *elaborate a chrono-typological sequence for the settlement development*' (Tozzi, 1978, p. 151) and three phases were identified. Microscopic analyses of the clay matrix were carried out and on the one hand tiny fragments of volcanic glass, and on the other hand Gypsum minerals were identified. These data allowed C. Tozzi (1968, p. 332) to conclude that the type of clay used at

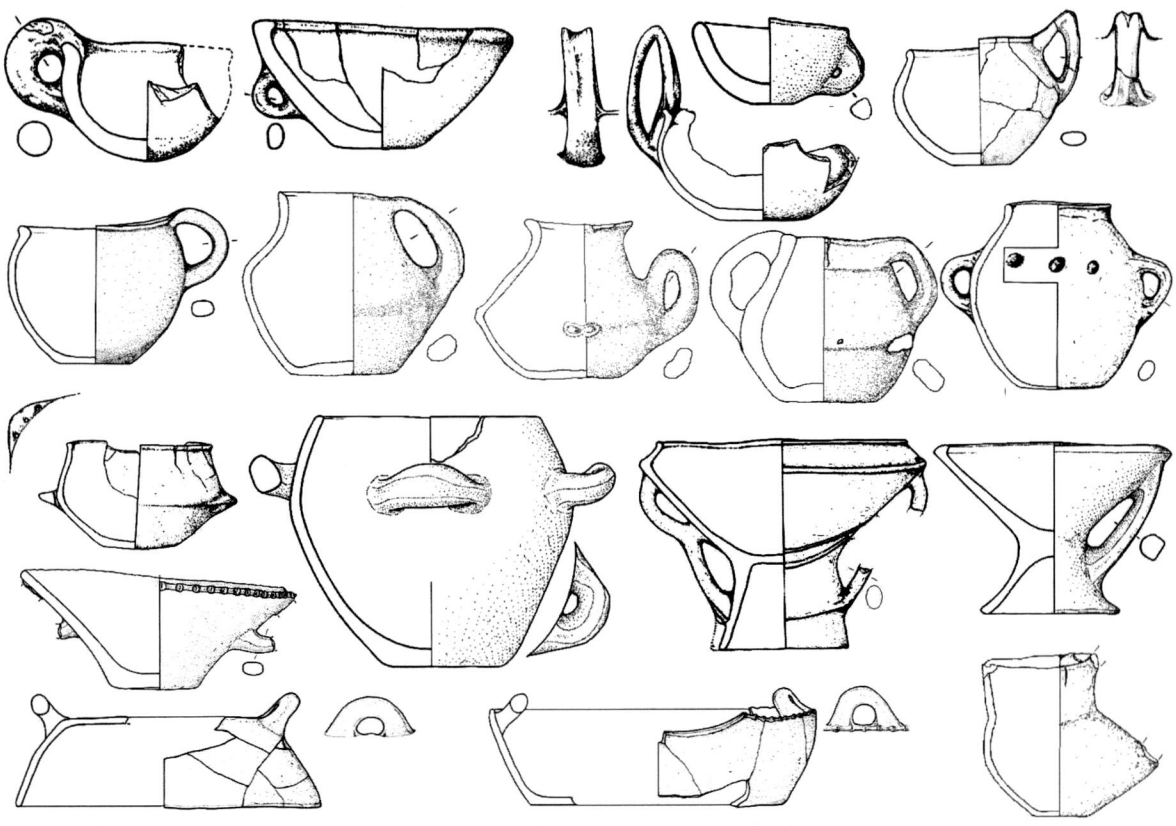

FIGURE 2. THE CERAMIC TYPES ASSEMBLAGE FROM MURSIA (FROM CATTANI, TUSA & NICOLETTI, 2012).

Mursia had come from Sicily or from the African North coasts and he tried to outline a more complex picture than the one sketched by P. Orsi.

In 2001 the Università Suor Orsola Benincasa di Napoli extended the researches to the D area, located on the NE side of the promontory. The study of the materials and the new architectural and stratigraphical evidences recognised the most ancient occupation of the settlement, adding in this way a further tile to the history of its diachronical development. The University of Bologna continued the excavations in the B area and the study of the new materials and contexts led to further chronological clarifications, creating an historical and cultural frame for the '*facies* di Mursia' in an unexpectedly complex central-Mediterranean perspective (Ardesia *et al.* 2006; Cattani, Tusa & Nicoletti, 2011; Nicoletti, 2009) (Figure 2). Unfortunately after the first microscopic analyses, no other systematic attempt to carry out other analyses on the compositions of the ceramic repertoire of the island was made. The study *Caratterizzazione mineralogico–petrografica di reperti ceramici provenienti dal settore B del villaggio dell'eta del Bronzo di Mursia*, recently published by Secondo *et al.* (2011) is the sole contribution in this direction.

1.2. Setting social complexity: materiality, archaeology of the settlement and mobility

In the light of the above-sketched picture, the typological study of the pottery was necessary to identify specific morphometric and stylistic characters and to set the chronology of the settlement and its phases (Ardesia & Cattani, 2011). At the same time also Manuela Secondo's petrographic and XRF analyses on 13 samples were useful to reach a better understanding of the several variables of the vascular repertoire, with particular regard to the composition of the ceramic bodies.

Although the fundamental characteristics useful for the distinction of the 'pantesca' *RTV* fabric from the 'castellucciana' pottery of the continent were recognised, further steps should still be made in this direction. The gap with the South-Italian Ionian area, where a long tradition of archaeometric studies and network analyses have certainly contributed to the reconstruction of the socio-cultural dynamics between the indigenous and foreign peoples since at least the '60s, is striking (see, among the others, Taylour, 1958; Vagnetti, 1983; Peroni, 1983; Bietti Sestieri, 1985; Kilian, 1983; Smith, 1987). The contributions on similar issues concerning Sicily are instead few and recent and they reconstructed the complexity of the social dialectics between the RTV groups and the 'castellucciani' ones on the basis of the discovery of stylistically different ceramic groups in the same contexts (Palio, 2006, p. 1243). O. Palio's hypothesis on the interaction between the two groups can be supported also by the spatial analysis of the settlements. The outcome seems to go in the direction of a demographic growth, especially in the Etna district (see Cultraro, 1991-1992), but also in the central and South Sicily (see McConnel & Bevan, 1999). F. Nicoletti (2000, p. 122) obtained those outcomes in a study on the district of the Monti Algar, the Easternmost part of the system of the Erei in central-East Sicily.

Similar demographic dynamics, although far from being scientifically verified, can be perceived also in the context analysed in this paper. The late Early Bronze Age settlement of Mursia (Pantelleria, TP) (18th-15th centuries BCE), set on the promontory between Cala di Modica and Cala dell'Alca (Figure 3). As shown in several contributions (Marazzi & Tusa, 2005; Ardesia *et al.* 2006; Cattani & Tusa, 2011), the site is characterised by a complex settlement development, mirrored both in the variety of patterns of use of the spaces in some structures and in the architectural dynamics (Figure 4).

The ceramic samples analysed in the research come especially from the B3 hut and 5 from the North zone of the B area. An astonishing dynamics was recognised for the frequentation of the B3 hut (Cantisani 2015). The reconstruction of the stratigraphical sequence, the analysis of the material culture formative processes, the study of the use of the spaces in connection with specific patterns of spatial distribution of the objects outlined as far as possible a dynamic and never discontinuous process of formation of the archaeological record (Figure 4). The use for which the structures

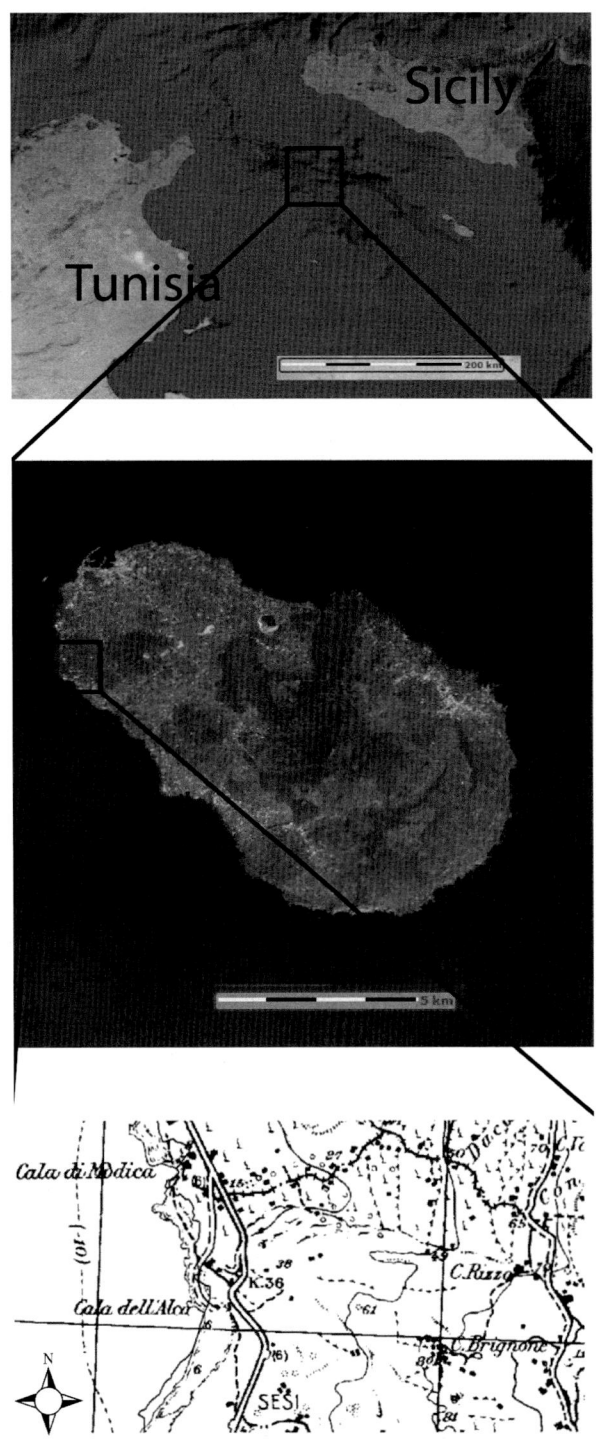

FIGURE 3. GEOGRAPHICAL SETTINGS AND MURSIA SITE LOCATION (SOURCE: ISPRA).

were designated, the renovations in which later structural elements were incorporated, the use and re-use of the previously used spaces, although fully inserted in the phase of the building moment of the oval huts in parallel lines in the B area (for *comparanda* see Ardesia *et al.* 2006; Marcucci, 2008; Ardesia *et al.* 2012; Cattani, Tusa & Nicoletti, 2011), show a continuous process of internal transformation of the single components. Further elements that testify the demographic growth of the population up to a maximum of 300 persons in the most recent phases have been presented in Cattani & Tusa (2011).

To sum up, the recognition of some fabric groups in the pottery repertoire of Mursia has surely contributed to increase the knowledge on the RTV pottery, but it is not yet sufficient. Specific studies aiming to understand first of all the social organisation on the basis of the production are still lacking and this must be considered the preliminary step towards the recognition of the material patterns of technological changes. At the same time a holistic perspective concerning the technological innovations, considered as possible outcomes of the cultural transfer is still lacking. Besides this, it is necessary to remember that such innovations could in theory underlie social, cultural and economic changes.

My paper, although further in-depth analyses are needed, aspires to be an original contribution to the recent Prehistory of Pantelleria. The existence on the island of a well-defined pottery production, characterised by specific technological features has been recognised thanks to a well-structured plan of enquiry. This perspective and the outcomes of the spatial analyses briefly summarised in this introduction made it possible to reach a hypothesis on the structure of socio-cultural dynamics that underlies the forms of interaction existing on an indigenous level.

2. Approach and significant questions

Since at least the first half of the '30s of the last century the social analysis of the processes of formation of the materiality connected to the development of the social complexity has been the object of

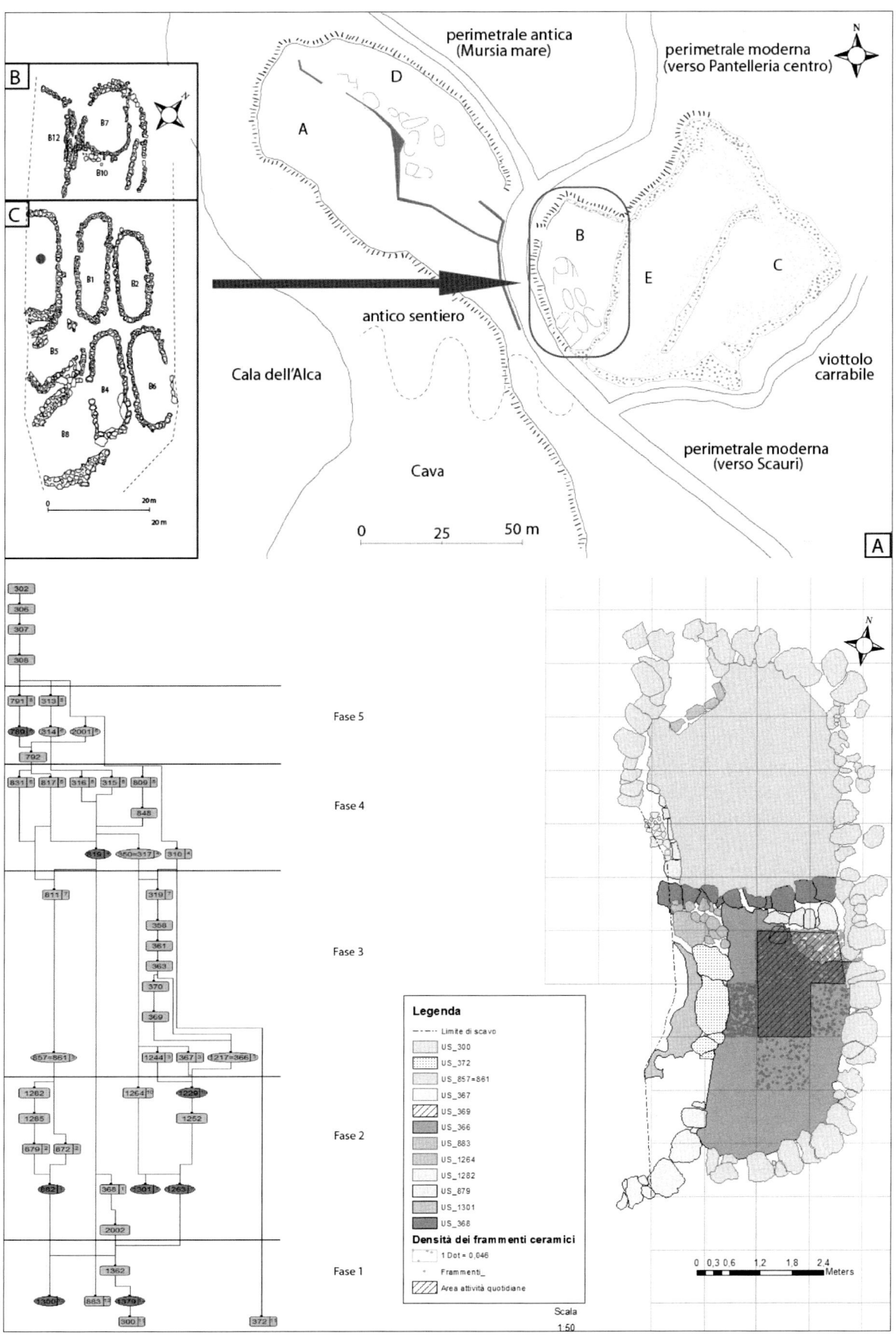

FIGURE 4. PARTICULAR OF THE INVESTIGATED AREAS [A) THE LOCATION OF B AREA; B) THE NORTH ZONE; C) THE SOUTH ZONE WITH LOCATION OF THE STRUCTURE B3]. UNDER THE PLANIMETRY ARE THE STRATIGRAPHIC SEQUENCE AND A MAP OF DISTRIBUTION PATTERNS OF CERAMICS WITHIN THE B3.

several publications. In Europe, after Marcell Mauss' pioneering studies (1934), several contributions followed until the elaboration of more specific theories, such as the Cultural Transmission (Shennan & Steel, 1999; Shennan, 2002; see for a synthesis Eerkens and Lipo, 2005; 2007) the one of the Agency (Dobres and Robb, 2005) or the one of the 'Archeologia della Produzione' (Mannoni & Giannichedda, 2003).

My paper aims to develop the subject of the connection between the spatial dynamics, the variability of the context of transmission and the outcomes of the technological analysis of the pottery thanks also to the typological analysis and that has interested especially the United Kingdom and US. I do not intend to present here a precise theoretical picture. Word limit restrictions and the limited quantity of the analysed data preclude an exhaustive discussion. Yet I would like to make clear the particular relevance of the settlement analysis. This aspect can be perhaps considered the most distinctive methodological feature of my research. Lacking the ethnographic data, often used in the fundamental studies of the Cultural Transmission, the reconstruction of the context both of transmission and contents must follow other routes. In this perspective the importance of the settlement archaeology, aimed to reconstruct the lost systemic context through the spatial analysis, must be recognised (see Doonan, 2001; Cutting, 2006).

Following the above-mentioned assertions, I tried to answer to the following questions:
- Can a specific pattern in pottery production be identified at Pantelleria?
- Could this pattern reflect the dynamism of the context of transmission and the opening to technological innovations?
- What kind of interaction could such a pattern hide?

3. Materials and methods

The first step was the typological study of about 209 potsherds from the all levels documented of the B3 dwelling. I worked following a consolidated tradition of studies on an already classified ceramic repertoire (for the criteria followed in the classification process see Ardesia *et al.* 2006; Ardesia & Cattani, 2011) and this has surely facilitated my work typologically. About 945 diagnostic fragments from all the settlement have been inserted into the database since today, and 693 belong to the B area. The amount of the ceramics here analyzed is therefore more than 1/3 of the diagnostic material from B area. The sample is, hence, quite representative. Secondly, I took into consideration an accurate study of the geo-morphological context. The outcomes of this part of the research will be presented further on. Finally petrographic analyses through the optical microscope Leitz ORTHOLUX II POL – BK were carried out on 14 samples taking into account specific morphometric and stratigraphical criteria to have a pottery production sample as much representative as possible. Firstly, I preliminary analysed the fractures using a magnifying lens. This procedure, carried out during the preliminary typological classification of the materials, made it possible to observe the macroscopic composition of the paste and to establish preliminary fabric groups: the generalised presence of non-plastic components of volcanic lithology were found. The geological homogeneous nature of the island was the reason to exclude the choice of the geological nature of the inert materials as a criterion for the macroscopic distinction. However the hypothetical presence of primary formation clay deposits in connection with the geothermal alterations of the mother rock in specific areas of the island were good reasons to consider the degree of homogeneity of the paste among the possible criteria. Basins containing primary formation deposits are made of homogeneous dirt as far as composition is concerned, but they show irregular granulometry of the inert components. Basins containing secondary deposits are instead characterised by sedimentations with a well-organised texture, although spurious from a compositional point of view. In this perspective I chose to consider both the consistency of the paste, linked to the degree of porosity, and the quantity of the more visible (to the naked eye) inert components. On the contrary, I did not took into consideration the surface finish of the fragments and the colours, because the first one is a further step of the *chaîne operatoire*, while the second parameter can be strongly modified by the kind of the firing process adopted.

4. Outcomes

4.1. Regional Tectogenesis and structural features of the island

The *graben* of Pantelleria is the outcome of the extensional tectonics that, since the Late Miocene, determined the outbreak of the process of rifting (Civile *et al.* 2010, p. 174) (Figure 5). The formation of the volcanic cone of Pantelleria must be set hence in this framework (Catalano *et al.* 2009). The volcanic activity determined around 114 Ka the outbreak of the most ancient caldera, the Vecchia Caldera (Mahood & Hildreth, 1986; Cornette *et al.* 1983; Civetta *et al.* 1988). Traces of the most recent caldera, the one of Zighidì can be detected, too. It dates back to about 45 ka and is a consequence of the eruption of the Tufo Verde (Civetta, 1998, p. 1456). Both the calderas are in the SE part of the volcanic cone.

Further tectonic structures identified on the island are the systems of fault (Figure 6). NNE-SSW and NW-SE oriented faults were documented (Tortorici, 2007, p. 304; Berrino, 1997). The first group is concentrated on the W side of the Montagna Grande and the fault planes are characterised by sub-vertical striae. The second group can be found in the Scauri area and in the SE coast of the island. In this case the fault planes are sub-horizontal or oblique (Tortorici *et al.* 2007, p. 304). An extensional process is the base for the formation of the tectonic structures of the first type, as demonstrated by the orientation of the fault planes (Civile, 2008; Berrino, 1997). The outbreak of the faults of the second group has been instead attributed to dip slip faults (Ibid.). The fault of Zinedì, on the W side of the Montagna Grande, from Punta Pozzolana to Grotta Calda on the S coast of the island, is part of the first group. The fault of Scauri instead is a dip slip one and extends in the immediate offshore of the island, creating the cliffs of the SE coast (Tortorici *et al.* 2007, p. 304-305). Several scholars (ibid.; Cello *et al.* 1985) agree that the main route followed by the magma flux corresponds to this system of faults. Therefore the proposed model (Cello *et al.* 1985) identifies two groups of eruptive centres, one in the NW part of the island and the other in the SE part. As demonstrated by the magmatic products, the first centre is characterised especially by the emission of basaltic lava, possibly facilitated by the thinning of the underlying continental crust as a consequence of extensional movements. On the contrary the absence of this kind of movements in the area of the most ancient calderas (the

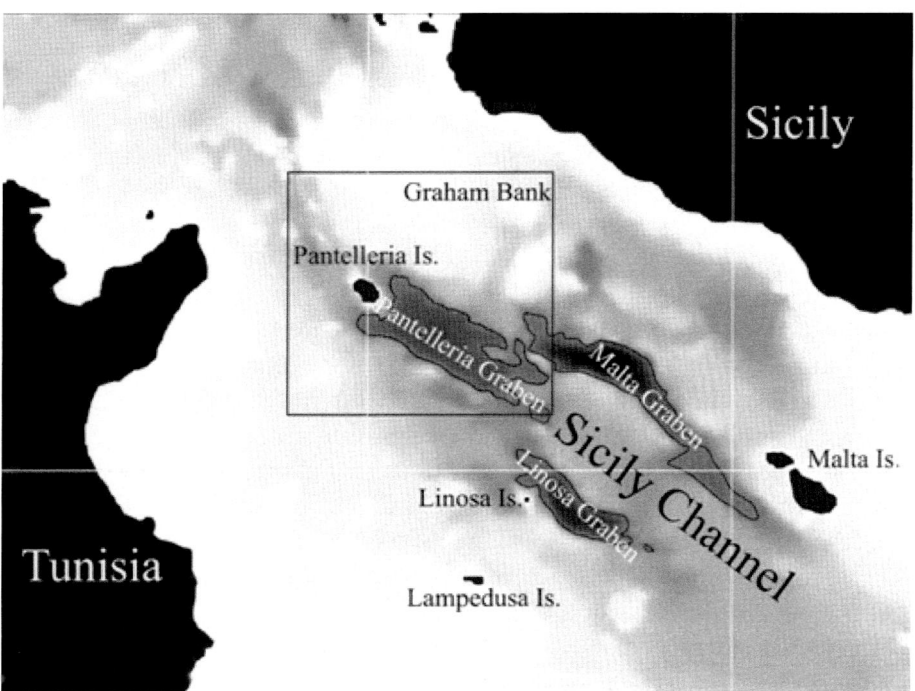

FIGURE 5. PANTELLERIA ISLE LOCATION WITHIN THE SCRZ (SOURCE: CIVILE *ET AL.* 2008).

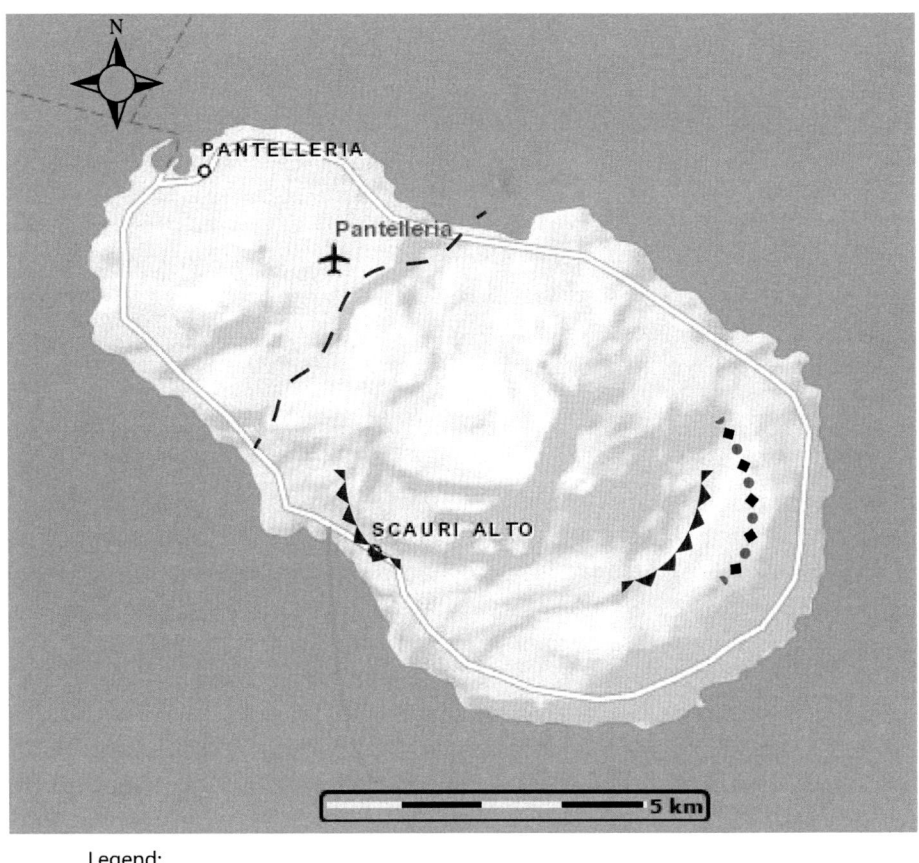

FIGURE 6. FAULTS AND CALDERA AREAS IN PANTELLERIA (ELABORATED BY THE AUTHOR. BASE CARTOGRAPHY FROM: ISPRA WEBGIS).

Legend:
▲▲▲ Serra Ghirlanda Caldera   — — Zinedì Fault
♦♦♦ Cinque Denti Caldera   ——— Scauri Fault

SE ones) and the greater thickness of the continental crust in connection with the main volcanic structures seem to suggest the existence of a rather superficial magma chamber, characterised by a moderate quantity of compact siliceous magma that can hinder the more liquid basic emission from the underlying mantle (Civetta *et al.* 1998). The petrological data seem to confirm this reconstruction (Giocanda & Landi, 2010).

On the basis of the previous arguments, the structural characteristics of the island and the differentiated systems of faults probably contributed to the definition not only of the physiography of the island but also and above all of the lithological characteristics of the two identified areas (Figure 7).

4.2. Lithology of the territory and petrographic characterisation of the volcanic rocks

The volcanism, I briefly illustrated in the previous paragraph, originated rocks exclusively of volcanic type and they form the substratum of the vegetation coverage of the island. As underlined by several geo-volcanological studies (Villari, 1974; Mahood & Hildreth, 1986; Orsi, 2003) through the reconstruction of the sequence of the magmatic activity, the lithology of the island is characterised by several groups of structural units, sedimented in 6 basically alkaline eruptive cycles that can be divided into two phases. The first phase precedes the deposition of the ignimbrite unity, classified under the label of Green Tuff event and happened around 45 KA BP. The second phase is subsequent. The litho-stratigraphic sequence of the first phase represents the first cycle, characterised by the deposition of several structural units of lava, pumice and tufa. The eruption of the so-called Green Tuff corresponded to the beginning of the second phase. The corresponding litho-stratigraphic sequence is characterised especially by the deposition of lava, pumice cones and by the formation of domes

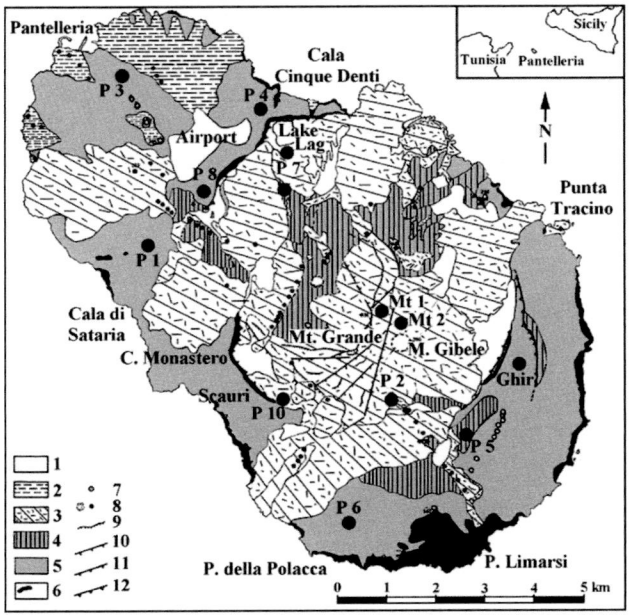

1: flood area
2: basaltic lava
3: Lava flows and cinder cones belonging to different silicic cycles
4: Pyroclastic deposits of pumice from different silicic cycles
5: Green Tuff
6: Silicic activity elder than 50 Ka BP
7: Eruptions elder than 50 Ka BP
8: Eruptions younger than 50 Ka BP

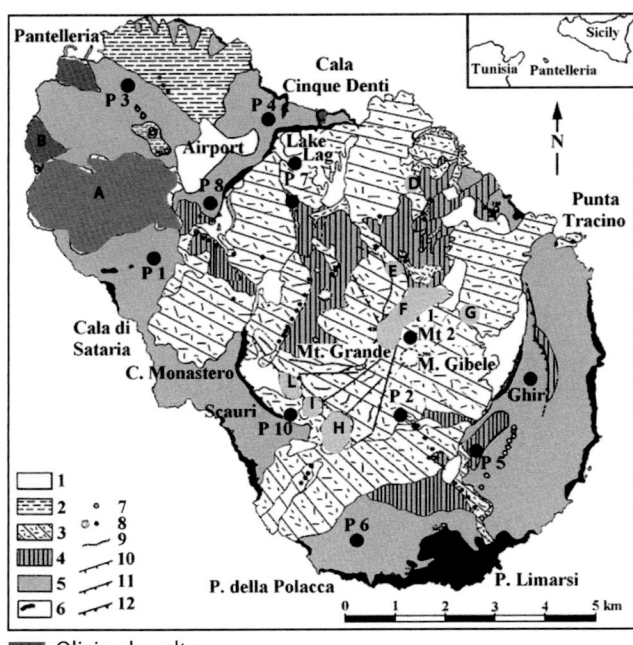

■ Olivine basalts
■ Soda-trachytes associated with pumice
░ Rhyolites
A: Gelkhamar flow
B: Mursia plain
C: Località Campobello
D: Cuddia Gadìr
E: Cuddia del Gallo and Cuddia del Moro
F: Fossa Carbonara
G: Cuddia Mueggen
H: Fossa del Rosso
I: Mount Gibbile
L: Mount Gibbile

that can be organised in five eruptive cycles.

The identified lithotypes are classified on the basis of the increase of the degree of acidity: olivinic basalts, hawaiites, 'pantelleritiche' trachytes or soda trachytes and peralkaline rhyolitic rocks (the so-called 'pantelleriti') (Villari, 1974; McDonald, 1974; Mahood & Hildreth, 1986; Civetta et al. 1988). The olivinic basalts have a porphyritic structure formed for the greater part of crystals of plagioclase containing anorthite (between 66 and 40%). In the hawaiites the plagioclase is more sodic and abundant. Crystals of olivine (10%) and clinopyroxene (8%), in addition to the pyroxenes are present. As indicated by the above-described structures, the olivinic basalts and the hawaiites can be found in the plain of Mursia and of Arenella, in Masira and Campobello localities.

The pinpointed 'pantelleritiche' trachytes are instead characterised by a porphyritic texture. Big crystals (35-40%) or anorthoclase are dipped in a microcrystalline matrix of alkaline feldspar, joined to small crystal of sanidine (not more than 3%) surrounded by aegirine-augite streaks and characterised by a weak pleochroism (Villari, 1974; Mahood & Hildreth, 1986). They can be found in the caldera rims and form the substratum of several volcanic domes, among which the ones of the Montagna Grande and of the Monte Gibele. The Monte Gelkhamar and its more recent satellites, are equally formed by soda trachytes rocks associated to pumice-stones. The peralkaline rhyolite produced in the last cycle is instead very different from the trachytic magma because of

FIGURE 7. THE ERUPTIVE CYCLES AND THE VOLCANIC STRUCTURES ABOVE; UNDER THE MAIN GEOLOGICAL LITHOTYPES ARE REPRESENTED (GRAPHICS FROM DI FIGLIA ET AL. 2007, RIELABORATED BY THE AUTHOR).

the aphanitic texture, characterised by a low percentage of small phenocrysts (15-20%) dipped in a usually vitreous matrix. Feldspars, poor in Ca, in the effusion variation of the Anorthoclase, poor as far as anorthite and albite are concerned (Civetta *et al.* 1998), are the main component. Pyroxene and olivine phenocrysts in the form of Fayalite are also attested. Quartz phenocrysts are rare (<2%). When the matrix is not vitreous, small sanidine, quartz and amphibole crystals are present, too. The domes of the Fossa del Rosso, Fossa Carbonara, Cuddia del Gallo, the two Monti Gibbile as well as the Cuddie of the Gadir and of Patite are made by peralkaline rhyolite.

4.3. The petrographic groups

Due to word limit restrictions, a synthetic table has been provided, the content of which is constituted by the sample code, the inerts, the percentage of them with respect to the groudmass and the wall thickness. On a general level the petrographic characterisation pinpointed that the non-plastic components are usually homogeneous in each group. The analysis of the texture pointed out the existence of two main structures: the granular one and the fluidal one. The rounded particles range between the angular and the blunted forms. The non-plastic part is defined especially by the altered alkali feldspar (such as the *Microcline*), sanidine, sodic plagioclase, quartz and other mafic minerals, such as the pyroxenes (Table 1). Some samples contain micaceous elements, such as the muscovite and the biotite. Some samples are characterised by the presence of trachytic or rhyolitic rock and by ACF (argillaceous clay fragments, see Smith 2008). Samples that seem to have suffered chemical-physical alterations *in situ*, as demonstrated by the presence of opaque minerals (magnetite and hematite), have been also detected.

Sample	% aplastic	Inert Type	Morphology	Thickness
C12_11	30	ACF., Ig.R., F.	Deep Bowl	10 mm
C12_09	30	ACF., Ig.R., P.	Olla	>10 mm
C12_26	30	ACF., Ig. R., F. and P.		
C12_24	25	Ig.R., F., P.		
C12_04	30	Ig.R., F.	Deep Bowl	>10 mm
C12_08	30	Ig.R.,	Bowl	6 mm
C12_07	30	ACF., F . and P.		
C12_05	30	Ig.F., F. and P.	Vase on pedestal	>10 mm
C12_17	30	ACF., Ig.R., F.	Olla	10 mm
C12_21		Ig.R., F. and P.	Olla	10 mm
C12_15	30	ACF., Ig.R., P.	Deep Bowl	10 mm
C12_20	30	ACF., Ig.R., P.	Deep Bowl	10 mm
C12_23	20	F., Ig.R.	Cup/Bowl	7 mm
C12_12		ACF., Ig.R., F.	Bowl	6 mm

TABLE 1. SAMPLE. PETROGRAPHIC CHARACTERIZATION (ACF = ARGILLACEOUS CLAY FRAGMENTS; IG.R. = IGNEOUS ROCK FRAGMENTS; F = K-FELDSPARS; P = PYROXENES).

On the basis of the petrographic data and as a consequence of the texture analysis, three petrographic groups were recognised. The first one, the Group A, is composed by potsherd whose paste is organised in a granular structure formed by inclusions of middle and small granulomtery and few bigger inclusions of various lithology. No fragments of rhyolitic rock were observed. However trachytic rock and K-feldspar, such as microcline, are at the same time present. The absence of mafic minerals must be noted. The colour of the ceramic paste is light brown and light grey, stating possibly in this way the use of clay with not particularly altered iron inclusions (see Shepard, 1956). The sherds C12_12 and C12_23 are part of this group. The sherds C12_09 and C12_26 equally contain fragments of trachytic rock, but they have a matrix with a fluidal texture and are associated to fragments of ignimbrite. The Group B consists of samples with a matrix with a fluidal texture, characterised by the presence, sometimes, of micaceous inclusions, K-feldspars and orthopyroxenes in addition to fragments of rhyolitic rock. A chaotic disposition of those inclusions, with different granulometries, was observed. They were however definitely in the minority compared to the plastic component. The form of the inclusions is angular or sub-angular. The colour of the paste changes from reddish brown to black and it is possibly connected to the presence of extremely altered iron inclusions. The sherds C12_04, C12_05, C12_08, C12_15, C12_20, C12_24 are part of this group.

The third group, called Group C, is composed by samples with a fluidal and homogeneous matrix, generally following an anisotropic behaviour. The non-plastic component of this group contains inclusions of various granulometry chaotically dipped in the paste without an apparent order and clearly fewer in comparison to the plastic component. Also these inclusions, unlike the ones of the first group, have an angular or sub-angular structure. The recurring rock fragments are trachytic and rhyolitic. The colour of the paste ranges between brown-reddish and black, probably indicating the presence of extremely modified iron inclusions, as a consequence of chemical-physical processes. The samples C12_07, C12_11 and C12_21 are part of this group.

5. Discussion: identifying an 'islander' pottery production

On the basis of the briefly above-described outcomes I recognised a pottery production on the island. I will hereinafter discuss the possible identified supply sources and then the technological characteristics originating from the recognised fabric groups.

5.1. Exploitation patterns

As far as the first point is concerned, on the one hand both the texture analysis and the petrographic characterisation and on the other hand the geological study seem to go in the direction of the existence of two different supply sources (Figure 8) and ceramic bodies (Figure 9). The structure of the matrix and the form of the inclusions of the Group A seem to be the outcome of processes connected to a sedimentary environment. The rounded or sub-rounded form, the rather homogeneous dimensions of the inclusions and the co-presence of different lithological components, such as quartz crystals, K-feldspars and trachytic fragments seem to be connected to transport phenomena, possibly connected to hydrology. The groups B and C are instead characterised by less homogeneous pastes from the granulometric point of view, as shown by the co-presence of fragments of rocks and minerals of various dimensions. Furthermore the angular inclusions seem to suggest an *in loco* alteration rather than process of transport (see Shepard, 1985).

In the geomorphological frame of the island two localities can be chosen on the basis of the geo-lithological characteristics and they can be identified with the two supply areas:
 – The hydrographic basin of the volcanic lake in the NW part of the island;
 – The intra-caldera territory in the SE part of the island.

In the first case the action connected to the formation of alluvial soils can have determined the creation of secondary clay deposits, homogeneous from the granulometric point of view but inhomogeneous

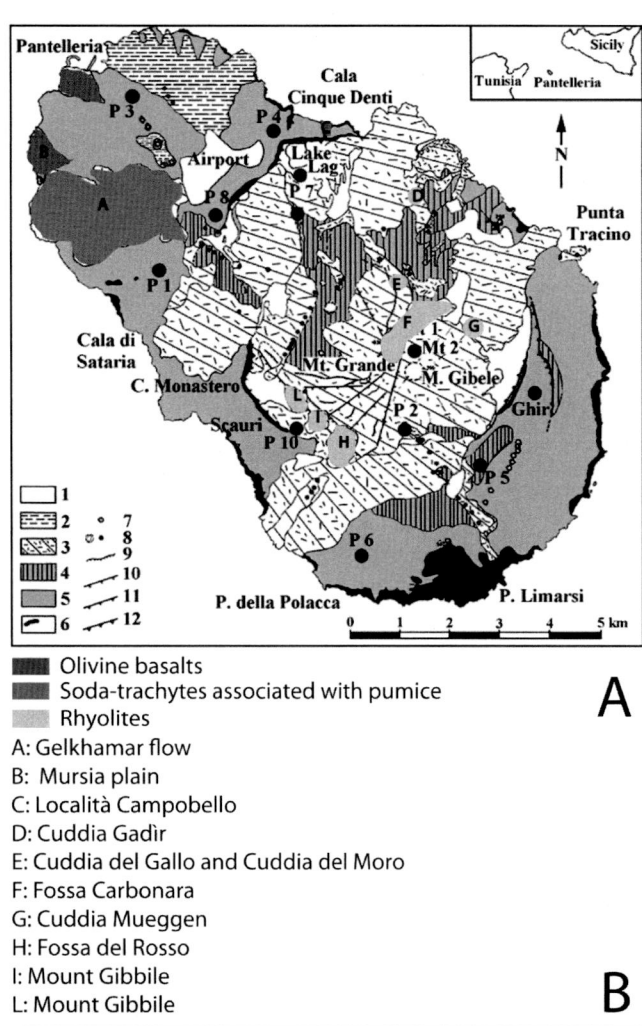

- Olivine basalts
- Soda-trachytes associated with pumice
- Rhyolites

A: Gelkhamar flow
B: Mursia plain
C: Località Campobello
D: Cuddia Gadìr
E: Cuddia del Gallo and Cuddia del Moro
F: Fossa Carbonara
G: Cuddia Mueggen
H: Fossa del Rosso
I: Mount Gibbile
L: Mount Gibbile

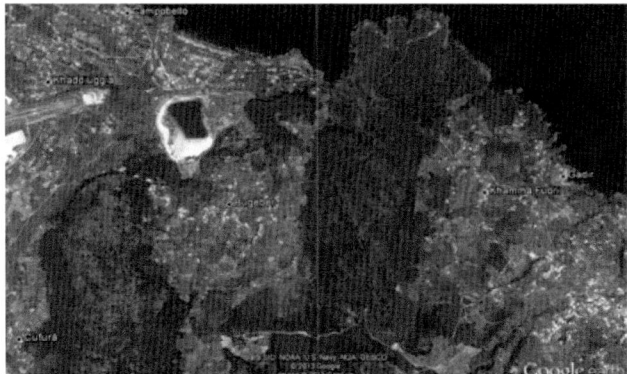

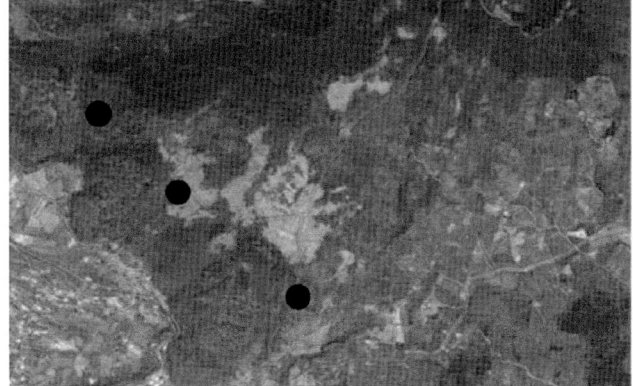

petrographically. The pastes of the Group A could have been created using the clay of the surrounding deposits.

The above-mentioned intra-caldera territory is instead an area with a high concentration of methane fluxes associated to the magmatic degassing (D'Alessandro et al. 2009). The lava is characterised by trachytic inclusions organised in rhyolitic mass (Mahood & Hildreth, 1986). The gasses, initially melted in a liquid solution, undergo a sudden evaporation as a consequence of the separation from the magma that turns into lava. The reaction causes the emission of CO_2, SO_2, SO_3, CL_2 and N_2 that are chemically responsible for the chemical-physical alterations in the mother rock. The rhyolites and the trachytes can therefore become friable and of a green-orange colour near the crackings from which the gasses come out. They are then transformed, through chemical reactions, in primary clays characterised by a homogeneous mineralogical component, rich in K-feldspars, sodic plagioclase and quartz. Therefore, in the second case, the para-volcanic phenomena connected to the geo-seismic activities located in the vicinity of the more accentuated tectonic structures could have caused alterations in the mother rock, especially of trachytic and rhyolitic types and the contemporary formation of primary clay deposits, whose presence has been by the way foreseen by Bellanca et al. (2000) in inland areas or near to the intra-caldera zone (Monastero, Montagna

FIGURE 8. RAW MATERIAL SOURCES LOCATION; A) THE GEOLOGICAL CONTEXT; B) THE LAKE BASIN WITH SECONDARY CLAY SEDIMENTS; C) FOSSA DEL ROSSO AND THE TWO GIBBILE MOUNTS WITHIN THE VECCHIA CALDERA, WITH PRIMARY CLAY SOURCES.

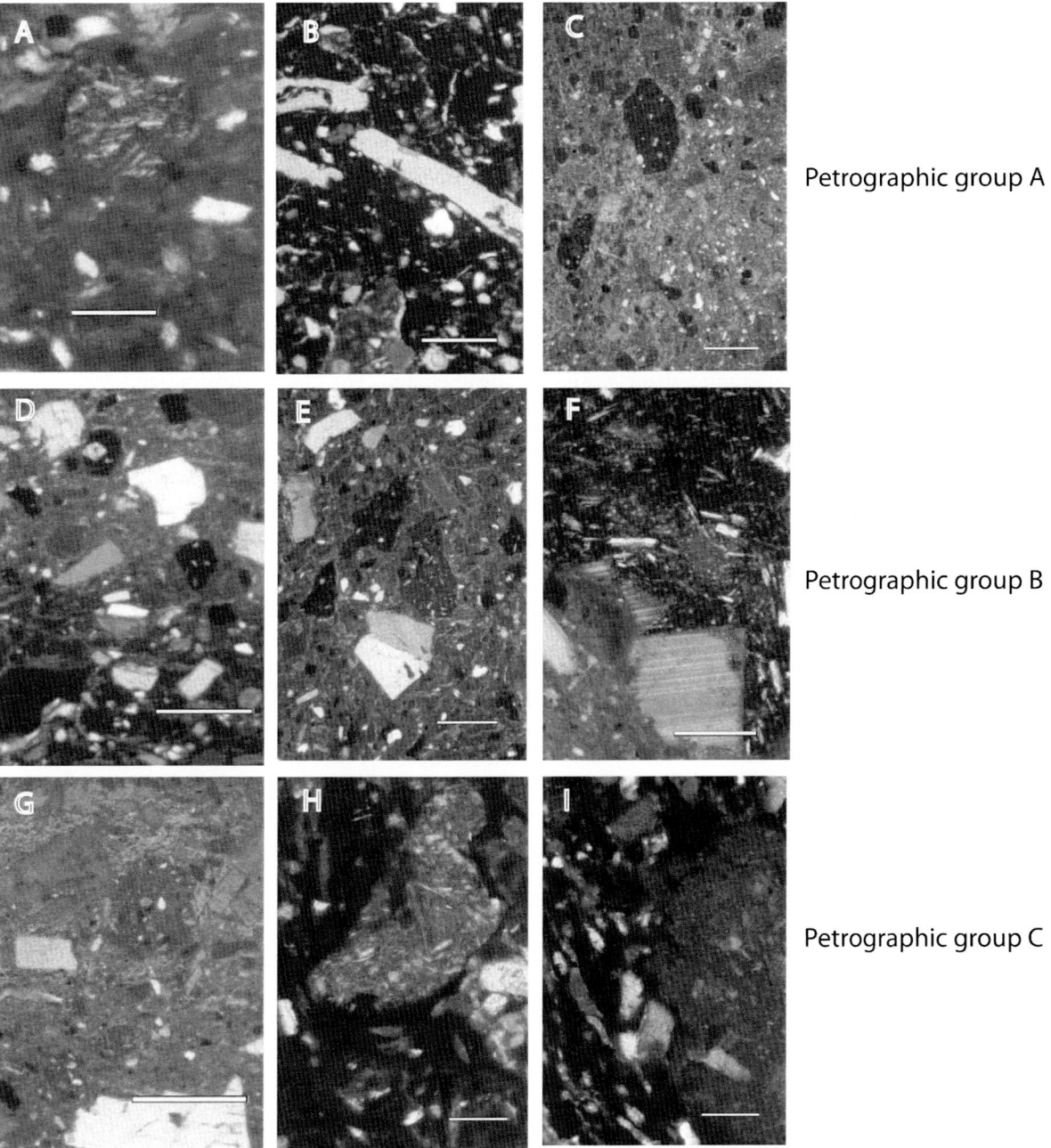

Figure 9. Thin section micrographs of the late Early Bronze Age pottery from Mursia. a) sample C12_09, with evidence of trachyte rock fragments, b) sample C12_12, with evidence of pseudomorphs, c) sample C12_23 with granular structure. Every sample owns rounded or sub-rounded particles. d) sample C12_04 with evidence micaceous elements within the paste and altered feldspars such as microclines, e) sample C12_15, with evidence of ACF and ryolithic rock fragments, f) sample C12_08 is characterized by the presence of ryolithic rock fragments and microclines. g) sample C12_07, with evidence of ACF and altered feldspar, h) and i) belong to sample C12_21, with evidence of both trachyte and ryolite.

Grande and Monte Gibele). The analyses of the acid soils carried out by Di Figlia *et al.* (2007) on the island show indeed that the major components connected to the chemical-physical alterations of the mother rock contain on the one hand K-feldspars and pyroxenes, on the other hand secondary products connected to the oxidation of the iron and of the titanium. The geothermal phenomena responsible for the chemical-physical alterations of the rhyolitic rocks and of the trachytes make it likely to define the area to the formations of the Fossa del Rosso and near the Monte Gibele and would justify the generalised presence of altered K-feldspars, such as the microcline in the ceramic fabric of the samples of the Groups B and C. The colour, sometimes reddish and sometimes black, could be justified by the presence of traces of secondary elements connected to the soil oxidation, such as magnetite and hematite, that are completely unknown in the samples of the Group A. The pastes of the rhyolitic *and* trachytic-rhyolitic groups (B and C) could have been therefore realised with primary clays from the SE intra-caldera area of the island.

5.2. Technological patterns

As far as the technological aspects derived from the typological and microscopic study of the ceramic paste are concerned, the following observations can be sketched. The Group A, produced with clay of secondary origin, probably contains both natural and intentionally added particles. The latter consist in angular fragments of trachytic rock that are not present in the lake basin. Without these particles, the fabric would have been richer as a consequence of the structural homogeneity, deriving from the transport processes and from the scarce permeability. This observation would explain the reason why the islanders might have decided to add the trachyte, rich in alkaline feldspar: first of all to balance the grade of plasticity of the paste and to improve its workability and secondly to lower the melting point, facilitating in this way the firing process of the pottery. Notwithstanding this, the fabric could not tolerate high thermal shock as a consequence of its permeability.

The Groups B and C, produced with clay of primary formation possibly contain only particles of natural origin, such as the ACF. They are rather similar to the grog as far as colour, structure and dimensions of the clasts are concerned. Nevertheless, the grog is usually abruptly shaped and pointy. The components I observed were instead extremely rounded. This paste is not particularly greasy instead, especially for the presence of oxides, K-feldspars and for a globally inhomogeneous structure. As a matter of facts it has natural vacuums and, maybe, traces of pseudomorphs (Figure 9, B). Considering all these aspects, the paste was rather permeable and, although more difficult to work, if compared to the one of the Group A, it was of refractory type. In this framework I noticed in a second moment that the vases identified as cooking pots or storing wares had been made with the clay of primary formation (pastes of groups B and C), naturally refractory and porous. The thermal shock resistance made it possible to use the pot on the fire without risking its integrity. The porosity itself affects heat conductivity, increasing the thermal shock resistance (Shepard, 1956, 126; Rice, 1987, 351). Besides, it might have help the transpiration through the walls, avoiding the accumulation of excessive humidity or the drying of the contents. Both the archaeometric and the morpho-typological data seem to suggest that the *ollae* (cooking pots or storing wares) were connected especially to the preparation of the food and/or to their storage. In detail, the Typological characteristics of the globular shape suggest that the vessels were used in connection with the transport of liquids or solid materials. The reduced dimensions, if compared to the ovoidal *ollae*, could facilitate the transport and the extroverted lip and *a colletto* rim made it possible to fix around the throat of the vase lids in perishable materials with a string, so to avoid the spillage of the content and to protect it from external factors. Technologically however, porosity might not have helped storing non solid materials in particular, since it usually increases permeability making the pot undesirable for boiling or storing liquids (see Rice, 1987, 231, 351). Such an inconvenience could still been overcome by post-fired surface treatment through polishing the exterior walls and so avoiding air to flow out. The other types, such as pitchers, deep bowls and cups were produced with the clay of secondary formation, characterised by a high degree of workability and by a minor porosity. The moulding of saddle-shaped handles and of more elaborated appendixes would have been simpler indeed.

6. Conclusions: disguising social complexity in late Early Bronze Age Pantelleria

A local socio-cultural dynamics, based on the hypothesis of an indigenous mobility, is possible through the analysis of the above-described outcomes.

First of all the existence of different material patterns of ceramic production can be identified thanks to a complex process of formation of the materiality. On the one hand this process is justified by precise supply strategies, based on at least two options connected to the choice of the raw material to be used in the preparation of the paste. On the other hand, the community behaviours, firmly connected to the accomplishment of everyday tasks, contributed to the production of a complex and dynamic material culture, that, although fully integrated in the styles and 'sense of taste' of the period, held a specific technological knowledge embedded in local traditions that are now difficult to discern. However the fact that the process of formation of such a materiality is linked to the existence of a specific pottery production on the island is unquestionable and it can be clearly distinguished from the one known on the continent, as a consequence of its local specificity, surely strengthened by the so-called insularity.

However, although at a first glance this concept seems to asseverate the idea of a conservatism of the local community and an isolation that hinders the mobility and the transfer of ideas, the data on the one hand of the spatial analyses of the settlement an on the other hand the presence of some foreign products in the site (see, for instance, Marazzi & Tusa, 2005; Nicoletti, 2009), testify a completely different perspective. The data presented in this paper go in this direction, too. These technological patterns do not constitute simply a set of logistic information. Considering the technological knowledge that underlies the process of formation of this materiality as a consequence of a transmission of information, the vitality of the original systemic context is evident. Unfortunately the recognition of a trail of that context is extremely difficult and the sole archaeological data speaks for it, obviously with the alterations due to the chronological gap. Notwithstanding this, as clearly attested by the spatial dynamicity of the site in general and by the hut B3 in particular, the complexity of the spatial and architectonical articulation in the use of the spaces and in their restorations, and its social context seem to go hand in hand with the complex formation of the here discussed material culture.

Also the concept of conservatism and isolation connected to insularity must be abandoned in the light of such evidences and, as suggested by Emma Blake: *'the concept of insularity must be revisited in the context of broader island-mainland, or inter-island relations'* (Blake & Knapp, 2005, p. 9; see Broodbank, 2000). As a matter of facts islands can be considered as ideas (Robb, 2001) and not only physiographic units without a socio-cultural identity. They are rather 'construction of the mind', mirrors of the socio-cultural identity that can be potentially changed by the above-mentioned connections and catalysts of the processes of formation of the materiality and of the cultural identity itself (Blake & Knapp, 2005; Broodbank, 2000).

In such a dynamic context of transmission, the chance that the prehistoric community of Mursia was favourably exposed not only to the introduction of foreign objects, as already known, but also and above all to new ideas is extremely plausible. But how can we identify technological inventions and creativity in the archaeological record? In other words, how can innovations be identified and, above all, why should the indigenous islanders have supported possible processes of innovation at least in connection with pottery production? Notwithstanding the until now limited analysis, I think that a path can be pointed out for future researches, as a consequence of the complex dataset here discussed and of some other evidences from Sicily. As briefly remembered in the introduction, phenomena of interaction between RTV groups and 'castellucciani' groups were reconstructed by O. Palio (2006). There is therefore no reason to avoid the adoption of a perspective based on the 'peer polity interaction' in this case, although some difficulties could emerge, such as, for instance, the difficulty in identifying structural homologies for such an old period in Sicily (see Renfrew, 1986, p. 4; Cherry, 1986, p. 19). But this issue surely deserves a further analysis that is impossible to tackle here. I therefore limit myself to suggest the possibility that the specific local natural refractory production of cooking pots might have been used as catalyst for the development of the social complexity. Whether, in this case, it shall be possible to speak of creative inventions and process of innovations still remains to be properly assessed through more research. Nevertheless it is clear that the islander potter chose to cope with the castelucciani potter by creating and developing a local refractory pottery production. Has been pointed out indeed that the 'castellucciani' pottery discovered in the site seem to have had the same refractory properties of the groups B and C (see for *comparanda* Secondo *et al.* 2011).

Finally, was this type of interaction strategy related to prestige reasons? A system of local interaction between the EBA community of Pantelleria and the Castelluccian groups could have developed through such an adaptive behaviour, as might be inferred by the presence of RTV-style objects such as that fragments recovered nearby Ramacca (e.g. Procelli *et al.* 2011, 1315 ff.) and the finds at Serral del Palco (Palio 2006).

Acknowledgements

The author is grateful to Mr. T. Azevedo, professor J. Baptista and all the Department of Geology, UTAD, Vila Real for their technical support; to professor D. Delfino and professor M. Cattani for their precious advise; to M.C. Biella, who revised the English text.

References

ARDESIA, V. 2007-2008. *La cultura di Rodì-Tindari-Vallelunga tra Pantelleria e la Sicilia nel quadro del Bronzo Antico siciliano*. Tesi di dottorato di ricerca. Università di Udine.

ARDESIA, V. & CATTANI, M. 2011. Tipologia ceramica e caratteristiche culturali della facies RTV. In *Dai Ciclopi agli Ecisti società e territorio nella Sicilia preistorica e protostorica. Atti della LXII Riunione Scientifica dell'Istituto Italiano di Preistoria e Protostoria*. Palermo. 16-19 Novembre 2006. Firenze: Istituto Italiano di Preistoria e Protostoria. pp. 775-789.

ARDESIA, V. *et al.* 2006. Gli scavi nell'abitato dell'età del Bronzo di Mursia, Pantelleria (TP). Relazione preliminare delle campagne 2001-2005. *Rivista di Scienze Preistoriche*. 56. pp. 1-75.

ARDESIA, V. *et al.* 2011. Le strutture produttive della capanna B6. In *Dai Ciclopi agli Ecisti società e territorio nella Sicilia preistorica e protostorica. Atti della LXII Riunione Scientifica dell'Istituto Italiano di Preistoria e Protostoria*. Palermo. 16-19 Novembre 2006. Firenze: Istituto Italiano di Preistoria e Protostoria. pp. 1185-1190.

BELLANCA, A. *et al.* 2000. Behaviour of major e minor elements during volcanic rock weathering e soil formation in the Pantelleria isle. Sicily Channel, Italy.*Mineraria Petrologica Acta*. 43. pp. 153-166.

BERRINO, G. 1997. Gravity changes e present-day dynamics of the isle of Pantelleria (Sicily Channell-Italy). *Journal of Volcanology e Geothermal Research*. 78. pp. 289-296.

BIETTI SESTIERI, A. M. 1985. *Contact, Exchange and Conflict in the Italian Bronze Age: the Myceneans and the Tyrrhenian Coasts*. B.A.R. (international series). 245. Oxford: Archaeopress.

BLAKE, E. & KNAPP, B. (eds.) 2005. *The Archaeology of Mediterranean prehistory*. Oxford: Blackwell publishing.

BROODBANK, C. 2000. *An Island Archaeology of the Early Cyclades*. Cambridge: Cambridge University Press.

CANTISANI, M. 2015. Le capanne B3 e B9 dell'abitato dell'età del Bronzo di Mursia (Pantelleria). In IpoTesi di Preistoria 7(1): pp. 49-70.

CATALANO, S. *et al.* 2009. Late Quaternary deformation on the isle on Pantelleria: new constraints for the recent tectonic evolutionof the Sicily Channel Rift (southern Italy). *Journal of geodynamics*. 48. pp. 75-82.

CATTANI, M.; TUSA, S. & NICOLETTI, F. 2011. Resoconto preliminare degli scavi dell'insediamento di Mursia. In *Dai Ciclopi agli Ecisti società e territorio nella Sicilia preistorica e protostorica. Atti della XLII Riunione Scientifica dell'Istituto Italiano di Preistoria e Protostoria*. Palermo. Novembre 2006. Palermo: Istituto Italiano di Preistoria e Protostoria. pp. 637-652.

CATTANI, M. & TUSA, S. 2011. Paesaggio agro-pastorale e spazio rituale nell'età del Bronzo a Pantelleria. In *Dai Ciclopi agli Ecisti società e territorio nella Sicilia preistorica e protostorica. Atti della XLII Riunione Scientifica dell'Istituto Italiano di Preistoria e Protostoria*. Palermo. Novembre 2006. Palermo: Istituto Italiano di Preistoria e Protostoria. pp. 803-816.

CELLO, G. et al. 1985. Transtensive tectonics in the Strait of Sicily: structural e volcanological evidence from the Isle of Pantelleri. *Tectonic.* 4. pp. 311-322.

CHERRY, J. 1986. Polities and Palaces: some problems in Minoan state formation. In: Renfrew, C. & Cherry, J. (eds.) *Peer polity interaction and socio-political changes.* Cambridge: Cambridge University Press.

CIVETTA, L. et al. 1988. The eruptive history of Pantelleria (Sicily Channel) in the last 50 ka. *Bulletin volcanologique.* 50. pp. 47-57.

CIVETTA, L. et al. 1998. The geochemistry of volcanic rocks from Pantelleria Isle, Sicily Channel: petrogenesis e characteristics of the mantle source region. *Journal of Petrology.* 39. pp. 1453-1491.

CIVILE, D. et al. 2008. Relationships between magmatism e tectonics in a continental rift: The Pantelleria Isle region (Sicily Channel, Italy). *Marine Geology.* 251. pp. 32-46.

CIVILE, D. et al. 2010. The Pantelleria graben (Sicily Channel, Central Mediterranean): An example of intraplate 'passive' rift. *Tectonophysics.* 490. pp. 173-183.

CORNETTE, Y. et al. 1983. Recent volcanic history of Pantelleria: a new interpretation *Journal of Volcanology e Geothermal Research.* 17. pp. 361-373.

CULTRARO, M. 1991-92. Distribuzione dei complessi delle culture di Castelluccio e di Thapsos nell'area etnea e ai margini della Piana di Catania. *Rassegna di Archeologia.* 10. pp. 762-763.

CUTTING, M. 2006. More than one way to study a building: approaches to prehistoric household and settlement space. *Oxford Journal of Archaeology.* 25. pp. 225-246.

D'ALESSANDRO, W. et al. 2009. Hydrothermal methane fluxes from the soil at Pantelleria island (Italy). *Journal of Volcanology e Geothermal Research.* 187 (3-4). pp. 147-157.

DI FIGLIA, M. et al. 2007. Chemical weathering of volcanic rocks at the isle of Pantelleria, Italy: Information from soil profile e soil solution investigations. *Chemical Geology.* 246. pp. 1-18.

DOBRES, M. A. & ROBB, E. R. 2005. 'Doing' Agency: introductory remarks on methodology. *Journal of Archaeological Method and Theory.* 12. pp. 159-166.

DOONAN, O. 2001. Domestic Architecture and Settlement Planning in early and Middle Bronze Age Sicily. *Journal of Mediterranean Archaeology.* 14, pp. 159-188.

EERKENS, J. W. & LIPO, C. P. 2005. Cultural Transmission, Copying Errors and the generation of variation in material culture and the archaeological record. *Journal of Anthropological Archaeology.* 24. pp. 316-334.

EERKENS, J. W. & LIPO, C. P. 2007. Cultural Transmission Theory and the archaeological record: providing context to understanding variation and temporal changes in material culture. *Journal of Archaeological Research.* 15. pp. 239-274.

GIOCANDA, A. & LANDI, P. 2010. The pre-eruptive volatile contents of recent basaltic and pantelleritic magmas at Pantelleria (Italy). *Journal of Volcanology e Geothermal Research.* 189 (1-2). pp. 191-201.

GOSSELAIN, O. P. 1992. Technology and style: potters and pottery among Bafia of Cameroon. *Man.* 27 (3). pp. 559-86.

KILIAN, K. 1983. Civiltà micenea in Grecia: nuovi aspetti storici e d interculturali. In *Magna Grecia e mondo Miceneo. Atti del ventiduesimo Convegno di Studi sulla Magna Grecia.* Taranto. 7th-11th October 1982. Napoli: Istituto per la Storia e l'Archeologia della Magna Grecia. pp. 93-95.

MAHOOD, G. A. & HILDRETH, W. 1986. Geology of the peralkaline volcano at Pantelleria, Strait of Sicily. *Bulletin volcanologique.* 48. pp. 143-172.

MANNONI, T. & GIANNICHEDDA, E. 1998. *Archeologia della produzione.* Torino: Einaudi.

MARAZZI, M. & TUSA, S. 2005. Egei in Occidente. Le più antiche vie marittime alla luce dei nuovi scavi sull'isola di Pantelleria. In *Emporia. Aegeans in the Central and Eastern Mediterranean. Proceedings of the 10th International Aegean Conference.* Athens. April 2004. Athens: Italian School of Archaeology. pp. 599-609.

MARCUCCI, S. 2008. La capanna B6 dell'abitato dell'Antica Età del Bronzo di Mursia, (Pantelleria-TP) e le strutture produttive domestiche. *IpoTesi di Preistoria.* 1. pp. 125-199.

MAUSS, M. 1934. Les techniques du corps. *Journal de Psychologie.* 32. pp. 5-20.

MacDonald, R. 1974. Tectonic settings e magma associations. *Bulletin volcanologique*. 38. pp. 575-593.

McConnel, B. E. & Bevan, B. W. 1999. Spatial analysis of a Castelluccian Settlement in Early Bronze Age Sicily. In: Tykot and Al. (eds.) *Social Dynamics of the Prehistoric Central Mediterranean*. London: Accordia Research Center.

Nicoletti, F. 2000. Indagini sull'organizzazione del territorio nella facies di Castelluccio. Il caso dei Monti Algar. *Sicilia Archeologica*. 98. p. 105-127.

Nicoletti, F. 2009. Mursia. Un emporio nel Canale di Sicilia alle soglie della Protostoria. In *Traffici, commerci e vie di distribuzione nel Mediterraneo tra Protostoria e V secolo B a.C. Atti del Convegno Internazionale*. Maggio 2009. Gela: Regione Siciliana. pp. 15-31.

Orsi, G. 2003. Geology e volcanism of Pantelleria: abstract. In *Seismic phenomena associated with volcanic activity. Annual workshop*. Pantelleria. September 2003.

Palio, O. 2006. La ceramica bruna tipo Rodì Tindari Vallelunga nei complessi castellucciani della fine del Bronzo Antico. In *Materie prime e scambi nella preistoria italiana. Atti della XXXIX Riunione Scientifica: nel cinquantenario della fondazione dell'Istituto italiano di Preistoria e Protostoria*. Firenze. 25-27 Novembre 2004. Firenze: Istituto italiano di Preistoria e Protostoria. pp. 1240-1245.

Peroni, R. 1983. Presenze micenee e forme socio-economiche nell'Italia protostorica. In *Magna Grecia e mondo Miceneo. Atti del ventiduesimo Convegno di Studi sulla Magna Grecia*. Taranto. 7th-11th October 1982. Napoli: Istituto per la Storia e l'Archeologia della Magna Grecia. pp. 211-284.

Procelli, E. et al. 2011. Ceramica ed utensili dal villaggio di Torricella. In *Dai ciclopi agli ecisti società e territorio nella Sicilia preistorica e protostorica (atti della XII riunione scientifica, San Cipirello (PA), 16-19 novembre 2006)*, pp. 1315-1319.

Renfrew, C. 1986. Introduction: peer polity interaction and socio-political change. In: Renfrew, C. & Cherry, J. (eds.) *Peer polity interaction and socio-political changes*. Cambridge: Cambridge University Press.

Rice, M. P. 1987. *Pottery Analysis. A sourcebook*. Chicago: University of Chicago press.

Robb, J. E. 2001. Island Identities: ritual, travel and the creation of difference in Neolithic Malta. *European Journal of Archaeology*. 4. pp. 175-202.

Secondo, M. et al. 2011. Caratterizzazione mineralogico – petrografica di reperti ceramici provenienti dal settore B del villaggio dell'Età del Bronzo di Mursia. In *La Ceramica e il mare. Atti della XII Giornata di Archeometria della Ceramica*. Genova. 10-11 aprile 2008. Roma: Aracne. pp. 29-39.

Shennan, S. 2002. *Genes, Memes and Human History. Darwinian Archaeology and Cultural Evolution*. London: Thames and Hudson.

Shennan, S. & Steel, J. 1999. Cultural Learning in Hominids: a behavioral ecological approach. In Box, H. O. & Gibson, K. R. (eds.) *Mammalian social learning: comparative and ecological perspective*. Cambridge: Cambridge University Press.

Shepard, O. A. 1956. *Ceramics for the archaeologist*. Washington: Carnagie Institution of Washington.

Smith, T. R. 1987. *Mycenean trade and interaction in the West Central Mediterranean -1600-1000 B.C.* B.A.R. (international series). 371. Oxford: Archaeopress.

Taylour, W. 1958. *Mycenean pottery in Italy and adjacent areas*. Cambridge: Cambridge University Press.

Tortorici, L. et al. 2007. Caratteri strutturali dell'isola di Pantelleria. *Rendiconti della Società geologica italiana*. 4. pp. 304-306.

Tozzi, C. 1968. Relazione preliminare sulla I e II campagna di scavi effettuati a Pantelleria. *Rivista di Scienze Preistoriche*. 23. pp. 315-388.

Tozzi, C. 1978. Nuovi dati sul villaggio dell'età del Bronzo di Mursìa a Pantelleria. *Quaderni de La Ricerca Scientifica*. 100. pp. 149-157.

Vagnetti, L. 1983. I Micenei in Occidente. Dati acquisiti e prospettive future. In *Forme di contatto e processi di trasformazione nelle società antiche. Atti del Convegno di Cortona*. Cortona. 24th to 30th May 1981. Pisa-Roma: Scuola Normale Superiore. pp. 165-181.

Villari, L. 1974. The isle of Pantelleria. *Bulletin volcanologique*. 38. pp. 680-724.

Bronze Age ceramics from Sardinia (Italy) – a technological study

Maria Giuseppina GRADOLI
'Ceramics Technology', School of Archaeology and Ancient History,
University of Leicester (UK)
mgg11@le.ac.uk

Abstract

215 Bronze Age ceramics from 7 Nuragic settlements (corridor nuraghi, single nuraghi, complex nuraghi and villages) in the Marmilla region, south-central Sardinia, were studied under the petrographic polarising microscope to verify whether their technological study could shed new light on the pattern of pottery production, consumption and exchange at an inter-site level among the archaeological settlements considered. The research was complemented by laboratory and field tests, such as the assessment of the 'chaine operatoire' different steps, the 'provenance raw materials study', the experimental archaeology, and the mineralogical analysis of the clays.

Key-words: *Ceramic Technology, Petrographic study, Bronze Age, Marmilla region, Sardinia*

Résumé

215 céramiques de l'âge du Bronze de sept sites Nuragiques dans la région Marmilla, centre-sud de la Sardaigne, ont été étudiés au microscope polarisant pétrographique de vérifier si leur étude technologique peut contribuer à l'explication de la structure de la production, la consommation et le commerce dans la zone d'étude. La recherche a été complétée par des tests de laboratoire et de terrain tels que l'évaluation des différentes étapes des 'chaine opératoire', la provenance des matières première, l'archéologie expérimentale et l'analyse minéralogique de l'argile trouvée sur le terrain.

Mots-clés: *technologie de la céramique, étude pétrographique, l'âge du Bronze, région Marmilla, Sardaigne*

Introduction

The present work is based on my current PhD research at the University of Leicester (UK), '*Dynamic Social Changes and Identity. A Petrological study of Bronze Age Ceramics from Nuragic Sardinia*', which studies 487 samples of domestic pottery from 7 different nuragic settlements of the Marmilla region, in south central Sardinia (Figure 1). They are (see Figure 1):

1. Corridor Nuraghe Brunku Madugui (Gesturi plateau), Middle Bronze Age;
2. Corridor Nuraghe Sa Fogaia (Siddi plateau), Middle Bronze Age;
3. Corridor Nuraghe Conca 'e Sa Cresia (Siddi plateau), Middle Bronze Age;
4. Single tower nuraghe Is Trobas (Lunamatrona), Middle Bronze Age;
5. Complex Nuraghe Genna Maria (Villanovaforru), Middle/Recent, Final Bronze Age, and Early Iron Age;
6. Complex Nuraghe Ortu Comidu (Sardara), Recent, Final Bronze Age, and Early Iron Age;
7. Complex Nuraghe Su Nuraxi (Barumini), Final Bronze Age/Early Iron Age;
8. Complex Nuraghe Arrubiu (Orroli), Middle, Recent, and Final Bronze Age. This nuraghe is not part of the Marmilla region but was chosen as an element of comparison with the region under study for three main reasons: the first is that it is one of the largest nuraghi on the southern part of the island. The second is its geographic setting on a basaltic plateau similar to those of Gesturi and Siddi, located approximately 25 kilometres further east. The third is the presence of a huge quantity of ceramics of all types and ages from which to select the samples to study.

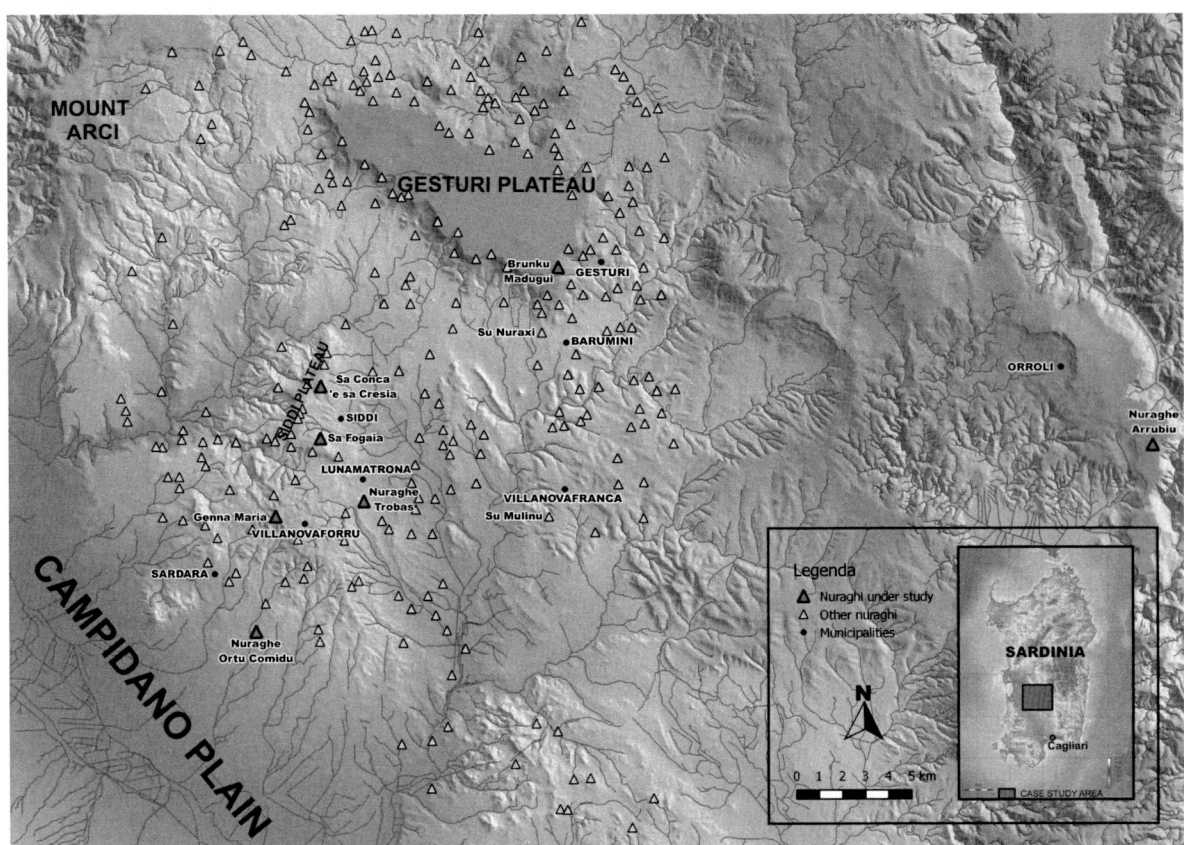

FIGURE 1. THE AREA UNDER STUDY. FROM LILLIU C. 1985; AND BADAS *ET AL.* 1989.
DRAWING: M. G. GRADOLI, AND V. G. ANARDU.

These settlements refer to the time span, locally called 'Nuragic Society', starting around the Middle Bronze Age, 1700-1365 BC, and continuing through the Recent Bronze Age, 1365-1200 BC, to the Final Bronze Age, 1200-1020 BC. Nuragic society derives its name from its most characteristic and unique buildings – *nuraghi* – truncated high round towers built of large blocks of local rock set without mortar in regular horizontal rows, and roofed by corbelled vaults (Lilliu 1959, 1982, 1987, 1988, 2005)

A growing complexity of architectural structures can be observed through time: the first Middle Bronze Age buildings were the so called '*corridor nuraghi*', long and low stone irregular platforms with an internal corridor, and one or few small chambers linked to it (Cossu 2003; Demurtas and Demurtas 1991; Moravetti 1991; Webster 1996).

Simple 'nuraghi towers', constituted by a 10-15 meter high circular room entered through a low and narrow passage, appeared during the Middle Bronze Age as well and spread, more or less regularly on the whole surface of the island, during the Recent Bronze Age. Sardinian archaeologists look at this period as the apex of Nuragic Civilization during which both 'corridor' and 'single tower nuraghi', were progressively enlarged with the addition of multi-tower complexes and hut villages. At the end of the Final Bronze Age (Figure 2) the most part of complex compounds were abandoned, or dismantled and just a few were converted into places of worship (Campus and Leonelli 2006 a and b; Dyson and Rowland 2007; Lo Schiavo *et al.* 2010; Perra 1997; 2009, 2013 and 2014; Usai 1995, 2003 and 2006; Webster 1996).

Figure 2. Complex Nuraghe Genna Maria at Villanovofarru.
Photo Municipality of Villanovaforru.

Methodology and principal research question

A broad theoretical context, based on both the physical and the social sciences, was defined to investigate the ancient ceramic technology, and its social meaning, both in the field and in the laboratory. This was possible through the study of the system: clay selection and refinement; fashioning techniques; firing temperature and atmosphere; mechanical and thermal proprieties; decoration techniques and surface treatment; availability and provenance of raw materials; and the social context in which the pottery was conceived and used, using also historical and ethnographic data, when available.

The methodology here used analyses ceramic fabric variability among selected common nuragic vessel forms in close connection with the domestic architectures in which they were found, and represents an innovation with respect to the previous studies of pottery in Sardinia, that have mainly focused on stylistic attributes, and their use in assessing a chronological typology (Antona *et ali* 1999; Bagella *et ali* 1999; Campus and Leonelli 2000, and 2006; Depalmas 2009 a, b, and c; Lilliu 1955, 1982, and 1986; Santoni 1994 and 2001). In particular, starting from these pre-existing typologies I am going to test them using the concept of 'technological style' and challenge their interpretation in terms of social organisation and chronological significance. In so doing, I shall be considering what follows:
1. *Ceramic petrology*, which is the systematic description of pottery materials, their compositions and organization in hand specimen and prepared samples or thin-sections, using a polarising microscope (Whitbread 1995). This will permit to divide the ceramics into 'fabric groups' or major ceramic technological styles in relation to each site and temporal phase of the nuragic culture. By comparing the different contemporary technological traditions for each cultural phase, patterns of continuity and diversity in vessel fabrics and fashioning techniques, through space and time, will be determined. The qualitative and quantitative description – or

'characterization analysis' – of these different components will be useful in the evaluation of their technological properties and their possible uses (Whitbread 1995: 368);

2. The *'chaine opératoire'* approach, which permits reconstruction of part, or the whole sequence of technical gestures and different physical and mental actions that potters performed in vessel manufacturing, starting from the way natural resources were acquired in the area, mixed together in different proportions, fashioned and then physically transformed by the process of firing into cultural commodities with specific proprieties and performance characteristics. This will help to recognise variations due to potters' personal choices, and the technological traditions within which they worked, which can then be isolated as different 'technological styles';

3. *Experimental archaeology* that will provide the opportunity to confirm potential hypothesis and conclusions with multiple trials and repeatable tests in a chemical/mineralogical laboratory and will be used for the reconstruction of the different steps of the *'chaine opératoire'*, the reproduction of the nuragic ceramic fabrics, and their comparison with the archaeological ones under study. On the assumption that pottery sherds encode both mineralogical information from the source and behavioural information from the potters (Rice 1987), the nuragic vessels from the same micro region, obtained from the same set of sources – different clays mixed together and inclusions – could be expected to be similar in composition (Arnold, Neff and Bishop 1991: 88);

4. *Raw materials provenance study* which, using analytical and geological approaches, helps in establishing whether the corpus of vessel sherds under study was produced using clays and other naturally or intentionally added materials obtained from the investigated area or far away from it. The presence of intentionally added materials, unfamiliar to the geology of the area under study, permits to assess the degree of non-local production among the nuragic settlements, pointing out at possible differentiation and exchange patterns within them. In fact, provenance studies provide a means to investigate how local groups might have connected with each other across a broader landscape, through networks of different geographical and temporal dimension, operating at a regional level. Moreover, comparing these results with the excavation data related to growing architectural complexity from the Middle to Final Bronze Age, it is possible to investigate whether observable architectural changes were accompanied by similar changes in the way pottery was manufactured, especially during the most important transitional periods.

The principal research question of this work is whether a technological study of a selected group of pottery coming from nuragic domestic structures (corridor nuraghi, single tower nuraghi, complex nuraghi and villages) within the region under study, can shed new light on the pattern of pottery production, consumption and exchange at an inter-site level among the archaeological settlements considered. It is important to consider that the word 'exchange' here refers to recurrent, independent, symmetrical and small-scale material transactions that served to reinforce intercommunity relationships (Zedeno 1994:16).

Petrographic analysis of the pottery

The petrographic analysis was carried out on 0.030 mm thick thin-sections taken by the sherds in their original state, using a Brunel SP-300-P polarising microscope equipped with a Canon 1100D camera. The method and terminology applied were those proposed by Whitbread 1989 and 1995. A descriptive vocabulary was used to better maintain objectivity during the data recording, and separate interpretation from description.

Two hundred and fifteens (215) ceramics, sampled during the years 2013 and 2014, have been studied up to now, and seven main fabric groups identified, subdivided into several relevant sub groups (Figure 3), as follows:
 1. Fabric group 1. Volcanic sand;

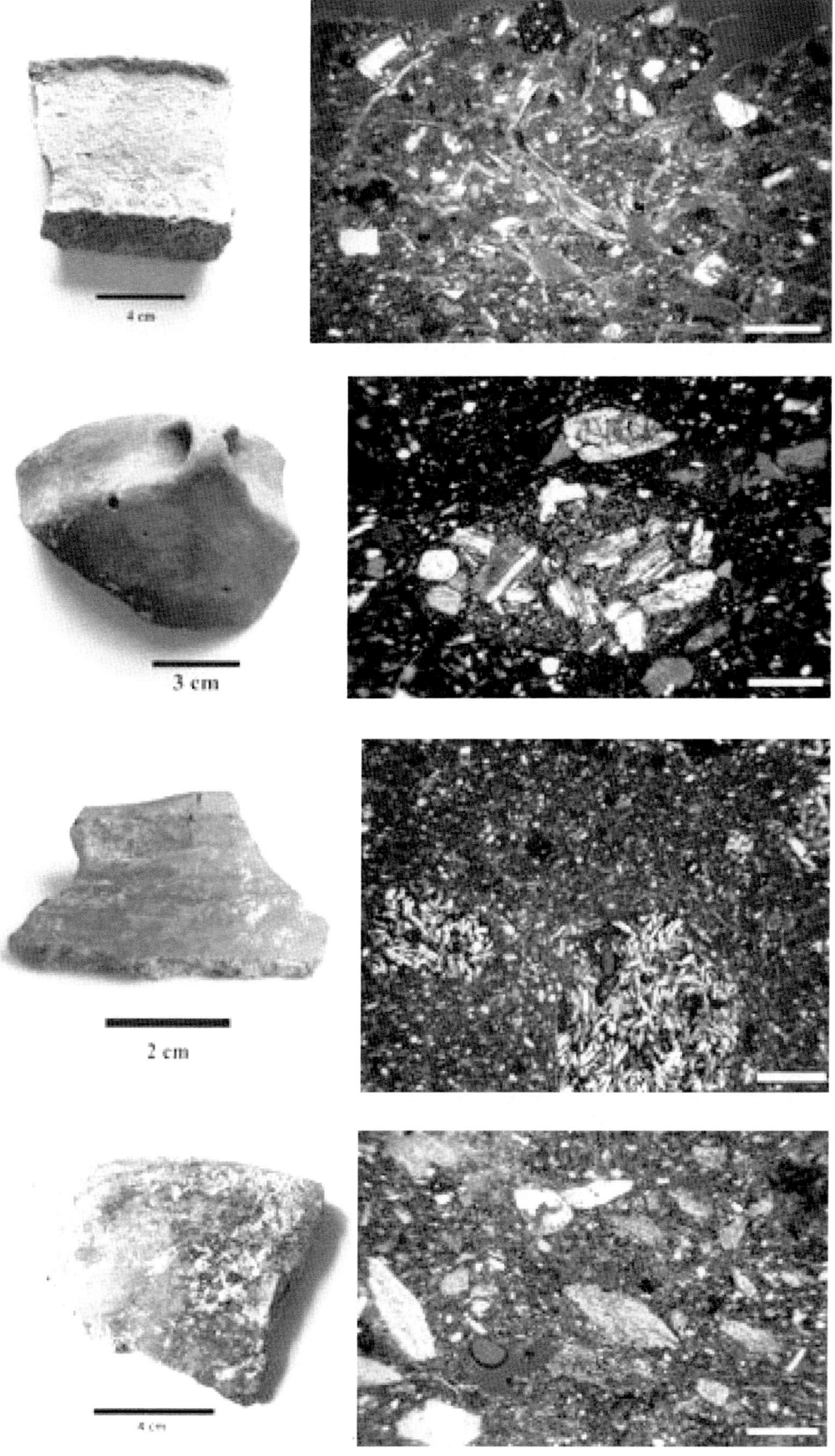

Figure 3. Middle and Recent Bronze Age pottery from the studied area. Scale bar 250 μm. Macro and photomicrographs: M. G. Gradoli.

2. Fabric group 2. Plutonic sand;
3. Fabric group 3. Metamorphic sand;
4. Fabric group 4. Mixed metamorphic and volcanic sand;
5. Fabric group 5. Carbonate sand with fossils;
6. Fabric group 6. Mineral sand;
7. Fabric group 7. Very weathered sand.

Two main fabric groups (the '*Volcanic Sand*' and the '*Mineral Sand*' ones) are the most representative of pottery manufacturing in the area. In particular, one can see how local potters used the same raw materials and therefore 'technological choices' with a great variety of micro-morphological characteristics and inclusion dimensions. These groups are present, at the same time and during the Middle/Recent Bronze Age among the settlements considered, and used to produce different categories of domestic vessels, such as pans, platters, large and small storage jars, large and small bowls as well as cups, made by producing a finer fabric. Moreover, these two fabric groups were the most common of those present in the area during the Pre-Nuragic period too, confirming a manufacturing continuity of several millennia in the tradition of the area, regardless of their varying use contexts (habitation or burial), shape and presence of peculiar decoration.

Within the '*Mineral Sand*' Group, fine, medium and coarse fabrics are present. In particular, coarse mineral sand was used since the Middle Bronze Age for manufacturing jars, thickened rim jars, necked jars, bowls, and carinated bowls at Sa Fogaia, Genna Maria, and Nuraghe Trobas. During the Recent Bronze Age the same shapes were produced at the Nuraghe Trobas, and the Nuraghe Arrubiu. Fine mineral sand was used for cups and bowls at the Brunku Madugui nuraghe during the Middle Bronze Age, and during the Recent Bronze Age at the Nuraghe Arrubiu the same fabric was used to manufacture necked jars, collared jars, and bowls.

The *Plutonic Group* is present during the Middle Bronze Age at Genna Maria, at Brunku Madugui, Conca 'e Sa Cresia, Genna Maria, and the Nuraghe Arubiu. A plutonic fabric is also present at Ortu Comidu during the Recent/Final Bronze Age, and even during the Pre-Nuragic period (Final Neolithic).

The *Metamorphic Group* is only present at the Nuraghe Arrubiu-Orroli, and this is, from a geological viewpoint, justified by the presence of the metamorphic Palaeozoic basement beneath the volcanic plateau, eroded and exposed in the north-eastern part by the Flumendosa River. During the Middle Bronze Age this metamorphic sand was used to manufacture pans, and bowls, while mixed metamorphic and volcanic sand was used to make some thickened rim jars. During the Recent Bronze Age necked jars, and large bowls were manufactured using this fabric, along with a collared jar produced using a mixture of metamorphic and volcanic sand.

The *Carbonate sand* with fossil shell and microfossils was used to manufacture light-coloured small vessels during the Middle Bronze Age at Brunku Madugui, Sa Fogaia, and Nuraghe Trobas; one similar vessel was found at Ortu Comidu representing the Recent/Final Bronze Age.

Very weathered ceramic samples are found in different fabrics: very weathered basaltic rock pieces were used at the Nuraghe Arrubiu during the Middle and the Recent Bronze Age for manufacturing pans and platters. Very weathered rock pieces with voids characterize jars, pans, and bowls found at Brunku Madugui during the Middle Bronze Age. Representing the same period jars, pans, platters, bowls, carinated bowls, and necked vessels are found at Conca 'e Sa Cresia. A very weathered carbonate sand was used during the Middle Bronze Age at Conca 'e Sa Cresia to manufacture pans, platters, and jars.

All samples studied under the petrological microscope seem to have been manufactured using clays with different amounts of natural inclusions. Fine and very fine sand might have been obtained through sieving or levigation of coarser ones. Only a few samples were intentionally tempered with grog.

Decoration on the external surface, while rarely present (11 samples out of 215 examined) consists of impressed vertical lines, a single row of dots, dots or impressions filling the internal part of an impressed triangle shape, and in one rare case some horizontal thin brown painted lines. The external and internal surface colours, reflect different firing conditions: red-reddish or orange, grey and black, light beige or brown denoting oxidising or reducing atmospheres or, more frequently, mixed firing conditions.

Surface treatment and finishing techniques vary as well. They are the following:
1. *'Textured or rough'*: vessels used on the fire, such as pans and platters, have corrugated or textured exterior surfaces thought to be able to better transmit heat but also to be easily grasped and moved around; their internal surfaces are smooth in the attempt to reduce surface permeability. Jars and storage vessels have corrugated or smoothed external surfaces and smoothed internal ones.
2. *'Brushing'*: this kind of surface treatment was sometimes observed in jars and the exterior part of cooking vessels;
3. *'Plain'*, rarely found both on the interior and the exterior surfaces;
4. *'Burnishing'*: different stages of the process were noted especially in Recent Bronze Age ceramics. Some very well burnished ceramics were found at the Conca 'e Sa Cresia corridor nuraghe during the Middle Bronze Age;
5. *'Smudging'*: during the Final part of the Middle Bronze Age/Recent Bronze Age this type of surface finishing starts to appear, becoming much more popular during the Final Bronze Age. This type of surface treatment interested those vessels called by the local author, 'Ceramica Nera Lustrata'- 'Black Lustrous Ceramic';
6. *'Slipped'*: sometimes, a black, or reddish slip, made of very fine clay, was applied to one or both the vessel surfaces, masking their original colours due to firing conditions. This is the case for the black slip applied over a reddish surface in some ceramics from Brunku Madugui (Gesturi), Nuraghe Trobas (Lunamatrona), and Nuraghe Arrubiu (Orroli).

Preliminary conclusions

As the study is still in progress, only the data for the Middle Bronze Age and part of those from the Recent Bronze Age of the Marmilla region are discussed, along with some additional information coming from the Recent/Final Bronze Age of the Nuraghe Ortu Comidu at Sardara.

The one hundred and twenty one (121) Middle Bronze Age ceramics of the Marmilla region, including the ones from the Nuraghe Arrubiu (Orroli), located on a basaltic plateau in the nearby Sarcidano region, permitted me to define patterns of ceramic production, consumption and exchange at an inter-site level in the area under study. In particular, considering architectural settlement type and distribution, the Marmilla region was inhabited by several small groups of people, sharing basic rules of pottery manufacturing, raw material choices and accessibility, and similar external vessel shapes. No precious or 'prestige vessel' or any kind of craft specialization or standardization was observed in their domestic assemblages, leading to the preliminary conclusion that during the Middle Bronze Age the same landscape was occupied by small, semi-independent households with a high degree of mobility, sharing and exchanging technological knowledge from distinct co-residential units through extensive 'cultural networks'. The same pattern seems confirmed for the corpus of the Recent Bronze Age ceramics studied to date.

Such a new scenario of the Middle and Recent Bronze Age way of living in the Marmilla region challenges previous interpretations of 'Nuragic social complexity' and the overestimated power enacted by local 'elites'. Social complexity, not only in Sardinia, was assimilated to hierarchy and power centralisation, which I believe do exist but must be visible on several analytical scales. Undue emphasis is often at the basis of vertical political differentiation assuming the existence of institutionalised, hereditary leadership, even when it is possible to interpret data available in terms of different forms of social organization and control (Kienlin, 2012: 18). Kienlin and Kohring, among others, suggest the use of a 'bottom-up' approach to understand social complexity and begin analysing complexity not from the elite viewpoint but using the notions of 'equality' or 'inequality' (Kienlin, 2012: 19; Kohring, 2011: 148). Equality is, actually, a utopian idea: in all human groups, people will differentiate between their fellow men and women on grounds of performance or other types of qualities, as equality or inequality is socially constructed. Nonetheless, hierarchy should not be confused with complexity because a group can be complex even without institutionalised ranking (Rowlands, 1995; Wynne-Jones and Kohring, 2007; Souvatzi, 2007). Authority and political power may operate at different levels, from households to kinship groups, through collective forms of decision-making in everyday life and in small-scale integrative units or via clans, lineages or larger entities such as the tribe (Kienlin, 2012).

In this research, I am concentrating on the analysis of ceramics from single households or different parts of the same household, exploring the inter-links between social knowledge systems and technical practises among 'communities of practise' from the same region. A community of practise is a group of people learning and sharing the same techniques of pottery manufacture and the same way of structuring their general meanings and understanding of the world (Wenger, 1998, cited by Korhing 2011). Such groups, to which people belong and into which they are incorporated, permit daily encounters, and sharing of practical and cosmological knowledge, recalling Bourdieu's consideration that the practices surrounding material culture establish social relationships (Bourdieu 1977, cited by Korhing 2011). Indeed, communities of practices frame encounters mediating between shared structuring principles and the individual-embodied '*chaine operatoire*'. In addition, they create a sense of shared identity by affirming links within and between communities (Kohring, 2011: 156). Such an approach demonstrates how, beyond the choice of specific raw materials from different collecting sites in replicating their own technological traditions, artisans from distinct co-residential units and maybe of different cultural affiliation in the Marmilla region shared knowledge about fabric preparation, typical of their peculiar 'communities of practise', and exchanged pottery, and other different items.

The investigation will continue by examining Recent Bronze Age ceramics from Nuraghe Genna Maria at Villanovaforru, and the Final Bronze Age ones from both Nuraghe Arrubiu, Genna Maria, and Su Nuraxi contexts, in order to verify whether the preliminary results discussed above may or may not be confirmed for the Final Bronze Age as well. In this regard, it can be useful to anticipate the results of the re-examination of 47 pottery thin-sections coming from the Nuraghe Ortu Comidu (Sardara), kindly provided by Dr Paul Nicholson, Department of Archaeology, University of Cardiff (UK). Considering their typology and microscopic characters, the excavators and the experts who studied the ceramics described two main different mineralogical homogenous fabric groups found in two different archaeological settings: the North area (N) of Recent-Final Bronze Age, and the South tower (S) of Final Bronze Age/Early Iron Age (Phillips, Nicholson, and Patterson 1986: 225). The Plutonic Fabric Group and its relevant sub groups, includes the ceramics coming from 'area N' – plan and carinated bowls and flat-based and footed vessels (Thomas and Nicholson 1994: 115) – which are all made by coarse or fine sand containing plutonic rock pieces. The ceramics coming from 'tower S' – deep jars, plain and carinated bowls, footed vessels and platters – (Thomas and Nicholson 1994: 115) were manufactured using coarse or well sorted loose sand without rock pieces.

These fabrics show a great variability in the use of raw materials and their micro-morphology: these observations, permitted me to infer that during the Recent/Final Bronze Age, pottery fabrics found in 'area N' and those used during the later period corresponding to the use of tower S, were collected from a different part of the landscape. The use of analytical methodology other than pottery petrology, for instance chemical analysis, would not have permitted this differentiation, as ceramics coming from both areas would have shown the same chemical and mineralogical composition even if the 'inclusions' present had a different material consistency. Nevertheless, these two different groups are present in all the nuraghi analysed since the Middle Bronze Age, and even during the Pre-Nuragic period, confirming the conservative tendency of the local pottery communities to keep using the same raw materials, easily available in that part of the landscape even if shape changed in the course of time.

References

ANTONA, A. *et al.* 1999. Criteri di nomenclatura e di terminologia applicati alla definizione delle forme vascolari nuragiche dal Bronzo Medio all'Età del Ferro. In D. Cocchi Genick (ed.), *Atti del Congresso di Lido di Camaiore*, 26-29 Marzo 1998, pp. 497-512.

ARNOLD, D. E.; NEFF, H. and BISHOP, R. L. 1991. Compositional analysis and sources of pottery: an Ethnoarchaeological Approach, *American Anthropologist*, New Series, Vol. 39, N. 1, pp. 70-90.

BAGELLA, S. *et al.* 1999. Forme vascolari del Bronzo in Sardegna. In D. Cocchi Genick (ed.), *Atti del Congresso di Lido di Camaiore*, 26-29 Marzo 1998, pp. 513-525.

BALMUTH, M. S. 1986. Studio Architettonico del nuraghe Ortu Comidu. In *'La Sardegna nel Mediterraneo tra il secondo e il primo millennio a. C.'*, Atti del II Convegno di studi 'Un millennio di relazioni fra la Sardegna e i Paesi del Mediterraneo', Selargius-Cagliari, 27-30 novembre 1986, pp. 219-223.

BOURDIEU, P. 1977. *Outline of a Theory of Practice*. Cambridge University Press.

COSSU, T. 2003. L'Età del Bronzo Medio: I primi nuraghi e l'occupazione dell'altopiano di Prenu 'e Muru. In T. Cossu *et al.* (eds.) *La vita nel nuraghe Arrubiu*, Comune di Orroli, Il Laboratrio della Conoscenza e della Memoria. Analisi dei protonuraghi nella Sardegna centro-occidentale, pp. 15-31.

CAMPUS, F.; LEONELLI, V. 2000. *La tipologia della ceramica nuragica. Il materiale edito*. Viterbo.

CAMPUS, F.; LEONELLI, V. 2006a. La Sardegna nel Mediterraneo fra l'età del Bronzo e l'età del Ferro. Proposta per una distinzione in fasi. In *Studi di Protostoria in onore di Renato Peroni*, Firenze: All'Insegna del Giglio Editore, pp. 379-392.

CAMPUS, F. and LEONELLI V. 2006b. I nuragici in Sardegna e nel Mediterraneo. In A. Boninu (ed.), *Il nuraghe Santu Antine di Torralba. Sistemi, Segni, Suoni*. Sassari, pp. 139-167.

DEMURTAS, L. and DEMURTAS, S. 1991. Analisi dei protonuraghi nella Sardegna centro-occidentale. In B. Santillo Frizel (ed.). *Arte Militare e Architettura Nuragica*. Proceedings of the First International Colloquium on Nuragic Architecture at the Swedish Institute in Rome, 7-9 December 1989. Acta Instituti Romani Regni Sueciae. Series 4, XLVIII, Stockholm, pp. 41-52.

DEPALMAS, A. 2009a. Il Bronzo medio della Sardegna. In Atti della XLIX Riunione Scientifica dell'Istituto Italiano di Presistoria e Protostoria, *La Preistoria e la Protostoria della Sardegna*. Cagliari, Barumini, Sassari 23-28 novembre 2009.

DEPALMAS, A. 2009b. Il Bronzo recente della Sardegna. In Atti della XLIX Riunione Scientifica dell'Istituto Italiano di Presistoria e Protostoria, *La Preistoria e la Protostoria della Sardegna*. Cagliari, Barumini, Sassari 23-28 novembre 2009.

DYSON, S. L. and ROWLAND, R. J. 2007. *Archaeology and History in Sardinia from the Stone Age to the Middle Ages. Shepherds, Sailors, & Coquerors*. University of Pensylvania Museum of Archaeology and Anthropology.

KIENLIN, T. L. 2012. Beyond Elites: an Introduction. In T. L. Kienlin, A. Zimmermann (eds.) *Beyond Elites. Alternatives to Hierarchical Systems in Modelling Social Formations*, pp. 15-32.

KOHRING, S. 2011. *Social Complexity as a Multi-Scalar Concept: Pottery Technology, 'Communities of Practice' and the Bell Beaker Phenomenon*. Norwegian Archaeological Review, Vol. 44, n. 2, 2011, pp. 145-163.

KOHRING, S. 2012. A Scalar Perspective on Social Complexity: Complex Relations and Complex Questions, in T. L. Kienlin and A. Zimmermann (eds.) *Beyond Elites. Alternatives to Hierarchical Systems in Modelling Social Formations*, pp. 327-338.

LILLIU, G. 1959. The Nuraghi of Sardinia, *Antiquity*, Vol. 23, Issue 129, pp 32-38.
LILLIU, G. 1962. *I Nuraghi, Torri Preistoriche della Sardegna*. Verona: La Zattera.
LILLIU, G. 1987. La Sardegna tra il II e il I millennio avanti Cristo. In Atti del I Convegno di studi 'Un millennio di relazioni fra la Sardegna e i Paesi del Mediterraneo', Selargius – Cagliari, 1987. *La Sardegna nel Mediterraneo tra secondo e il primo millennio a.C.;* pp 13-32.
LILLIU, G. 1988. *La Civiltà dei Sardi dal Paleolitico all'Età dei Nuraghi*. Torino: Nuova ERI, 3rd edition.
LILLIU, G. 2005. *I Nuraghi torri preistoriche della Sardegna*. Nuoro: Ilisso.
MORAVETTI, A. 1991. Sui Protonuraghi del Marghine e della Planargia. In B. Santillo Frizel (ed.). *Arte Militare e Architettura Nuragica*. Proceedings of the first International Colloquium on Nuragic Architecture at the Swedish Institute in Rome, 7-9 December 1989. Acta Instituti Romani Regni Sueciae. Series 4, XLVIII, Stockholm, pp. 185-197.
LO SCHIAVO, F. *et al.* 2009. Sardegna: le ragioni dei cambiamenti nella Civiltà Nuragica. In *Scienze dell'Antichità, Storia Archeologia, Antropologia 15*, Edizioni Quasar di Severino Tognon S.r.l.; pp. 265-289.
LO SCHIAVO, F. *et al.* 2010. Le ragioni dei cambiamenti nella civiltà nuragica. In M. Frangipane, Renato Peroni, A. Cardarelli (eds.), *Nascita, declino e crollo delle società tra la fine del IV e inizio del I millennio a.C.;* Atti del Convegno di Studi, Roma 15-17 giugno 2006. Scienze dell'Antichità, 5, 2009, Roma.
PERRA, M. 1997. *From deserted ruins: an interpretation of Nuragic Sardinia*. In Europaea, Journal of Europeanists, 3, 2, pp. 49-76.
PERRA, M. 2009. *Osservazioni sull'evoluzione sociale e politica in età nuragica*. Rivista di Scienze Preistoriche LIX, pp. 355-368.
PERRA, M. in press. *Tempi che cambiano, luoghi che si trasformano: i mutamenti nei nuraghi tra l'età del Bronzo ed il primo Ferro*.
PHILLIPS, P.; NICHOLSON, P.; PATTERSON, H. 1986. La ceramica nuragica di Ortu Comidu. In *'La Sardegna nel Mediterraneo tra il secondo e il primo millennio a.C.'*, Atti del II Convegno di studi 'Un millennio di relazioni fra la Sardegna e i Paesi del Mediterraneo', Selargius-Cagliari, 27-30 novembre 1986, pp. 225-232.
RICE, P. M. 1987. *Pottery Analysis: A Sourcebook*. Chicago, Illinois: University of Chicago Press.
ROWLANDS, M. 1995. A Question of Complexity. In D. Miller, M. J. Rowlands, C. Tilley (eds.), *Domination ad Resistance*. One World Archaeology 3, London: Routledge 1995, pp. 29-40.
SANTONI, V. 2001. *Il nuraghe Su Nuraxi di Barumini*, Quartu S. Elena.
SOUVATZI, S. 2007. Social Complexity is not the same as Hierarchy. In S. Kohring, S. Wynne-Jones (eds.), *Socialising Complexity: Structure, Interaction and Power in Archaeological Discourse*. Oxford: Oxford Oxbow, 2007, pp. 37-59.
THOMAS, J.; NICHOLSON, P. 1994. *Refiring Experiments on Material from Nuraghe Ortu Comidu (Sardara): some Aspects of Ceramic Technology*. In Quaderni della Soprintendenza Archeologica di Cagliari e Oristano, n. 11, 1994, pp. 115-139.
USAI, A. 1995. Note sulla società della Sardegna nuragica e sulla funzione dei nuraghi. In N. Christie (ed.), *Settlement and Economy in Italy 1500 BC to AD 1500*. The Fifth Conference of Italian Archaeology, Oxford, pp. 253-259.
USAI, A. 2003. Sistemi insediativi e organizzazione delle comunità nuragiche nella Sardegna centro-occidentale. In *Le comunità della preistoria italiana. Studi e ricerche sul neolitico e l'età dei metalli*, Atti della XXXV Riunione Scientifica IIPP (Lipari 2000), pp. 215-224.
USAI, A. 2006. Osservazioni sul popolamento e sulle forme di organizzazione comunitaria nella Sardegna nuragica. In *Studi di protostoria in onore di Renato Peroni*, Firenze, pp. 557-566.
WEBSTER, G. S. 1996. *A Prehistory of Sardinia*. Sheffield: Sheffield Academic Press.
WENGER, E. 1998. *Communities of Practice: Learning, Meaning and Identity*. Cambridge: Cambridge University Press.
WHITBREAD, I. K. 1995. *Greek Transport Amphorae. A petrological and Archaeological Study*. The British School of Athens, Flitch Laboratory Occasional Paper, 4.

Wynne-Jones, S. and Kohring, S. 2007. *Socialising Complexity: Structure, Interaction and Power in Archaeological Discourse*. Oxford: Oxford Oxbow.

Zedeno, M. N. 1994. *Sourcing Prehistoric Ceramics at Chodistaas Pueblo, Arizona: The Circulation of People and Pots in the Grasshopper Region*. Anthropological Papers N. 5, Tucson: University of Arizona Press.

A preliminary archaeometric study of eneolithic anthropomorphic statues from Nurallao (central Sardinia, Italy)

Marco SERRA[*]
Dipartimento di Storia, Beni Culturali e Territorio – Università di Cagliari;
Consorzio per la Promozione delle Attività Universitarie del Sulcis-Iglesiente (AUSI);
Centro di Ricerca per l'Energia, l'Ambiente e il Territorio (C.R.E.A.TE)
marco.serra@unica.it

Valentina MAMELI and Carla CANNAS
Dipartimento di Scienze Chimiche e Geologiche, Università di Cagliari;
Consorzio Interuniversitario Nazionale per la Scienza e
Tecnologia dei Materiali (Cagliari Unit)
valentina.mameli@unica.it; ccannas@unica.it

Abstract

A visual and instrumental multi-technique approach has been carried out on 10 geological samples collected from the fossiliferous limestone of the Villagreca Unit, in Nurallao (central Sardinia, Italy), in which the likely prehistoric quarry of Perda Tellada is located. Macroscopic examinations and chemical measurements by non destructive ED-XRF, ICP-OES and ICP-MS have been performed on the geological material. This study has allowed us to determine the geochemical intra-source variability of the lithic raw material. Furthermore, the mineralogical investigation by PXRD and the ICP-OES data on geological samples, have led us to define some technological properties of the local limestone. Conversely, on 13 eneolithic anthropomorphic limestone sculptures from the archaeological site of Aiodda-Nurallao ('menhir statues' of III millennium BC), nine without any scientific edition and five published, according to conservative requirements we have achieved only non destructive ED-XRF measurements and visual observations. Through the comparison between artifacts and lithological outcrop's analytical data, we have been able to define the precise original source of the raw materials employed for the prehistoric megaliths, establishing spatial relationships between the stone sources and the sites where the sculptures had been found.

Key-words: *Sardinia, Copper Age, menhir, provenance study, technological properties*

Résumé

Une approche multi-technique, autoptique et instrumentale, a été effectuée sur 10 échantillons géologiques recueillies à partir du calcaire fossilifère de la formation de Villagreca, dans Nurallao (centre de la Sardaigne, Italie), dans lequel il y a la carrière de pierre probablement préhistorique de Perda Tellada. Sur le matériau géologique, ont été utilisés une étude macroscopique et des techniques d'analyses chimiques telles que ED-XRF par approche non destructive, ICP-OES et ICP-MS. Cette étude nous a permis de déterminer la variabilité géochimique de la matière première lithique. En outre, l'investigation de minéralogie par PXRD et les données ICP-OES sur des échantillons géologiques, nous ont conduits à une définition de certaines propriétés technologiques de calcaire local. Sur 13 sculptures anthropomorphes chalcolithique de calcaire du site archéologique de Aiodda-Nurallao ('statues-menhirs' du III millénaire a. J.C.), neuf sans aucune édition scientifique et cinq publié, selon les exigences conservatrices nous avons obtenu que des mesures de fluorescence non destructifs et observations autoptiques. Grâce à la comparaison entre les artefacts et les donnés analytiques des affleurements lithologiques, nous avons été en mesure de définir la source d'origine précise des matières premières utilisées pour les mégalithes préhistoriques et d'établir des relations spatiales entre les sources de pierre et les sites où les sculptures avaient été trouvés.

Mots-clés: *Sardaigne, Chalcolithique, menhir, étude de la provenance, propriétés technologiques*

---

[*] Corresponding author.

FIGURE 1. GEOGRAPHIC SETTING OF NURALLAO.

1. Introduction

This study has been carried out on the territory of the small mountain village of Nurallao (CA), located in central-southern Sardinia (Italy).

Nurallao (403 m on the sea level), is situated between the Campidano plain and the inland regions of Sardinia. Starting from the north, Nurallao borders the municipalities of Laconi (OR), Isili (CA), Nuragus (CA) and Genoni (OR). This territory extends for about 35 km² and has two different geomorphological dominions. The most extensive one is located in the south-east of the country and consists of an alluvial flat-hilly area now mainly devoted to agriculture and pastoralism. Arranged in a semicircle around the north-eastern limits of the plain, there is a large limestone hill called Su Taccu. Near this sedimentary plateau, flow the rivers called Rio Casteddu, Rio Sarcidanu and Gutturu Ispadula, major tributaries of the Flumini Mannu, and the artificial lake of Is Barrocus (Fig. 1).

In 1979 a group of Sardinian archaeologists investigated the Bronze Age burial of Aiodda-Nurallao (Fig. 2a). During the excavations, a number of anthropomorphic limestone sculptures ('menhir statues') were found in the grave walls. They had probably belonged to a nearby a eneolithic sanctuary of III millennium BC and were reused as a building material by Nuragic people during the II millennium BC (Atzeni 1982 30-31). Some of these megaliths were removed from the burial site and now are exposed at the 'Giovanni Antonio Sanna' National Archaeological Museum of Sassari. Only the studies concerning the sculptures Aiodda I-VI were published (Sanges 1985; 2001a; 2001b; Cicilloni 2008 244-249) while the other nine, labelled by the authors with cardinal numbers, are presented for the first time in this study. The statues show a typical ogival profile, a plano-convex section and a generalised masculine connotation, clearly evident from the upside down anthropomorphic representation and the dagger with single or double triangular blade (Fig. 2b), probably symbols of a

FIGURE 2. AIODDA-NURALLAO: SOUTHERN VIEW OF THE NURAGIC BURIAL (A);
MENHIR STATUES CALLED AIODDA I (B), AIODDA IV (C) AND AIODDA 13 (D).

warrior caste (Atzeni 1982 30-32; Arnal, Arnal and Demurtas 1983 147-148). Solely Aiodda IV has a mysterious V-shaped engraving, while a large circular symbol is represented on the central portion of the Aiodda 13 sculpture (Fig. 2c-d).

An ancient quarry of limestone blocks, that was probably exploited during the prehistoric age, were discovered near the tomb of Aiodda, in the Perda Tellada's area (Fig. 3).

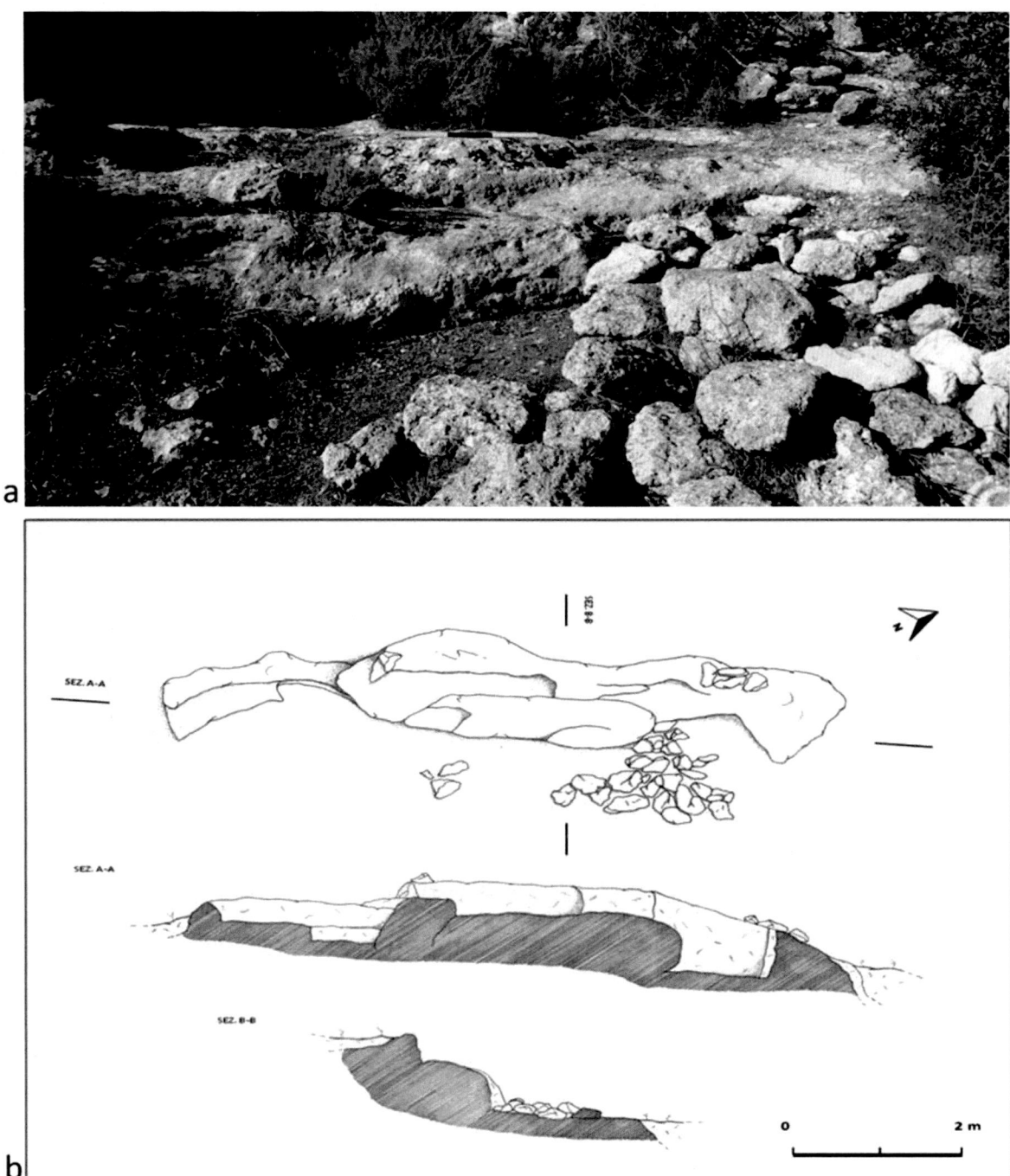

FIGURE 3. EASTERN VIEW (A), LAYOUT PLAN AND CROSS SECTIONS (B) OF THE PERDA TELLADA'S LIMESTONE QUARRY.

Until today, these statues and ancient quarry have not been subjected to any archaeometric investigation. The present study shows the characterization, the technological properties and the origin of the raw materials used for the production of the eneolithic sculptures of Nurallao. It involves visual examinations and instrumental archaeometric measurements both on geological materials and archaeological artifacts.[1]

---

[1] This study is a part of the doctoral research conducted on the eneolithic anthropomorphic statues of Sardinia by Dr. M. Serra under the supervision of G. Tanda, Full Professor at the University of Cagliari.

2. Geological setting

During the Cenozoic geological era, in the lapse of time between the Oligocene and the late Miocene (33-5 Ma), two different marine sedimentary cycles, which led to the formation of a 1000 m thickness carbonate deposit, took place in the territory of Nurallao (Fig. 4). The continental sediments of Riu su Rettori was originated during the first sedimentary phase. This geological unit is made of calcareous-arenaceous benches rich in quartz, schist, dolomia and fossils of corals and echinoderms (Assorgia *et al.* 1998 15; Frau and Meloni in press). Above this continental deposits outcrop the sandstones of Serralonga (Nurallao Unit), located in the south-east of the town of Nurallao. They include lenses of conglomerates, breccias and fine-grained sandstones. During the development of the sedimentary process, in the western sector of Nurallao a carbonate platform of fossiliferous limestone emerged. Today it's called Villagreca Unit (Pomesano Cherchi 1968 258; ISPRA 2011).

On the second miocenic sedimentary cycle (Lower Miocene), in the middle territory of Nurallao the Gesturi Unit took place. It's composed of marlstones with interbedded fossiliferous sandstones (Cherchi 1974; ISPRA 2011).

Finally, the formation of alluvial plains that made up a good part of the southern territories of Nurallao, dates back to the Quaternary geological era (Frau and Meloni in press).

Among the mentioned lithologies, only the Villagreca one owns the requirements sought by the ancient builders. It is revealed by the identification of this raw material on all prehistoric monuments

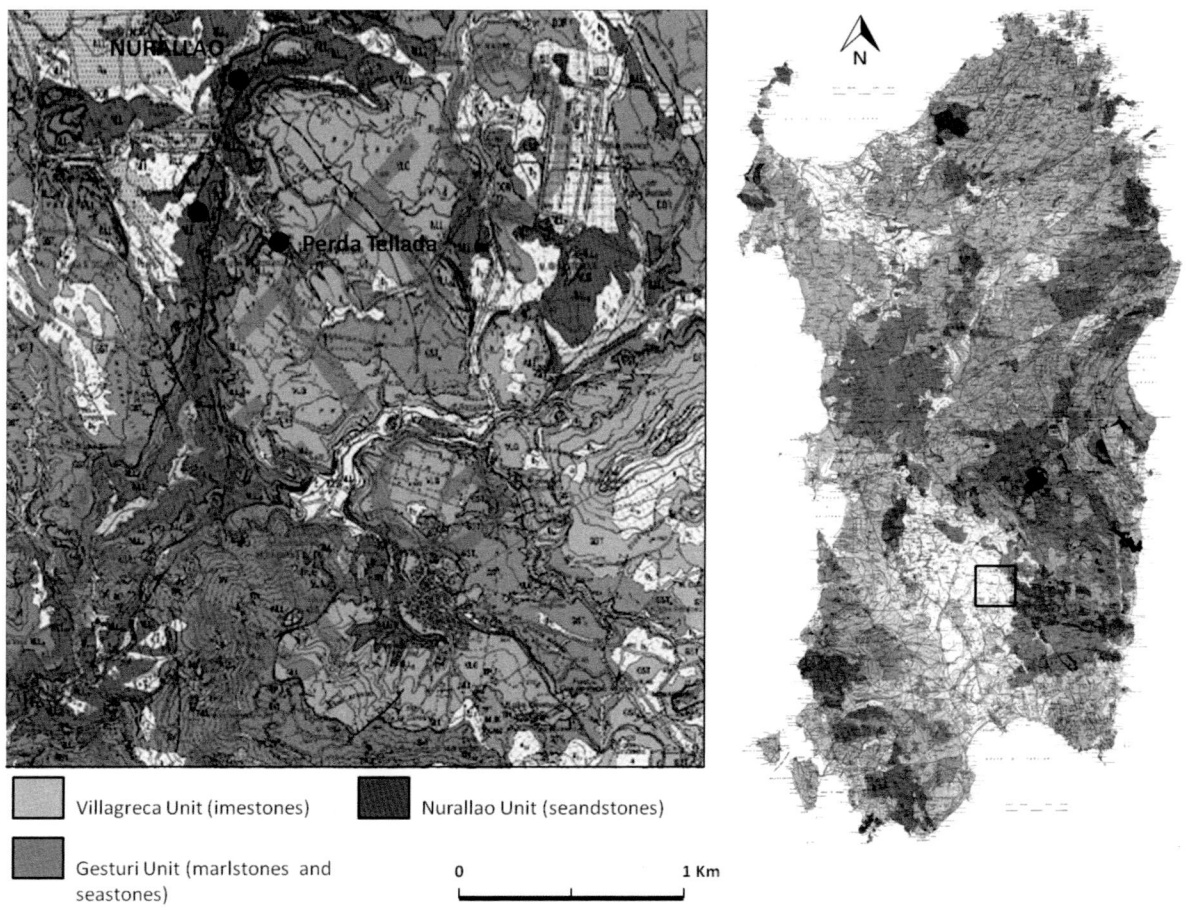

FIGURE 4. GEOLOGICAL SETTING OF NURALLAO (AFTER BARCA *ET AL.* 1997, RIELAB.).

of Nurallao. This phenomenon is probably due to the low compactness of the lithotype, which involves its good workability.

3. Materials and methods

3.1. Geological sampling

The geological sampling was performed on the bioclastic limestone of the Villagreca Unit (Pomesano Cherchi 1968 258; ISPRA 2011), labelled in this study with 'VLG', that covers an area of about 8 km² in the territory of Nurallao. It has been inscribed within a prospecting transect (4 x 2 km) oriented along the North-South direction. During the definition of the geological sampling plan, we have preferred to oust the extreme southern appendix of the calcareous autcrop, certainly unrelated to the production of the eneolithic local sculptures, as evidenced by the total lack of the macro-fossil fauna instead present on the artifacts.

Much geoarchaeological literature has proclaimed the chance of creating reliable characterizations of limestone lithologies with a little geological sampling, due to the compositional homogeneity of this rocks (Middleton and Bradley 1989; Harrell 1992 203). However, we have opted for a considerable number of samples, in order to achieve a more complete geochemical representativeness of the Villagreca raw material. Therefore, we have collected 10 stone specimens, removed from the ancient quarry of Perda Tellada (VLG_C1-2) and the rest of the outcrop (VLG_C3-10) (Fig. 5). The samples have been georeferenced with a global positioning systems based on the WSG84 geodetic datum (cfr. Fornaseri, Malpieri and Tolomeo 1975 113).

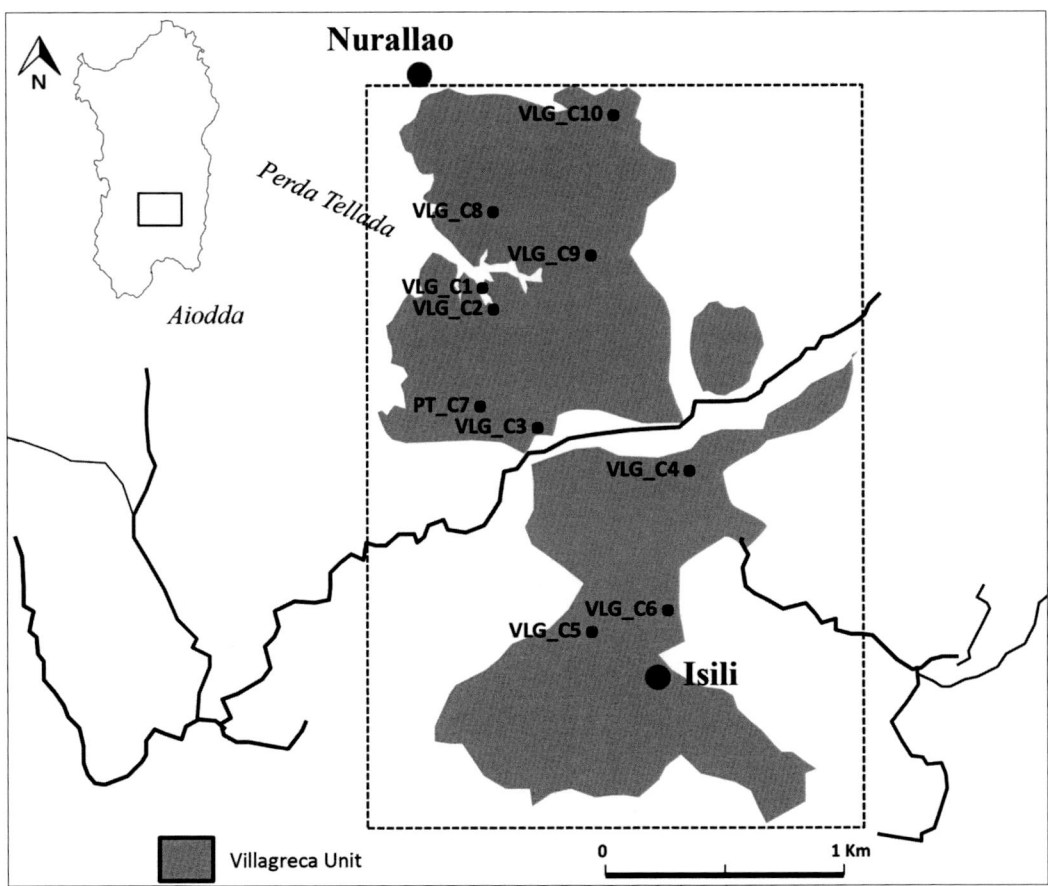

FIGURE 5. GEOLOGICAL SAMPLING PLAN OF THE VILLAGRECA LIMESTONE.

3.2. Archaeological sampling

All the menhir statues of Nurallao had been found in the nuragic tomb of Aiodda, 200 m away from the limestone quarry of Perda Tellada that is located on the northern portion of the calcareous outcrop of Villagreca. Thirteen eneolithic sculptures reused as building material in the Bronze Age burial, have been subjected to archaeometric investigation. The analyses have been done in the 'Giovanni Antonio Sanna' National Archaeological Museum of Sassari. Unfortunatelly, the archaeological sampling couldn't include the remaining sculptures located *in situ* in the grave walls of Aiodda (Saba 1993 154-155; 2000 128-129), due to the impossibility to transport the instruments on the field.

3.3. Visual and instrumental analysis

3.3.1. Geological samples

The first analytical level on the Villagreca limestone has been conducted by visual observation (Shotton and Hendry 1979 76). This approach has allowed us to describe the macroscopic structural features of the lithology and to evaluate the preliminary relationships between the geological outcrop and the statues' raw material.

The lithotype analyses have been conducted by non destructive ED-XRF. The measurements have been performed on three different points of each lithic sample. Qualitative and semi-quantitative chemical data was been obtained by ED-XRF.

An addictional screening on the ED-XRF data has been performed (Shotton and Hendry 1979 77; Lundblad, Mills and Hon 2008 3; Shackley 2011 19). Two samples from the Perda Tellada quarry (VLG_C1, 2) have been chosen. Two others lithic fragments from the Villagreca Units (VLG_C7, 10) have been selected through the random sampling technique (Orton 2000 20). An aliquot of all these samples, approximately 5% in weight, has been milled by an orbital shaker with a tungsten carbide jar, in order to avoid the contaminations caused by still jars (Jones, Bailey and Back 1997 931; Djindjian 2002 341; Samuel *et al.* 2007 298). The powders have been analysed by ICP-OES spectrometer. In these samples some discriminant trace elements were hardly detectable by optical spectrometry, so we have decided to quantify them by ICP-MS spectrometer. The results have confirmed the ED-XRF data.

Finally, the same powdered geological samples (VLG_C1-2, VLG_C7, VLG_C9-10) have been also subjected to mineralogical investigations carried out by means of PXRD. It should be noticed that crystalline structure rules some stones properties, such as hardness, durability and workability, certainly interesting for prehistoric man during the selection and exploitation of lithic raw materials (Bevan 2007 40; Rubinetto *et al.* 2013 20).

3.3.2. Archaeological artifacts

According to conservative limitations, on the sculptures we have performed exclusively visual inspections and non destructive ED-XRF measurements. The use of a portable equipment allowed us to analyse the artifacts inside the museum, avoiding the difficult transport of the statues. Once again, we have measured three points on the main artifacts' surface, to collect qualitative and semi-quantitative data on their elemental composition. Therefore, the experimental data have been processed in order to characterize the sculptures' raw materials and to investigate their connections with the geological limestone of Villagreca.

3.3.3. Analytical data: instruments and software

ED-XRF analyses have been carried out by means of the spectrophotometer ASSING LITHOS 3000, through the following experimental conditions: acquisition time 600 s; voltage 25 kV; electric current 150 μÅ; collimator diameter 5 mm; distance from the sample 10 mm. These settings have been applied both on geological and archaeological materials. For the qualitative attribution of the ED-XRF picks, the software Assing Lithos, supplied with the spectrophotometer, has been used. The analytical intensities have been calculated through the European Synchrotron PyMCA 4.6.0 software (Solé et al. 2007).

For the ICP-OES (spectrometer Perkin Elmer OPTIMA 5300 DV) and ICP-MS (Perkin Elmer ELAN DRC-e) analyses the SARM 2 international standard (South Africa Reference Materials) made of Transvaal syenites, have been used. The ICP-OES and ICP-MS elemental concentrations have been calculated by WinLab32 and Elan software.

For all the PXRD measurements, we have utilized the $\theta - 2\theta$ Seifert X-3000 diffractometer, equipped with a Cu Kα source (λ=1.54056 Å). The analytical conditions have been the following: voltage 40 kV; electric current 40 mÅ; angular range from 10° to 65° 2θ; goniometer step 0.05 θ/s; acquisition time 1 h. Phase identification was carried out by means of the Analyze software.

For the comparison between the geological and archaeological materials, we have used the semi-quantitative data obtained by non destructive ED-XRF analyses, the only one available for both the sampling categories. We have chosen to use the intensity ratios of the identified chemical elements. This method has allowed us to avoid the risks of using the pure intensities provided by the software (PyMca 4.6.0), certainly influenced by factors such as the matrix effect and the roughness of the irradiated surfaces (Warashina, Kamaki and Higashimura 1978 284; Catelani, Corbella and Colombi 1979 397; Jones, Bailey and Back 1997 936; De Francesco et al. 2006 534; Lundblad, Mills and Hon 2008 3).

Through binary scatter plots of the intensity ratios, we have established the effective links between the statues and their stone sources (cfr. Banning 2000 28).

4. Results

4.1. Characterization of the geological samples

4.1.1. ED-XRF analysis

The ED-XRF measurements performed on the Villagreca limestone geological samples, have revealed an elemental set always composed of K, Ca, Ti, Mn, Fe, Sr (Tab. 1a). For each chemical element the average intensity on three measurements and the related standard deviation have been calculated. Firstly, these semi-quantitative data have been related to the Ca intensity (the main analyte). Subsequently, these ratios have been linked to each other by binary scatter plots. Through this procedure we have recognized three discriminant variables which have shown a clear intra-source variability among the geological samples. In fact, the ratios K/Ca vs Sr/Ca, Ti/Ca vs Mn/Ca and Ti/Ca vs Sr/Ca have been able to segregate the two lithic fragments collected from the quarry of Perda Tellada from the other ones (Tab. 2a). This partition of the Villagreca limestones into two geochemical sub-groups, has been due to a greater concentrations of K and Ti in the Perda Tellada's samples than in the rest of the geological other ones.

4.1.2. ICP-OES/ICP-MS analysis

The previously detected geochemical intra-source variability, has suggested us to perform an analytical verification of the phenomenon, using ICP-OES and ICP-MS. For this purpose we have analysed the powdered samples from the Perda Tellada's quarry (VLG_C1-2) and two others geological ones randomly selected (VLG_C7, 10).

For all the measurements, the analytes detected by the ICP have been Mg, Al, Si, K, Ca, Ti, Mn, Fe, Rb, Sr. Quantitatively, Ca has been the major element, Mg, Al, Si, Fe the minor elements and Mn,

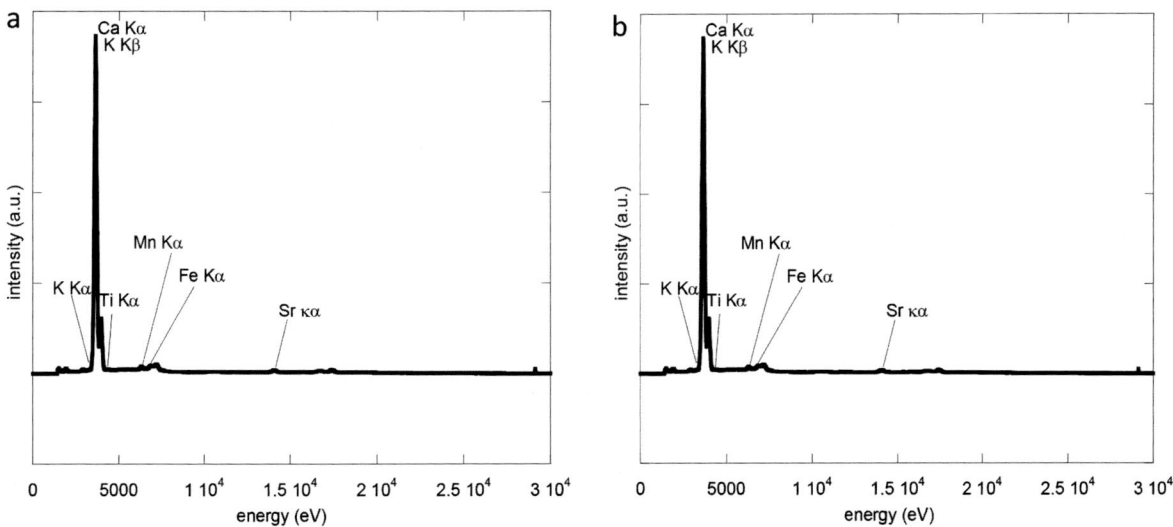

TABLE 1. ED-XRF SPECTRA OF A VILLAGRECA GEOLOGICAL SAMPLE (A)
AND A MENHIR STATUE OF AIODDA (B).

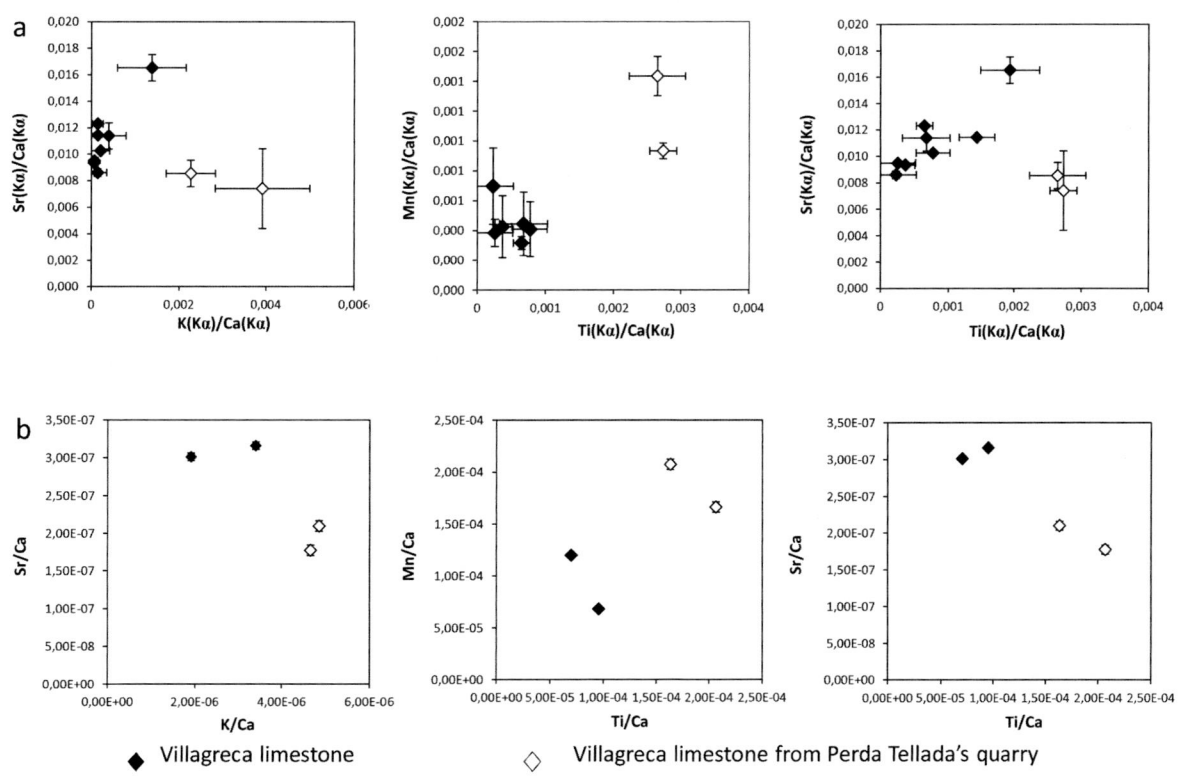

TABLE 2. GEOCHEMICAL INTRA-SOURCE VARIABILITY OF THE VILLAGRECA UNIT: SCATTER PLOTS OF
THE ED-XRF INTENSITIES RATIOS (A) AND ICP-OES/ICP-MS CONCENTRATIONS (B).

K, Ti, Rb, Sr the trace elements. The binary graphics of K/Ca vs Sr/Ca, Ti/Ca vs Mn/Ca and Ti/Ca vs Sr/Ca (the same discriminant variables used for the ED-XRF intensity ratios' scatter plots) have confirmed the existence of the two geochemical sub-groups suggested by the ED-XRF data (Tab. 2b).

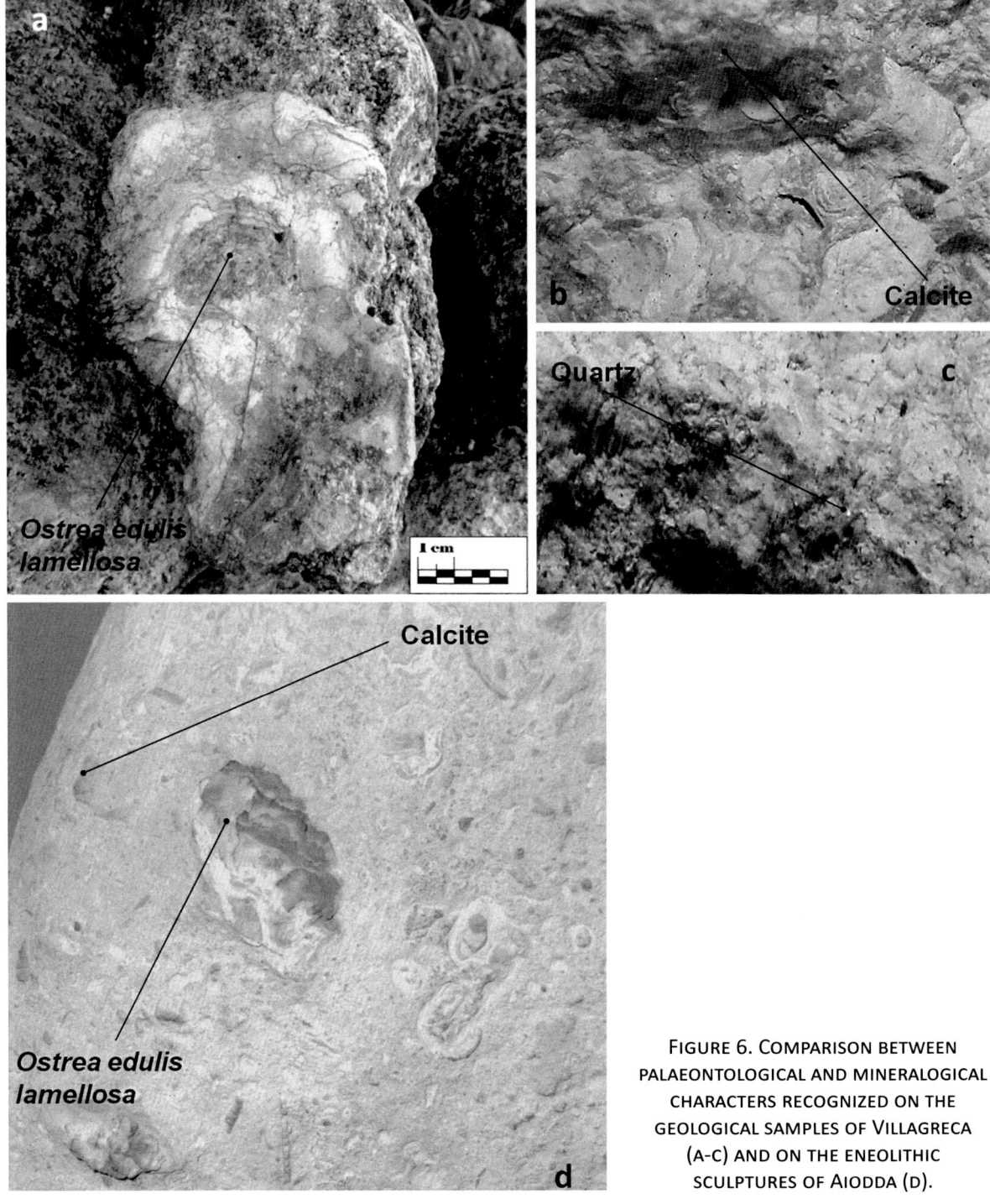

FIGURE 6. COMPARISON BETWEEN PALAEONTOLOGICAL AND MINERALOGICAL CHARACTERS RECOGNIZED ON THE GEOLOGICAL SAMPLES OF VILLAGRECA (A-C) AND ON THE ENEOLITHIC SCULPTURES OF AIODDA (D).

From the technological point of view, the very low concentration of silicon found in all the samples analysed by ICP (about 1%), has suggested the good workability of this raw material, which has probably led its extensive use in ancient times.

4.2.3. Mineralogical properties: PXRD analysis and visual examination

The macroscopic inspection of the Villagreca limestone has allowed us to see its fine structure with fossiliferous inclusions of corals, bryozoans and *Ostrea edulis lamellosa*. This white-gray rock has revealed calcitic phenocrysts and subordinated siliceous ones (Fig. 6a-c). It has also shown a high porosity responsible of a low firmness of the lithology (cfr. Atzeni, Pia and Sanna 2010 26).

The PXRD analyses have been performed on the samples VLG_C1-2, VLG_C7, VLG_C9-10. According to our visual observations, the measurements have revealed a main mineralogical phase of calcite ($CaCO_3$) with subordinate quartz (SiO_2) (Tab. 3), confirming the status of 'soft-stone' also suggested by the the low silicon percentages detected by ICP. This data have contributed to uphold our conclusions about the workability previously proposed for this stone.[2] However, the high workability matched to a limited life of the raw material, that is responsible for the strong erosion of the Aiodda menhir statues' iconographic elements.

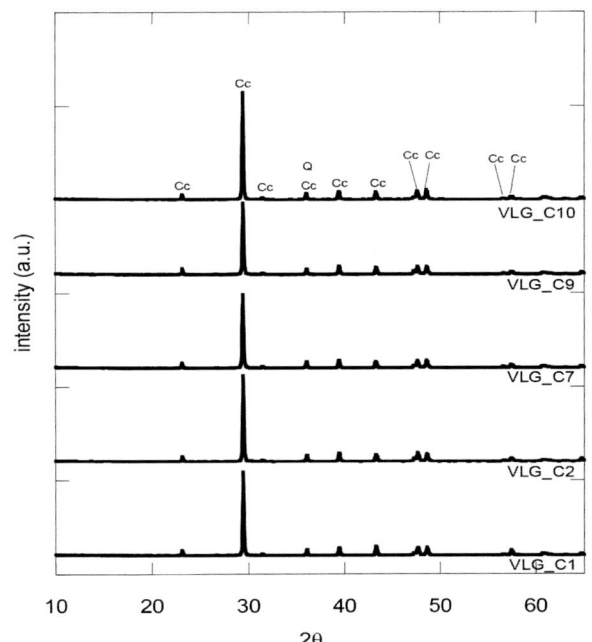

GEOLOGICAL UNIT	CRISTALLOGRAPHIC PHASES	CHEMICAL FORMULA	PDF CARD
Villagreca Unit	**Calcite**	$CaCo_3$	72-1652
	Quartz	SiO_2	82-511

TABLE 3. PXRD PATTERNS OF THE VILLAGRECA GEOLOGICAL SAMPLES (CC: CALCITE; Q: QUARTZ).

4.2. Archaeological artifacts

4.2.1. Chemical and mineralogical properties: non-destructive ED-XRF analysis and visual examination

The non destructive ED-XRF measurements has been performed on three different points of each statue. The chemical composition of the sculptures has revealed the same elemental set identified by ED-XRF on the Villagreca geological material: K, Ca, Ti, Mn, Fe, Sr (Tab. 1b). Once again, we have calculated the average value and the standard deviation of the three intensities obtained for each chemical element, in order to achieve the K/Ca vs Sr/Ca, Ti/Ca vs Mn/Ca and Ti/Ca vs Sr/Ca binary scatter plots. The comparison between ED-XRF semi-quantitative data obtained on geological and archaeological samples, has allowed us to determine the Aiodda sculptures' stone source. Chemical relations have enabled us to establish the provenance of 12 out of 13 analysed sculptures (Tab. 4). They have shown the affinity between the 11 statues (Aiodda I, II, IV, V, 3, 7, 8, 10, 11, 13, 15) and the limestone of the Perda Tellada's quarry, located near the Aiodda grave in which the artifacts had been found. The sculpture called Aiodda 9 has ended up coming from an indefinite part of the Villagreca's outcrop. It has not been possible to determine a reliable attribution of Aiodda VI, due to its unclear link with the geochemical fingerprint of the Villagreca limestone.

The fabric, the macroscopic mineralogical properties and the paleontological observations of the statues' raw material, have shown a microcrystalline matrix, several calcitic phenocrysts, low silica minerals and macro-fossil species of coastal environment (Fig. 6d), according to the features previously detected on the Villagreca limestone.

---

[2] The lithology of Villagreca may be scratched by a copper tip, according to the 3th level of the Mohs hardness scale of minerals (Bevan 2007 42 fig. 4.1; Goffer 2007 87-88).

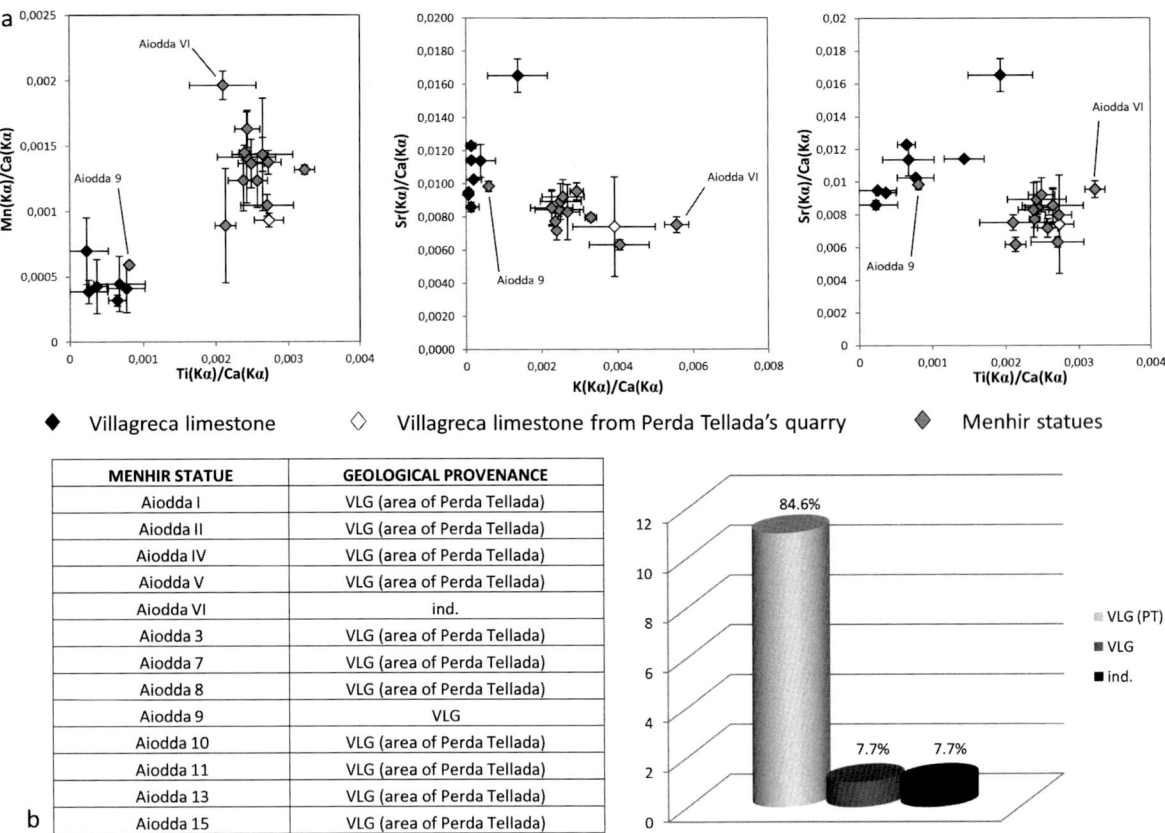

TABLE 4. SOURCE PROVENANCE OF THE ANTHROPOMORPHIC SCULPTURES OF AIODDA: SCATTER PLOTS OF THE GEOLOGICAL SAMPLES AND MENHIRS ED-XRF INTENSITY RATIOS (A); SYNOPTIC TABLE AND HISTOGRAM OF THE MENHIRS' PROVENANCE.

5. Discussion and conclusions

Chemical analyses led us to detect important differences within the limestone outcrop of Nurallao (Villagreca Unit). The precise origin of the raw materials employed for the production of the eneolithic menhir statues of Aiodda was found thank to those intra-source variability. The analytical and visual relationships between geological and archaeological samples have surely revealed the use of the Villagreca limestone for the anthropomorphic sculptures' manufacturing. The frequent link between the artifacts and the Perda Tellada's limestone outcrop, has suggested to identify the here located ancient quarry as the preferential source of the megaliths. According to this interpretation, the extraction site could be dated back to the Copper Age, as well as the menhirs (cfr. Saba 2001 133).

The exploitation of local geo-materials has revealed an ancient supply strategy in agreement to the economic resources' optimization often observed by scholars on others european megalithic contexts in which long distance raw materials procurements were usually excluded (cfr. Thorpe et al. 1991 147-150; Pirson, Toussaint and Frèbutte 2003 152-155; Williams-Thorpe et al. 2006 42; Rubinetto et al. 2013 21-22). The erection of the sculptures near the Perda Tellada quarry seems to follow the same criteria.

The chemical and mineralogical data have shown a clear trend in selecting raw materials easy to work by means of ancient technologies. This fact reveals precise petrologic knowledge, certainly acquired by the eneolithic craftsmen of Nurallao through 'trial and error' empirical methods.

References

ARNAL, J.; ARNAL, S. and DEMURTAS, S. 1983. Les statues-menhirs sardes. *Bulletin du musee d'anthropologie prehistorique de Monaco* 27, 123-150.

ASSORGIA, A.; BARCA, S.; PORCU, A.; SPANO, G.; BALOGH, K. and RIZZO, R. 1998. The oligocene-miocene sedimentary and volcanic succession of central Sardinia, Italy. *Romanian Journal of Stratigraphy* 78, 9-23.

ATZENI, C.; PIA, G. and SANNA, U. 2010. *I materiali dell'edilizia storica. Storia, tecnologia, applicazioni*. Roma, ARACNE editrice.

ATZENI, E. 1982. Menhirs antropomorfi e Statue-Menhirs della Sardegna. *Annali del Museo Civico di La Spezia* II, 9-63.

BANNING, E. B. 2000. The archaeologist's laboratory. The analysis of archaeological data. Interdisciplinary Contributions to Archaeology, XVIII. New York, Kluwer Academic Publishers.

BARCA, S.; CARMIGNANI, L.; OGGIANO, G.; PERTUSATI, P. C. and SALVADORI, I. 1997. *Carta Geologica della Sardegna, scala 1:200,000*. Firenze, Litografia Artistica Cartografica.

BEVAN, A. 2007. *Stone vessels and values in the Bronze Age mediterranean*. New York, Cambridge University Press.

CATELANI, D.; CORBELLA, A. and COLOMBI, A. 1979. *Chimica analitica quantitativa*. Milano, Editrice Scientifica Guadagni.

CHERCHI, A. 1974. Appunti biostratigrafici sul Miocene della Sardegna (Italia). In Actes du V Congres du Neogene Mediterranee (Lyon, septembre 1971). *Mémoire du Bureau de Recherches Géologiques et Minières* 78, 433-445.

CICILLONI, R. 2008. Le statue-menhir della Sardegna: aspetti tipologici. In G. Tanda and C. Lugliè eds.; *Il Segno e l'Idea. Arte preistorica in Sardegna*. Cagliari, CUEC, pp. 155-271.

DE FRANCESCO, A. M.; BOCCI, M.; CRISCI, G. M.; LO VETRO, D.; MARTINI, M.; TOZZI, C.; RADI, G.; SARTI, L.; CUDA, M. T. and SILVESTRINI, M. 2006. Applicazione della metodologia analitica non distruttiva in Fluorescenza X per la determinazione della provenienza delle ossidiane archeologiche del Progetto 'Materie Prime' dell'IIPP. In *Materie prime e scambi nella preistoria italiana*. Atti della XXXIX riunione scientifica dell'Istituto Italiano di Preistoria e Protostoria (Firenze, 25-27 Novembre 2004). Firenze, IIPP, pp. 531-548.

DJINDJIAN, F. 2002. Population et échantillonnage. In J. C. Miskovsky ed.; *Géologie de la Préhistoire, méthodes, techniques, applications*. Paris, Géopré, pp. 341-348.

FORNASERI, M.; MALPIERI, L. and TOLOMEO, L. 1975. Provenance of pumices in the north coast of Cyprus. *Archaeometry* 17, 1, 112-116.

FRAU, A. and MELONI, S. (in press). Inquadramento geologico e strutturale dell'area della XIII Comunità Montana. In *Aspetti geologici e dissesto idrogeologico*, pp. 6-17. Available on: http://www.13cm.it/.

GOFFER, Z. 2007. *Archaeological chemistry*. New York-Chichester-Weinheim-Brisbane-Singapore-Toronto, Wiley Interscience.

HARRELL J. A. 1992. Ancient Egyptian limestone quarries: a petrological survey. *Archaeometry* 34, 195-212.

ISPRA, 2011. *Carta geologica d'Italia 1:50,000*. Foglio n. 540, Mandas.

JONES, G.; BAILEY, D. G. and BACK, C. 1997. Source provenance of andesite artefacts using non-destructive XRF analysis. *Journal of Archaeological Science* 24, 929-943.

LUNDBLAD, S. P.; MILLS, P. R. and HON, K. 2008. Analysing archaeological basalt using non-destructive energy-dispersive X-ray fluorescence (EDXRF): effects of post-depositional chemical weathering and sample size on analytical precision. *Archaeometry* 50, 1, 1-11.

MIDDLETON, A. P. and BRADLEY, B. 1989. Provenancing of egyptian limenstone sculture. *Journal of Archaeological Science* 16, 475-488.

ORTON, C. 2000. *Sampling in archeology*. Cambridge, Cambridge University Press.

PIRSON, S.; TOUSSAINT, M. and FRÈBUTTE, C. 2003. Les matières premières des mègalithes de Belgique: état de la question. *Notae Praehistoricae* 23, 147-172.

Pomesano Cherchi, A. 1968. Studio biostratigrafico del Miocene della Sardegna centro-meridionale (Campidano-Marmilla orientale-Sarcidano). *Giornale di Geologia* 35, 3, 255-276.

Rubinetto, V.; Appolonia, L.; de Leo, S.; Serra, M. and Borghi, A. 2013. A petrographic study of the anthropomorphic stelae from the megalithic area of Saint-Martin-de-Corléans (Aosta, northen Italy). *Archaeometry*, doi: 10.1111/arcm.12053.

Saba, A. 1993. Le nuove statue-menhir. *Bollettino di Archeologia* 19-21, 151-158.

Saba, A. 2000. Le statue-menhir di Isili (NU). *Studi Sardi* XXXII, 111-164.

Saba, A. 2001. Le stele figurate di Isili. In M. Sanges ed.; *L'eredità del Sarcidano e della Barbagia di Seulo: patrimonio di conoscenza e di vita*. Cagliari, Punto e Basta, pp. 39-42.

Samuels, K. E.; Broxton, D. E.; Vaniman, D. T.; Woldegabriel, G.; Wolff, J. A.; Hickmott, D. D.; Kluk, E. C. and Fittipaldo, M. M.; 2007. Distribution of dacite lavas beneath the Pajarito Plateau, Jemez Mountains, New Mexico. In B. S. Kues, S. A. Kelley and V. W. Lueth eds.; *Geology of the Jemez Mountains Region II*. Guidebook of 58th Field conference, New Mexico Geological Society (April 21, 2006). Socorro: New Mexico Bureau of Geology and Mine Resources, pp. 296-307.

Sanges, M. 1985. La tomba megalitica di Aiodda-Nurallao (Nuoro). In *Settimana dei beni culturali, 1975-1985: 10 anni di attivita nel territorio della provincia di Nuoro*. Catalogo della mostra (Nuoro, piazza Asproni, casa Buscarini 3 dicembre 1985). Nuoro, Cooperativa grafica nuorese, pp. 36-38.

Sanges, M. 2001a. Documenti archeologici del territorio di Nurallao. In M. Sanges ed.; *L'eredità del Sarcidano e della Barbagia di Seulo: patrimonio di conoscenza e di vita*. Cagliari, Punto e Basta, pp. 86-87.

Sanges, M. 2001b. La tomba megalitica di Aiodda. In M. Sanges ed.; *L'eredità del Sarcidano e della Barbagia di Seulo: patrimonio di conoscenza e di vita*. Cagliari, Punto e Basta, pp. 88-89.

Shackley, M. S. 2011. An Introduction to X-Ray Fluorescence (XRF) Analysis in Archaeology. In M. S. Shackley ed.; *X-ray Fluorescence Spectrometry (XRF) in Geoarchaeology*. New York-Dordrecht-Heidelberg-London, Springer, pp. 7-44.

Shotton, F. W. and Hendry, G. L. 1979. The developing field of petrology in archaeology. *Journal of archaeological science* 6, 75-84.

Solé, V. A.; Papillon, E.; Cotte, M.; Walter, Ph. and Susini, J. 2007. A multiplatform code for the analysis of energy-dispersive X-ray fluorescence spectra. *Spectrochimica Acta* (Part B) 62, 63-68.

Thorpe, R. S.; William-Thorpe, O.; Jenkins, D. J. and Watson, J. S. 1991. The geological sources and transport of bluestones of Stonhenge, Wiltshire, UK. *Proceedings of the Prehistoric Society* 57, 2, 103-157.

Warashina, T.; Kamaki, Y. and Higashimura, T. 1978. Sourcing of sanukite implements by X-ray fluorescence analysis II. *Journal of Archaeological Science* 5, 283-291.

Williams-Thorpe, O.; Jones, M. C.; Potts, P. J. and Webb, P. C. 2006. Preseli dolerite bluestones: axe-heads, Stonehenge monoliths and outcrop sources. *Oxford Journal of Archaeology* 25, 1, 29-46.

Early Iron Age pottery in south-western Iberia – archaeometry and chronology

Michał KRUEGER
Instytut Prahistorii, Uniwersytet im. Adama Mickiewicza w Poznaniu
krueger@amu.edu.pl

Dirk BRANDHERM
School of Geography, Archaeology and Palaeoecology, Queen's University Belfast
d.brandherm@qub.ac.uk

Abstract

Our current knowledge about the beginnings of the Early Iron Age in the south-western part of the Iberian Peninsula remains rather limited. The chronology and the nature of the first contacts between Phoenicians and Tartessians are among the unsolved issues plaguing the archaeology of Iberia's Early Iron Age. This paper argues that through systematic spectrographic analysis of pottery specimens from Tartessian sites (Setefilla and eleven other sites) it is possible to tackle these issues. Our methodology is based on both destructive and non-destructive analysis of ceramic samples. For the latter a highly sensitive portable X-ray fluorescence device is employed. The paper is also concerned with the strong need for a reliable ^{14}C-based chronology for the development of Tartessian material culture. A new approach for refining our chronological framework for this period is proposed that aims at providing us with a better grasp of the development of interactions and interdependences between the Phoenicians and the Tartessians over time.

Key-words: *archaeometry, pXRF spectrometry, chronology, Iron Age, Iberian Peninsula, western Andalusia*

Résumé

Nos connaissances sur les débuts de l'âge du Fer dans la partie sud-ouest de la péninsule Ibérique demeurent aujourd'hui encore plutôt insuffisantes. La chronologie et la nature des premiers contacts entre Phéniciens et Tartéssiens sont parmi les questions non résolues de l'archéologie de l'Âge du Fer en Ibérie. Ce travail démontre que, grâce à l'analyse spectrographique systématique des spécimens de poterie provenant de sites tartessiens (Setefilla et onze autres sites), il est possible de aborder ces questions. Notre méthodologie est basée sur l'analyse soit destructive, soit non destructive des échantillons de céramique. Pour ce dernier procédé, un dispositif de fluorescence à rayons X portable hautement sensible a été utilisé. Cet article aborde aussi l'importanceé d'une chronologie fiable basée sur des datations ^{14}C pour le développement de la culture matérielle tartessiénne. Une nouvelle approche permettant d'affiner le cadre chronologique de cette période est proposée, elle vise à fournir une meilleure compréhension du développement des interactions et interdépendances entre les Phéniciens et les Tartessiens au cours du temps.

Mots-clés: *archéométrie, spectrométrie pXRF, chronologie, âge du Fer, péninsule Ibérique, Ouest de l'Andalousie*

The purpose of this paper is to present a brief overview of an ongoing research project[1] on the beginnings of the Early Iron Age in the south-western part of the Iberian Peninsula. The start of the Iron Age is characterized by the presence of Phoenician traders on the Mediterranean and Atlantic coasts of ancient Iberia. Over the course of the last century, archaeological museums in Andalusia have accumulated an enormous body of wheel-made and hand-made Early Iron Age pottery. Unfortunately, our knowledge about relations between the Phoenicians and the locals is not increasing in proportion to the collected material evidence. Despite a long tradition of research on cultural contact in Iberia's Early Iron Age, basic problems still remain unsolved: the chronology and the nature of the first contacts between the Phoenicians and the native inhabitants of western Andalusia, the Tartessians.

---

[1] The project is financed by the Polish National Science Centre (grant number DEC-2013/09/B/HS3/00630).

The colonial impact on Tartessian society is often perceived as a unidirectional process in which the locals are passive consumers of imported goods. Such simplistic models go hand in hand with a lack of knowledge about patterns of long-distance trade between the Phoenicians and the locals. Currently, the origin of foreign artefacts found in local contexts in most cases remains uncertain (Fig. 1). To overcome theses problems, two informal research groups were established: one at Queen's University Belfast which will be responsible for the chronological part of the project, and the other at Adam Mickiewicz University in Poznań, working on archaeometric provenance determination of pottery.

To understand any historical process, a reliable chronological framework needs to be established first. Therefore, one of the objectives of the project is to create a reliable ^{14}C-based chronology for the Early Iron Age in south-western Iberia. This is to be achieved through a multi-disciplinary analysis of chronologically relevant data from the site of Setefilla, located in Seville province (Aubet 1975; 1978; Aubet *et al.* 1996). This site has been chosen because it was well excavated and provides a rich cultural assemblage, spanning most of the Early Iron Age, allowing us to combine site stratigraphy, seriation of grave assemblages and ^{14}C dating of cremated human bone to build a detailed chronological sequence that would be applicable also to other Tartessian sites. In particular, it offers the chance to distinguish between burials belonging to the precolonial phase of the indigenous LBA/EIA culture from later tombs that date to the phase of colonial contact with the Phoenicians. The

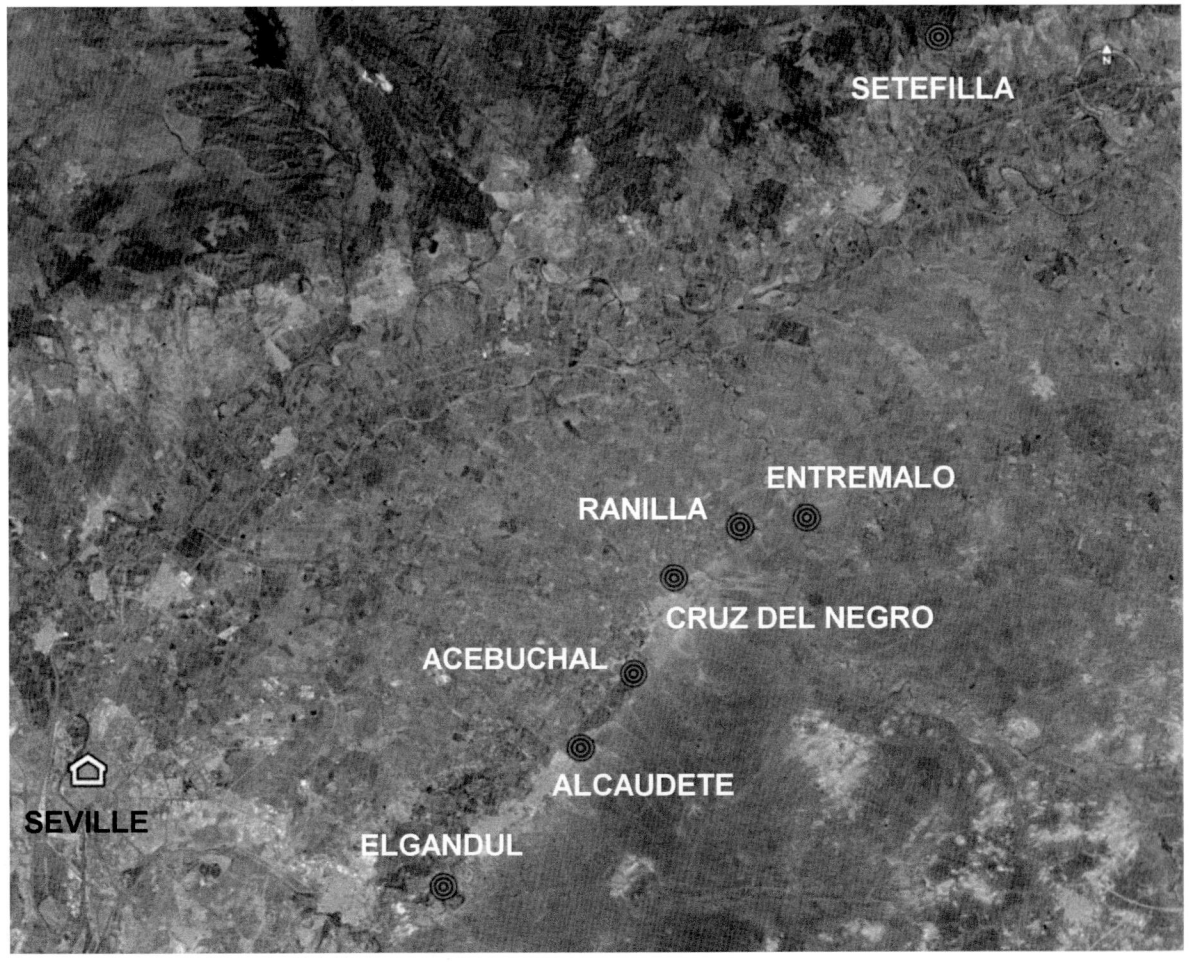

FIGURE 1. MAIN SITES OF THE LOWER GUADALQUIVIR STUDIED WITHIN THE PROJECT (BACKGROUND: GOOGLE EARTH).

fact that in 18 graves from different stratigraphical layers at the site Phoenician wheel-made pottery was found together with local grave goods provides an opportunity to tie in the development of indigenous material culture with a wider inter-regional sequence. Moreover, we are planning to also analyse samples from Cruz del Negro (Maier 1992; 1999) and Rabadanes (Pellicer, Escacena 2007), two further sites located in western Andalusia. According to conventional typo-chronology, all sites mentioned date to the beginning of the Early Iron Age. However, a better-founded and more precise chronology is urgently needed, to address questions concerning the development of the relationship between indigenous communities and newcomers from the Eastern Mediterranean.

Currently, the absolute chronology of the Late Bronze Age / Early Iron Age transition in SW Iberia to a large extent remains dependent on the dating of Eastern Mediterranean imports, mainly Phoenician pottery types, ultimately tethered to the historical chronologies of Geometric Greece and the Near East. This continues to hold true regardless of recent challenges to this model on the basis of new ^{14}C determinations from sites at both ends of the Mediterranean, and also regardless of the eventual outcome of the ongoing debate concerning the validity of the underlying historical chronologies (Brandherm 2006; 2008a; 2008b; Gilboa 2013; Toffolo *et al.* 2013).

What is really needed is a reliable chronology for indigenous settlements and their material culture that no longer depends on 'importing' dates from the Phoenician homeland or elsewhere. Only this will allow us to achieve a better understanding of the development of local communities and of their interaction with any new arrivals from the Eastern Mediterranean. A new basis for the dating of Phoenician imports on its own will do little to alleviate this continued need.

Consequently, the first objective of the present project consists in building a sound chronology for the Late Bronze Age and Early Iron Age in SW Iberia. This is to be achieved through multivariate analysis of chronologically relevant data from a number of key sites, mainly from Setefilla. Additional data will be drawn from other, broadly coeval sites in the Guadalquivir valley. This will allow us to obtain dates for pottery types poorly represented or altogether lacking at Setefilla, in order to minimize the effect of site-specific idiosyncrasies on our chronological model.

Our methodology to build a reliable chronological framework for the Late Bronze Age / Early Iron Age transition in SW Iberia draws on a number of recent advances in radiocarbon dating techniques: the potential to obtain reliable ^{14}C dates from cremated bone samples, enhanced AMS dating precision, and the use of advanced Bayesian statistics to model sets of radiocarbon dates based on known constraints. For the purposes of this project these constraints are provided by stratigraphic evidence and seriation data. It is expected that used in conjunction, these techniques will allow us to overcome some of the present problems posed by the shape of the calibration curve in the 750-400 cal BC range, the so-called 'Hallstatt plateau'.

Cremation cemeteries with poor preservation or recovery of organic matter other than cremated bone, such as Setefilla, in the past have been extremely difficult to date by scientific means, including radiocarbon dating. Suitable ^{14}C dating techniques only started to be developed from the late 1990s onwards (Lanting *et al.* 2001; Naysmith *et al.* 2007). Since then, radiocarbon measurement of bioapatite from cremated bone samples has become a recognized standard method, now routinely employed by a number of AMS research laboratories. This opens up new possibilities to refine our chronological framework for this period, with the aim of providing a better grasp of the development of interdependencies between the Phoenicians and the Tartessians over time. While the relative sequence of funerary assemblages from Setefilla could be established with reasonable confidence, suggestions regarding their absolute chronology vary widely. Thus the earliest burials from the site are dated to c. 800 BC or even more explicitly the late 9th century BC by some authors, while others would have them beginning only about a century later (Bendala 1992; Torres 1996; Beba 2008). This margin of uncertainty poses significant problems for the correct interpretation of social phenomena materialized in the archaeological record at Setefilla (Fig. 2). With a low chronology, a plausible

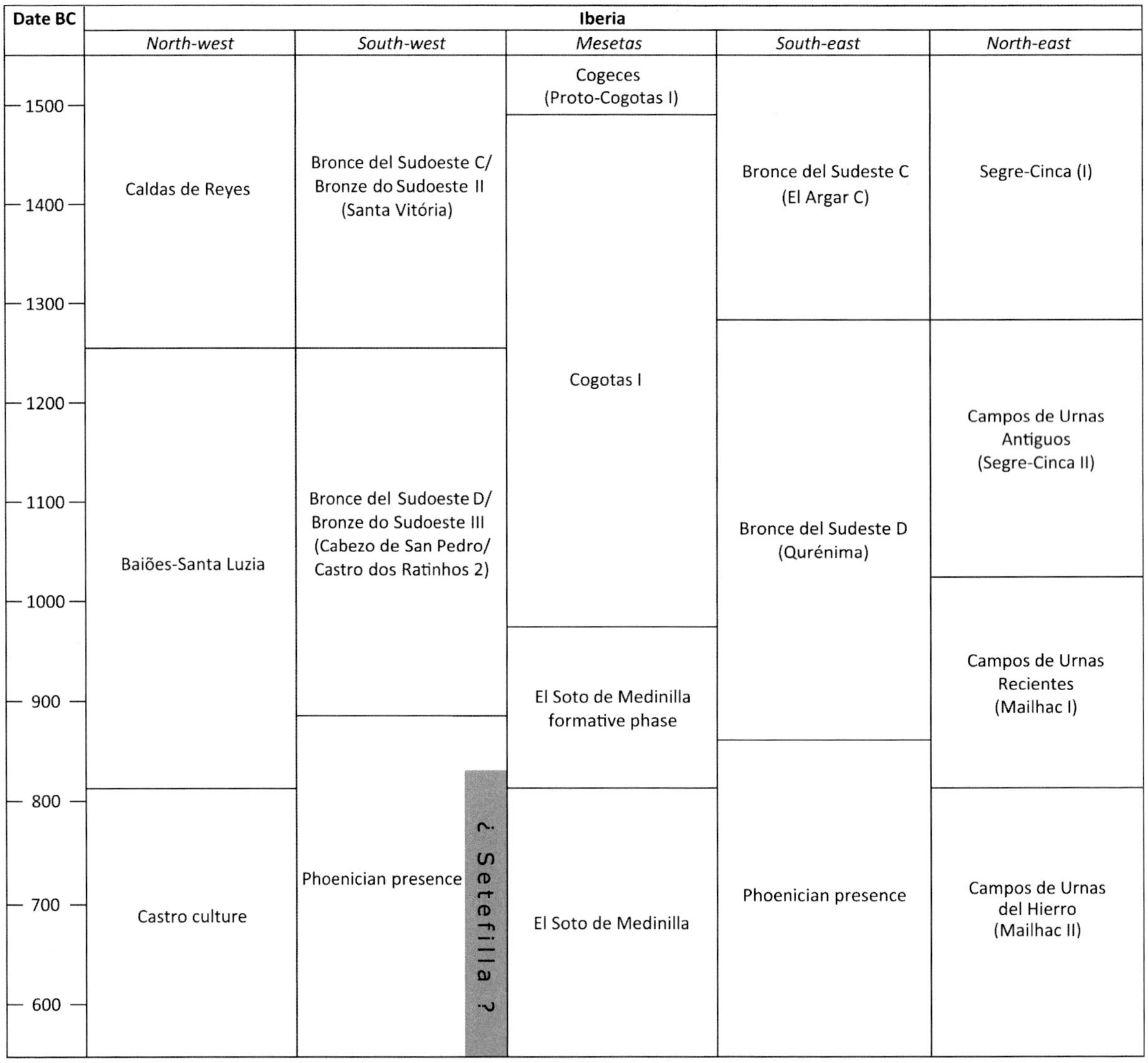

Date BC	Iberia				
	North-west	South-west	Mesetas	South-east	North-east
1500	Caldas de Reyes	Bronce del Sudoeste C/ Bronze do Sudoeste II (Santa Vitória)	Cogeces (Proto-Cogotas I)	Bronce del Sudeste C (El Argar C)	Segre-Cinca (I)
1400					
1300			Cogotas I		
1200	Baiões-Santa Luzia	Bronce del Sudoeste D/ Bronze do Sudoeste III (Cabezo de San Pedro/ Castro dos Ratinhos 2)		Bronce del Sudeste D (Qurénima)	Campos de Urnas Antiguos (Segre-Cinca II)
1100					
1000					
900			El Soto de Medinilla formative phase		Campos de Urnas Recientes (Mailhac I)
800	Castro culture	Phoenician presence	¿Setefilla? El Soto de Medinilla	Phoenician presence	Campos de Urnas del Hierro (Mailhac II)
700					
600					

FIGURE 2. CHRONOLOGICAL RANGE FOR CREMATION BURIALS FROM THE SETEFILLA FLAT CEMETERY AND TUMULI A AND B PREVIOUSLY PROPOSED WITHIN THE IBERIAN LATE BRONZE AGE AND EARLY IRON AGE (MODIFIED AFTER ROBERTS ET AL. 2013, FIG. 2.5).

case could be made for viewing the reintroduction of archaeologically visible burial rites to southern Iberia in the Early Iron Age as inspired by Phoenician funerary practice, following a nearly total lack of evidence for either inhumation or cremation burials during the Late Bronze Age. On the other hand, with the confirmation of an early date such a reading would likely become untenable, adding to increasing evidence for 'precolonial' indigenous burial practices from other parts of southern Iberia (González 2002; Lorrio 2008). The application of Bayesian statistics to radiocarbon dates from burial contexts at Setefilla is hoped to open up the way forward to establishing a more accurate and more reliable chronology against which the contours of social change during the Early Iron Age in this part of the Western Mediterranean may be outlined (Buck 2004).

A further obstacle which any attempt to establish a radiocarbon-based chronology for the period in question will have to overcome lies in the severe limitations imposed by the uniquely flat stretch in the calibration curve know as 'Hallstatt plateau'. Conventional approaches to calibration so far have not been able to offer a satisfactory solution to this problem, but drawing on the evidence from Setefilla a possible workaround may be available.

Based on conventional estimates it is expected that the burial sequence at the site spans the 9th to 7th centuries BC. Both a steep section in the calibration curve towards the end of the 9th and continuing into the early years of the 8th century as well as a peak in the curve during the second half of the 7th century are not subject to the usual problems experienced with the 'Hallstatt plateau'. They should be easily identifiable in any sufficiently large series of high-precision radiocarbon determinations spanning this period, and would provide fixed points to which the rest of the Setefilla sequence can be anchored, based on a combination of stratigraphic evidence with seriation data (O'Brien and Lyman 1999). Seriation of grave assemblages from Setefilla will be conducted using the PAST software package (Hammer et al. 2001).

Finally, stratigraphic evidence and seriation data will also be used to inform Bayesian modelling of AMS dates from Setefilla. It is envisaged to model the dates using both uniform-phase and normal-distribution approaches, and to subsequently check the outcome from these against each other as well as against existing models (Blaauw 2010; Blaauw and Christen 2011). Despite the considerable challenges posed by the shape of the calibration curve for this period, it is expected that the application of Bayesian statistics to radiocarbon dates from Setefilla will open up the way forward to establishing a more accurate and more reliable chronology against which to outline the contours of social change during the Early Iron Age in this part of the Western Mediterranean.

The basic principles of this method can be considered well understood and have successfully been applied to data sets from the period in question on a number of occasions (Bronk Ramsey 2009a; Finkelstein and Piasetzky 2010). With archaeological data of a comparable nature to those from Setefilla – Scythian Early Iron Age barrows with multiple burials for which the outline of a stratigraphical sequence could be established – this method has already been shown the potential of overcoming at least some of the problems posed by the 'Hallstatt plateau' (Van der Plicht 2004).

The second objective of our project is to determine the provenance of allegedly imported pottery from Tartessian sites. The actual origin of these alleged ceramic imports has not yet been securely established, and identifying their role in regional exchange networks will prove crucial for a better understanding of Early Iron Age society. In recent years, new provenance studies conducted on Phoenician pottery from SW Iberia have provided us with a much better understanding of production centres and trade connections across the Mediterranean (Behrendt and Mielke 2011; Behrendt et al. 2012). However, the relevant research was very much focussed on material from 'colonial' Phoenician sites, which is why despite the considerable advances made in this field, most questions regarding exchange and interaction between the Phoenicians and indigenous communities remain unanswered. We argue that through systematic spectrographic analysis of pottery specimens it is possible to gain useful insights into the diachronic interdependencies between Phoenician colonies and indigenous settlements. The origin of pottery is conventionally determined according to its morphological features. However, considerable uncertainty still persists in such determinations. Luxury products like wheel-made cups or plates could have been imported from the Levant, from the Phoenician colonies or produced locally. By using archaeometric techniques, a better understanding of regional production patterns and exchange networks can be achieved. The methodology is based on both destructive and non-destructive analysis of ceramic samples. Thanks to a highly sensitive, portable X-Ray Fluorescence analyser (Fig. 3) we expect to be able to establish the origin of raw materials used in the making of this pottery and therefore reveal whether wheel-made vessels are long-distance imports or just result from a practice of imitation. As the reference database for the raw clays is in the process of being created by different archaeologists and geologists working in Andalusia, our main method to determine the origin of pottery is the definition of fabric groups based on statistics. Statistical analysis of the results from nearly 300 samples permits to mark out groups with different chemical composition. Although at this stage we are not able to establish the exact provenance of every sherd, it is feasible to identify singular groups of possible foreign origin. It should be added that field XRF analysis of raw clays was undertaken in the surroundings of Setefilla, our key site.

pXRF analysis is a non-destructive method which permits to identify the chemical composition of a wide range of materials and does not require any extraction of samples, enabling analysis on-site in museum storage rooms, which eliminates problems of access to collections, the need for sample-export permits, and significantly reduces total project costs. The use of pXRF units is becoming more and more common in archaeology. The significance of pXRF analysis in archaeometry is unquestionable: it preserves the physical integrity of artefacts, enables access to large data sets and ensures the capability for rapid analysis (Goren *et al.* 2011; Shackley 2011; Forster *et al.* 2012; Bonizzoni *et al.* 2013). Above all, this method is extremely useful for providing information on the production and exchange of ancient ceramics (Ownby 2012). However, it is not the only technique used in the archaeometric part of the project. Low-tech fabric analysis will be conducted as a complementary technique in order to determine fabric groups. In this approach, invented in the 1960s at Leiden University, there is no need to use advanced equipment, nor specific 'know-how' (Franken and Kalsbeek 1969). Using this technique, the surface of the samples is polished by using sandpaper. The flat surface of a sample then permits to carry out further steps, i.e. optic microscope analysis and the identification of inclusions, porosity and matrix of the clay.

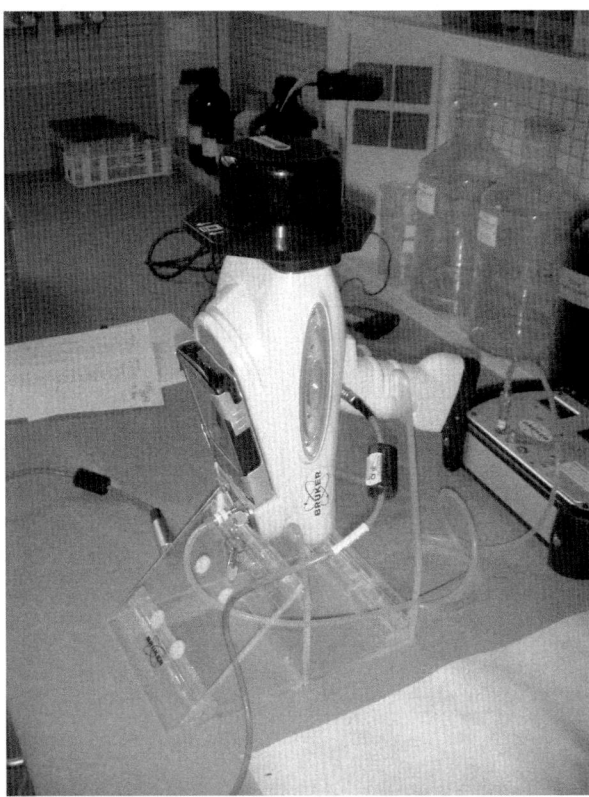

FIGURE 3. THE XRF SPECTROMETER IN THE FACULTY OF CHEMISTRY OF THE ADAM MICKIEWICZ UNIVERSITY IN POZNAŃ (PHOTO: M. KRUEGER).

In the case of Tartessos, the results of the provenance study will provide crucial information, allowing us to better understand the economic structure of the Tartessian region at the beginning of the Iron Age in SW Iberia. For the purposes of the project, a Bruker Tracer III SD spectrometer has been purchased. The use of the same type of instrument and similar measurement protocols employed by other teams working in the region will provide inter-project consistency, avoiding problems otherwise expected from the use of varied equipment and techniques. Over the last couple of years, a German team has started working on determining the provenance of Phoenician pottery from ancient Iberia, conducting a project entitled 'Archaeometric Investigation of Phoenician Pottery from the Iberian Peninsula' (Behrendt, Mielke 2014). Their research, however, is aimed at answering different questions and primarily studies pottery from coastal Phoenician sites rather than from inland indigenous contexts. Our project, at the moment focused on sites in the Guadalquivir valley, will complement this research.

Apart from non-destructive investigations, laboratory analysis of a test sample will be conducted as well, in order to cross-check results. Using pXRF to analyse ceramic samples with already known composition is the standard approach in this type of research. The destructive analysis of strong acids decomposition will be conducted at Adam Mickiewicz University using atomic spectrometers (atomic absorption analysis and the new analytical technique of microwave-induced plasma atomic emission spectroscopy). Thanks to multivariate data analysis it will be possible to establish whether the analysed artefacts are of local origin or not. It is expected that this will provide us with new insights into the network of interconnections that existed between Phoenicians and indigenous communities. The results of the large-scale provenance study undertaken as part of the present project will provide crucial information, allowing us to better understand the economic structure of our study area at the beginning of the Iron Age. Apart from being of crucial importance for the identification of economic networks, this research will also have considerable impact on our understanding of the political and social organization of indigenous Early Iron Age communities. New interpretive models place considerably less emphasis on the role of centralized power and elite control in the transformation of indigenous society following contact with the Phoenicians than has previously been the case, and instead shift focus on the agency of commoner households (Delgado 2013).

As the investigations are still in the initial stage, no results from the project are available at the moment. Therefore, we can only provide some preliminary information on our sampling strategy. Sampling was carried out during the summer of 2014 in three Andalusian institutions: in the Archaeological Museum in Seville, in the University of Seville and in the Casa-Museo Bonsor in Mairena del Alcor. Pottery from 20 Tartessian sites located in western Andalusia, mainly in the Guadalquivir valley were analysed by a portable XRF spectrometer. In total, 860 analyses were conducted directly in the relevant museums. Where possible, pXRF readings were taken on a broken edge. Where this was not feasible, the surface of the sherd was always cleaned prior to analysis. Special attention was paid not only to so-called Phoenician pottery, but also to items normally perceived as local, like *á chardón* and Cruz del Negro type vessels. What is more, 49 samples for destructive analysis were obtained from Setefilla, due to the significance of this site in establishing an accurate chronological framework. The link between chronology and chemical composition is the reason why the pottery from Setefilla has been chosen as the main reference group for further spectroscopic analysis of pottery from other Tartessian sites. At present, a data base of the archaeometric information is being prepared and the statistical analysis of the data will be carried out soon to obtain provenance classification. The results will be compared with the outcome of work undertaken by the German team.

In conclusion, we are hoping to integrate the analysis of samples from Setefilla and imported objects in a comprehensive analysis of the material culture within the social and territorial organization of the Lower Guadalquivir region. The planned research could shed completely new light on the beginning of the Iron Age in SW Iberia. The ongoing investigations will have important implications for our understanding of the development of this region during the transitional period between the Late Bronze Age and Early Iron Age, when for the first time indigenous communities were exposed to new social and economic models originating from the Eastern Mediterranean. Solving the problem of the origin of 'imported' items by determining their chemical composition and the problem of chronology through AMS dating can mark a significant breakthrough in our understanding of historical transformations in south-western Iberia.

Acknowledgements

We would like to thank our colleagues at the Casa-Museo Bonsor in Mairena del Alcor, Museo Arqueológico de Sevilla, Real Academia de la Historia in Madrid, Universidad de Sevilla, Universidad Autónoma de Madrid, and Universidad Pompeu Fabra in Barcelona for crucial information and their support in obtaining samples.

References

AUBET, M. E. 1975. *La necrópolis de Setefilla en Lora del Río, Sevilla*, Barcelona, CSIC.
AUBET, M. E. 1978. *La necrópolis de Setefilla en Lora del Río, Sevilla (Túmulo B)*, Barcelona, CSIC.

Aubet, M. E. 1989. La Mesa de Setefilla. La secuencia estratigráfica del corte 1. In: Aubet, M. E. (ed.), *Tartessos. Arqueología protohistórica del Bajo Guadalquivir*, Sabadell, Ausa, 297-338.

Aubet, M. E. 1982. Los enterramientos bajo túmulo de Setefilla (Sevilla). *Huelva Arqueológica* 6, 49-70.

Aubet, M. E.; Barceló, J. A. and Delgado, A. 1996. Kinship, Gender and Exchange: the Origins of Tartessian Aristocracy. In: *The Iron Age in Europe 12, XIII International Congress or Prehistoric and Protohistoric Sciences Forlì – Italia – 8/14 September 1996*, Forlì, A.B.A.C.O. Edizioni, 145-161.

Beba, S. 2008. *Die tartessischen 'Fürstengräber' in Andalusien*. Bochumer Forschungen zur prähistorischen Archäologie 1, Rahden, Leidorf.

Behrendt, S. and Mielke, D. P. 2011. Provenienzuntersuchungen mittels Neutronenaktivierungsanalyse an phönizischer Keramik von der Iberischen Halbinsel und aus Marokko. *Madrider Mitteilungen* 52, 139-237.

Behrendt, S.; Mucha, H.-J.; Bartel, H.-G. and Mielke, D. P. 2012. Zur Problematik der multivariaten statistischen Analyse umfangreicher p-RFA-Datenmengen phönizischer Keramik. In: Schlütter, F.; Greiff, S. and Prange, M. (eds.), *Archäometrie und Denkmalpflege 2012. Jahrestagung an der Eberhard-Karls-Universität Tübingen 28.-31. März 2012*. Metalla Sonderheft 5, Bochum, Deutsches Bergbau-Museum, 157-159.

Behrendt, S.; Mielke, D. P. 2014. Archaeometric Investigation of Phoenician Pottery from the Iberian Peninsula. In: Bieliński P. *et al.* (eds.) *Proceedings of the 8th ICAANE*, Wiesbaden, Harassowitz, 635-643.

Bendala, M. 1992. La problemática de las necrópolis tartésicas. In: Blánquez, J. and Antona, V. (eds.), *Congreso de Arqueología Ibérica: las necrópolis*, Madrid, Universidad Autónoma de Madrid, 27-36.

Blaauw, M. 2010. Methods and code for 'classical' age-modelling of radiocarbon sequences. *Quaternary Geochronology* 5, 512-518.

Blaauw, M. and Christen, J. A. 2011. Flexible paleoclimate age-depth models using an autoregressive gamma process. *Bayesian Analysis* 6, 457-474.

Bonizzoni, L.; Galli, A.; Gondola, M.; Martini, M. 2013. Comparison between XRF, TXRF, and PXRF analyses for provenance classification of archaeological bricks. *X-Ray Spectrometry* 42(4), 262-267.

Brandherm, D. 2006. Zur Datierung der ältesten griechischen und phönizischen Importkeramik auf der Iberischen Halbinsel. Bemerkungen zum Beginn der Eisenzeit in Südwesteuropa. *Madrider Mitteilungen* 47, 1-23.

Brandherm, D. 2008a. Erneut zur Datierung der ältesten griechischen und phönizischen Importkeramik auf der Iberischen Halbinsel. *Madrider Mitteilungen* 49: 115-144.

Brandherm, D. 2008b. Greek and Phoenician potsherds between East and West: a chronological dilemma? In: Brandherm, D. and Trachsel, M. (eds.), *A New Dawn for the Dark Age? Shifting Paradigms in Mediterranean Iron Age Chronology – L'âge obscur se fait-il jour de nouveau? Les paradigmes changeantes de la chronologie de l'âge du Fer en Méditerranée. Union Internationale des Sciences Préhistoriques et Protohistoriques – Actes du XV Congrès Mondiale (Lisbonne, 4-9 septembre 2006)*, vol. 9. BAR International Series 1871, Oxford, Archaeopress, 149-174.

Bronk Ramsey, C. 2009. Bayesian analysis of radiocarbon dates. *Radiocarbon* 51 (1), 337-360.

Buck, C. E. 2004. Bayesian chronological data interpretation: where now? In: Buck, C. E. and Millard, A. R. (eds.), *Tools for Constructing Chronologies: crossing disciplinary boundaries. Lecture Notes in Statistics* 177, London, Springer, 1-24.

Delgado Hervás, A. 2013. Households, merchants, and feasting: socioeconomic dynamics and commoners' agency in the emergence of the Tartessian world (eleventh to eight centuries B.C.). In: Cruz Berrocal, M.; García Sanjuán, L. and Gilman, A. (eds.), *The Prehistory of Iberia: debating early social stratification and the state*, New York-London, Routledge, 311-336.

Finkelstein, I. and Piasetzky, E. 2010. Radiocarbon dating the Iron Age in the Levant: a Bayesian model for six ceramic phases and six transitions. *Antiquity* 84, 374-385.

FORSTER, N.; GRAVE, P.; VICKERYB, N.; KEALHOFER, L. 2011. Non-destructive analysis using PXRF: methodology and application to archaeological ceramics. *X-Ray Spectrometry* 40, 389-398.

FRANKEN, H. J.; KALSBEEK, J. 1969. *Excavations at Tell Deir 'Alla I. A stratigraphical and analytical study of the Early Iron Age pottery*, Leiden: Brill.

GILBOA, A. 2013. À-propos Huelva: a reassesment of 'early' Phoenicians in the West. In: Campos, J. M. and Alvar, J. (eds.), *Tarteso. El emporio del metal*, Córdoba: Almuzara, 311-342.

GONZÁLEZ PRATS, A. 2002. *La necrópolis de cremación de Les Moreres – Crevillente, Alicante, España – s. IX-VII AC.;* Alicante, Universidad de Alicante.

GOREN, Y.; MOMMSEN, H.; KLINGER, J. 2011. Non-destructive provenance study of cuneiform tablets using portable X-ray fluorescence (pXRF). *Journal of Archaeological Science* 38, 684-696.

HAMMER, Ø.; HARPER, D. A. T. and RYAN, P. D. 2001. PAST: paleontological statistics software package for education and data analysis. *Palaeontologia Electronica* 4 (1), 1-9 <http://palaeo-electronica.org/2001_1/past/issue1_01.htm]

KRUEGER, M. 2011. *Estructura social tartésica a través del ejemplo de la necrópolis de Setefilla (Lora del Río, Sevilla)*, Barcelona, unpublished PhD thesis Universidad Pompeu Fabra.

LANTING, J.; AERTS-BIJMA, A. T. and VAN DER PLICHT, J. 2001. Dating of Cremated Bone. *Radiocarbon* 43 (2A), 249-254.

LORRIO, A. J. 2008. *Qurénima. El Bronce Final del Sureste de la Península Ibérica. Bibliotheca Archaeologica Hispana* 27 (=Anejo al Revista Lucentum 17), Madrid, Real Academia de la Historia.

MAIER, J. 1992. La necrópolis tartésica de 'La Cruz del Negro' (Carmona, Sevilla): excavaciones de 1900 a 1905. *Cuadernos de Prehistoria de la Universidad Autónoma de Madrid* 19, 95-141.

MAIER, J. 1999. La necrópolis de La Cruz del Negro (Carmona, Sevilla), ayer y hoy. *Madrider Mitteilungen* 40, 97-114.

NAYSMITH, P.; SCOTT, E. M.; COOK, G. T.; HEINEMEIER, J.; VAN DER PLICHT, J.; VAN STRYDONCK, M.; BRONK RAMSEY, C.; GROOTES, P. M. and FREEMAN, S. P. 2007. A Cremated Bone Intercomparison Study. *Radiocarbon* 49 (2), 403-408.

O'BRIEN, M. J. and LYMAN, R. L. 1999. *Seriation, Stratigraphy, and Index Fossils. The Backbone of Archaeological Dating*, New York, Plenum Publishers.

OWNBY, M. F. 2012. The Use of Portable X-ray Fluorescence Spectrometry for Analyzing Ancient Ceramics, *Archaeology Southwest Magazine* 26 (2) [http://www.archaeologysouthwest.org/pdf/pXRF_essay_ownby.pdf]

PELLICER CATALÁN, M. and ESCACENA CARRASCO J. L. 2007. Rabadanes. Una nueva necrópolis de época tartésica en el Bajo Guadalquivir. *Lucentum* 26, 7-21.

ROBERTS, B.; UCKELMANN, M. and BRANDHERM, D. 2013. Old Father Time: the Bronze Age chronology of Western Europe. In: Fokkens, H. and Harding, A. (eds.), *The Oxford Handbook of the European Bronze Age*, Oxford, Oxford University Press, 17-41.

SHACKLEY, M. S. 2011. An Introduction to X-ray Fluorescence (XRF) Analysis in Geoarchaeology. In: Shackley, M. S. (ed.), *XRay Fluorescence Spectrometry (XRF) in Geoarchaeology*, New York, Springer, 7-44.

TOFFOLO, M. B.; FANTALKIN, A.; LEMOS, I. S.; FELSCH, R. C. S.; NIEMEIER, W.-D.; SANDERS, G. D. R.; FINKELSTEIN, I. and BOARETTO, E. 2013. Towards an absolute chronology for the Aegean Iron Age: new radiocarbon dates from Lefkandi, Kalapodi and Corinth. *PLoS ONE* 8 (12): e83117 doi:10.1371/journal.pone.0083117.

TORRES ORTIZ, M. 1996. La cronología de los túmulos A y B de Setefilla. El origin del rito de la cremación en la cultura tartésica. *Complutum* 7, 147-162.

VAN DER PLICHT, J. 2004. Radiocarbon, the Calibration Curve and Scythian Chronology. In: Scott, E. M.; Alekseev, A. Y. and Zaitseva, G. (eds.), *Impact of the Environment on Human Migration in Eurasia. Proceedings of the NATO Advanced Research Workshop, held in St. Petersburg, 15-18 November 2003*. NATO Science Series 4, 42, London, Springer, 45-61.